SOUL
PSYCHOLOGY:

Keys to Ascension

Joshua David Stone, Ph.D.

THE EASY-TO-READ ENCYCLOPEDIA
of the SPIRITUAL PATH
✦ Volume II ✦

D0055026

Published by
Light Technology Publishing

Cover design by
Fay Richards

ISBN 0-929385-56-X

Published by
Light Technology Publishing
P.O. Box 1526
Sedona, AZ
86339

Printed by

MISSION
POSSIBLE
Commercial
Printing

P.O. Box 1495 • Sedona, AZ 86339

Introduction

One of my greatest interests in this lifetime has been the study of what I am now calling monadic or spiritual psychology. There are tens of thousands of self-help books on psychology and human relationships; however, there are very few books that integrate the soul and spirit into the picture. This has been my greatest focus of interest. This book represents the distillation of my life's research, study, and work in this area.

I have attempted to make this subject very clear, right to the point, and easy to understand. The book is extremely comprehensive and, in combination with my first book, *The Complete Ascension Manual: How to Achieve Ascension in This Lifetime,* it sets forth the basics of soul and monadic psychology.

It must be understood that there are three levels of self-actualization: There is personality-level self-actualization, soul-level self-actualization, and lastly there is monadic or spiritual-level self-actualization. These two books provide the basic understanding, tools, and maps for achieving all three levels of what might collectively be called God-realization.

Most of the books in the average bookstore are focusing on personality-level self-actualization. The new wave in the field of psychology is transpersonal, or soul, psychology, which will then lead to monadic psychology for the more advanced students of the path.

The entire understanding of psychology is completely changed when the soul is properly integrated. It has been said that personality-level self-actualization brings happiness; soul-level self-actualization brings joy; monadic- and spiritual-level self-actualization brings bliss. It is toward this goal that I humbly direct my life's work in understanding soul and spiritual psychology.

Joshua David Stone, Ph.D.

Dedication

I would like to dedicate this book to my father, mother, and sister. Earth life can be a very tough school and without a supportive and loving family, life becomes that much harder. By the grace of God, this lifetime I was born into a most wonderful family.

Without their most generous loving support on spiritual, mental, emotional, Earthly, and financial levels throughout my life, I would not be the person I am today and you would not be reading these books. In truth, I would have long since passed over to the spiritual world.

Words cannot put into proper expression the feelings of gratitude and love I feel for these three wonderful beings. It has been my honor to know them, and I am sure our love and friendship will continue long beyond the short span of this incarnation.

Contents

1

The Development of Personal Power and the Functioning of the Conscious and Subconscious Minds

*The single most important aspect of
achieving psychological and spiritual health
is learning to own your personal power*

Dr. Joshua David Stone

The conscious mind is the reasoning mind, whereas the subconscious mind is the nonreasoning mind. The superconscious mind is the all-knowing mind.

The conscious mind is the captain of the ship, computer programmer, decision-maker, gardener. If the conscious mind is the captain, then the subconscious mind is the shipmate below the deck who follows whatever orders the captain gives. The subconscious mind is the computer or tape recorder.

The subconscious mind is the soil. If the conscious mind is the gardener, the gardener plants the seeds (thoughts), and the soil grows whatever kind of seed is planted – a weed or a beautiful flower. The subconscious mind will store information and follow orders whether the orders are rational or irrational. The subconscious mind doesn't care, as it has absolutely no reasoning ability.

The subconscious mind is a paradox. It has no reasoning ability and yet it does have an incredible number of amazing abilities and intelligence factors. The best metaphor for understanding this is that of the computer.

The Three Minds

The
Superconscious
Mind
or
Higher Self

The
Conscious
Mind
or
Middle Self

The
Subconscious
Mind
or
Lower Self

The Spiritual Mind
1. Can be contacted through:
    a. Meditation
    b. Dreams
    c. Journaling
    d. Intuition
2. Can help us only if we ask for assistance. Does not interfere with our free choice on a conscious level.

The Reasoning Mind
1. Executive Director
2. President of the personality
3. Captain of the ship
4. Computer programmer
5. Gardener
6. Decision-maker
    a. Will power, discipline, discernment, discrimination, concentration, reasoning.

The Non-Reasoning Mind
1. Works on impressions, stimulus/response.
2. Is a memory bank and file of thoughts, feelings, memories, imagination, habit patterns, impulses, desires, instincts.
3. Operates physical body.
4. Creates most dreams.
5. Creates vital force.
6. Works twenty-four hours a day.
7. Functions according to the law of attraction.
8. Examines, classifies, stores information.
9. In metaphorical terms is the computer, garden, engine room.
10. Plays a key role in the prayer process.
11. Controls the inner senses (visualization).
12. Radiates senses.
13. Creates threads of energy that contact both objects and other people.
    a. Can leave body and follow those threads (as in the use of pendulums, psychometry, psychokinesis).
    b. Can send vital force and thought forms along these threads (as in telepathy and prayer).

A computer is an incredible piece of equipment, yet it doesn't care whether it's programmed to solve the energy crisis or to create a nuclear war. The subconscious does whatever it is programmed to do, no matter what. A good example is the way the subconscious mind completely runs the physical body. This can be proven by the effects of hypnotic suggestions given to a person concerning the body. The subconscious mind has the ability to create perfect health or create cancer. It will create whatever it is programmed to do. No one consciously programs cancer, but many people unconsciously program cancer into their bodies through self-hatred, victim consciousness, revenge, giving up, and so on. The ideal is to tell yourself or your subconscious mind that you are in perfect, radiant health and that every day in every way you are getting healthier and healthier.

The subconscious mind works separately from the functioning of the conscious mind. It works twenty-four hours a day, seven days a week, three hundred and sixty-five days a year while you are sleeping and awake, and it never gets tired. It is constantly doing whatever it has been programmed to do.

The Intelligence Factor of the Subconscious Mind

The basic function of the subconscious mind is to store information. It is the storehouse and memory bank of all your thoughts, feelings, imaginings, habit patterns, impulses and desires. From the time you were a little infant, you have been receiving programs from your parents, grandparents, peers, teachers, ministers, extended family and television programs. When you are a child, your reasoning mind has not developed enough to be able to discriminate and thereby protect you from negative programming. As a child, you are totally open, so your subconscious mind can be filled with mental poisons, faulty thinking and faulty beliefs. Just as the body can be filled with physical toxins from poor eating, the subconscious is filled with mental toxins from negative programming and education.

The subconscious mind also creates most dreams, although there are occasions when the superconsciousness creates dreams. A dream is basically a mirror of the way you think, feel, and act during your conscious daily life. A dream is like a newspaper you receive every night, depicting the organization and dynamics of your internal energies.

The difference between dreams and a real newspaper is that dreams are in the universal language of symbols. To understand your dreams is to understand that every part of a dream is, in reality, a part of you. By examining the relationship of the symbols you can gain insight into and understanding of the patterns that are manifesting in your life. A dream is an automatic process that the subconscious mind brings to you as feedback. This feedback is essential because very often you are manifesting patterns in your life that you are not consciously aware of manifesting.

The subconscious mind can also be termed the habit mind. It stores all habits, both positive and negative. A lot of people think habits are bad. This is not true. You want to change only bad habits, while creating good habits.

A good example of this is learning to drive a stick shift car. At first, it takes a lot of conscious effort and will power but soon shifting is done without your having to think about it. If you didn't have a subconscious mind to store your developed abilities, shifting would always require great focus and concentration.

There is a basic psychological law that says it takes twenty-one days to cement a new habit into the subconscious mind. You can learn something in a day, but to engrave a habit in the subconscious mind takes twenty-one days. This ability of the subconscious mind to store habits allows you to grow continually and to develop new abilities without worrying about old ones.

The subconscious mind is where the law of attraction operates. The subconscious mind is continually attracting things to and repelling things from you according to what has been programmed into it. A master is someone who uses this law to his own conscious benefit.

The subject of money and prosperity provides a good example. If you have the belief in your subconscious mind that you will never have money, you won't. If, on the other hand, you believe you will, your subconscious mind will attract those opportunities and possibilities to you. Whatever you want in life, you can affirm and visualize in your subconscious mind, and the subconscious mind will attract and magnetize it to you.

Carl Jung spoke of this when he talked about the collective unconscious. The subconscious mind is interconnected with all other subconscious minds. You might say that all the sons and daughters of God have one great subconscious mind.

The subconscious mind also has the ability to sense radiations of energy. You automatically use this ability in your daily life. It can be used specifically in areas such as water dowsing, or water witching. The subconscious can be programmed to search for any physical substance, not just water. It can sense the energy radiation of any substance for which it is programmed to search.

The subconscious mind is also the seat of psychic abilities. The subconscious has five inner senses that are the subtler counterparts of your five external senses: inner sight (clairvoyance), inner hearing (clairaudience), inner smell, inner taste, and inner touch.

When you dream you have your five senses available to you. How can this be if you are sleeping? It is because you are utilizing the five inner senses of the subconscious mind. You have psychic abilities and can develop them further. It is just a matter of practice and proper training, as with any external ability.

How the Conscious Mind Works in Relationship to the Subconscious Mind

The key function of the conscious mind is to be the computer programmer, protector and master of the subconscious mind. The subconscious mind is meant to be the servant or servomechanism of the conscious mind but is not meant to direct it. If you don't understand these psychological laws, you are likely to let your subconscious mind run you. Why would you let a nonreasoning mind run your life? Strangely enough, this is what most people do. When this happens you can become a victim and have a lot of problems.

When a thought, feeling or impulse arises in the subconscious mind, it is the job of the conscious mind to use its powers of reasoning and discrimination to check that thought at the gate. If the thought or impulse is positive and spiritual, you let it into your mind. If it is negative, you push it out.

Psychological health is the process of letting into your mind positive, spiritual, balanced thoughts. Psychological health is like physical health. If you want to be physically healthy, you put healthful food into your body. If you want to be psychologically healthy, you put healthful thoughts into your mind. By pushing the negative thoughts out of your mind, you are refusing them energy. This is much like a plant that is not being watered. It eventually withers and dies from lack of water (attention and focus). The second step is to affirm the opposite and positive thought. This is called positive thinking and the use of positive affirmations. By continually disregarding the negative thought and affirming the positive thought, a new habit is formed in the subconscious mind. The old habit dies because you are not giving it energy; and the new habit is formed because you are continually affirming and thinking positively. Within twenty-one days this new habit can be formed.

You must remember that the subconscious is filled with many old tapes that you accepted when you were young. If the conscious mind isn't making choices, then all this old programming from early childhood is affecting your present life.

Development of the Outer Bubble, or Shield, to Protect You from Other People's Negative Energy

Just as it is essential to develop an inner bubble to protect yourself from your own subconscious mind, it is also essential to develop an outer bubble, or shield, to protect yourself from other people's negative energy. Always remember that if you don't take responsibility for this, then the subconscious mind or other people will run your life. The ideal is to be the cause, creator and master of your own life.

Let's take the example of someone criticizing or judging you. The ideal is to be surrounded by an imaginary bubble, shield, or Light so that when criticism comes toward you, it hits the bubble or shield and slides off like water off a duck's back. You make a conscious choice as to whether to let it into your subconscious mind or not. It must be understood that this bubble is a semipermeable bubble. In other words, it allows positive energy in but keeps negative energy out.

If you don't have this bubble of protection available to you at all times, then you can be victimized by another person's comments, statements, or energy. There is a time to be open and a time to be closed. It is necessary to close down and protect yourself if other people are being negative. If someone threw an actual physical spear at you, I am sure you would physically try to get out of the way if you could. You don't want the subconscious mind to run your life and you don't want other people to run your life either.

Another way of saying this is that you want to respond instead of react. To respond is to choose how to deal with the incoming energy. To react is to let the incoming energy go right into the subconscious mind, solar plexus, or emotional body and to lash back. If someone judges or attacks you and you let it in, you will either be hurt and withdrawn and cry, or you will lash back. You are letting another person be the cause of your emotions. You want to cause your emotions.

A different way of saying this is that you are letting yourself be hypnotized. I am licensed as a hypnotist, as well as being a licensed counselor. However, most of my work consists not of hypnotizing people but of de-hypnotizing them. Many people are in a state of self-hypnosis, and I am trying to get them out of it. You are under hypnosis when you are a victim. You are hyper-suggestible when you don't make choices as to how you want to respond. In reality, you are invulnerable, psychologically. This is a very profound statement. To be invulnerable means that you can't be emotionally hurt unless you choose to be.

My Favorite Metaphor of All

My favorite metaphor likens psychological health to physical health. If a person you know catches a cold or the flu, you certainly don't want to get it. You do everything in your power not to get it. You take extra vitamin C. You tell yourself you are not going to get sick. You eat well and try to get enough sleep. In other words, you build up your resistance. If you keep your resistance up, you don't get sick.

Doctors and nurses don't catch all the sicknesses of their patients. How come? Because there is no such thing as a completely contagious disease. There are only people with low resistance.

This analogy is exactly the same on the psychological level. There is no such thing as a contagious psychological disease. There are only people with low resistance. How do you keep your psychological resistance up so you don't catch the infectious diseases of anger, depression, jealousy, judgment, attack, grudges, hatred, and so on? You keep your psychological resistance up by maintaining a positive mental attitude.

The protective bubble is one positive attitude technique. Other key techniques are maintaining your personal power, maintaining unconditional self-love and self-esteem, and maintaining your trust in God.

These are a few of the main attitudes. In following chapters I will explore some of the others. The point is that you are here in this world to set a better example. You are here to raise other people up, not to let yourself be sucked down. In essence, the Earth is like a hospital that is run by the patients and in which there are very few healers or doctors. The purpose of life is to *be* a healer.

When you allow other people to victimize you, you have become one of the patients again, and then you are in need of healing. This is okay. The lesson is to get back to your centered self and become healer again as soon as you can, for that is the mission in this lifetime.

The Development of Personal Power: the First Golden Key

Of all the attitudes that need development in the healthy personality, none is more important than personal power, or the development of will. The techniques in this book will not work without personal power. Personal power, or will, is the guiding force of the healthy personality.

Personal power is an attitude. You can choose to hold an attitude of weakness or of strength as you begin each day. Your power is the energy that you use to carry out your decisions. For example, let's say you want to exercise at three o'clock. When three o'clock comes, it is a good bet that you will need your power to make yourself do what you have committed yourself to do.

Your power is also needed to control your subconscious mind. Your subconscious mind will run the show unless you own your own power, so personal power is the enforcing agent of the conscious mind. Personal power, in its external usage, is assertiveness.

Personal power is also very much tied in with decisiveness. If you are not decisive, then the subconscious mind or other people will make your decisions for you. The subconscious mind has no reasoning, and other people's decisions are not always in your best interests.

How can you be the master of your life if you do not own your power? You know that God has power. The fact is that you are a cocreator and mini-god, so you have power, too. God helps those who help themselves; you can't help yourself if you don't own your power.

There is and has always been total personal power available to you. Personal power is nothing more than energy in your physical body and subconscious mind that you are using to control your life.

Part of owning your power is being a spiritual warrior in life. The will to live is really the will to fight. Yoga teaches that life is not only a school but also a battlefield. You are trying to get to the top of a mountain. Progress entails taking three steps forward and slipping back two until the top is reached. This is the nature of life for everyone on the spiritual path. The most important thing is not to be a quitter. Paramahansa Yogananda, the great Indian sage, said, "A saint is a sinner who never gave up." Part of owning your power is to keep plugging away. It is having faith in God's power, as well as your own power. When all outer security is stripped away, you always know that you have your power and God's power available to you. This is true security.

Your power is the energy you use to take risks. If you don't own your power, you are going to have a hard time maintaining your bubble of protection. Your power is what allows you to "fake it until you make it." Your personal power, in essence, is your center. When you are in charge you feel more centered.

When you use your power over a long period of time you have what is called discipline. Owning your power is what allows the conscious reasoning mind to stay in control and not be overwhelmed by subconscious or environmental forces. When you don't own your power you get depressed.

There are two opposing forces in life: good and evil, light and darkness, positive and negative, illusion and truth, egotistical thinking and spiritual thinking. Power is the weapon with which to fight the negative and identify with the positive. As Edgar Cayce said, "There is no force in the universe more powerful than your will or power."

The conscious reasoning mind, with the will or power, directs all incoming forces. Without power you would be overwhelmed. In an extreme state of giving up your power, you can become psychotic. The conscious mind can abdicate all responsibility, and the subconscious mind and the environment take over.

You don't have to be afraid of your power because you are going to use it only in a loving way — to serve God, yourself and other people. When you are in your power you feel good, you are challenging and asserting yourself.

When you don't have your power, life is clobbering you. The essence of what I am trying to teach in my work is that you are the cause of your reality. To create what you want, you must own your power.

How Do You Claim Your Power?

You claim your power by choosing, every morning, to affirm that you have it. The diagram at the end of this chapter lists some personal power affirmations that will cultivate this energy. I have also included some emotional-invulnerability affirmations to build your protective bubble, since this shield is so much involved with owning your power.

Edgar Cayce, the great "sleeping" prophet, made another important statement involving power. He talked about the importance of developing positive anger, and I emphasize the word positive. Positive anger is controlled anger that is not directed at other people or yourself but, rather, at the dark force that is trying to push you down. It is used to catapult you toward the Light and positivity.

There is enormous power tied up with anger. The idea is to channel this power constructively. Jesus turned to one of his disciples when he started to complain and said, "Get thee behind me, Satan." I think positive anger has to do with having some real emotion behind your power.

When you say the affirmations you must say them with real emotional power or they won't work. As soon as you mean business the subconscious will become your servant. You have to *make* it serve you, not ask it to serve you. It should also be noted here that God is not going to control your subconscious mind for you, no matter how much you pray. That is not His job. That is your job.

Every morning when you get up, you can claim your power and commit yourself to becoming the master of your life. You can be loving, serve God, have a great day, and let nothing in this universe stop you from your appointed tasks. Once you have established your power, then you can pray for God's help and do some affirmations and visualizations to program your subconscious mind the way you want it to work for you. This is the ultimate power in the universe.

You must realize the power that is at your disposal. How can you not win this war? How can you not eventually get to the top of the mountain? How can you not be successful with all this power? Add to this the fact that you are each a son or daughter of God, in truth, and are all one with God. Can God and the sons and daughters of God lose a battle with Satan, which is another name for ego, illusion, negative thinking?

My Two Favorite Spiritual Affirmations

1. God, my personal power, and the power of my subconscious mind are an unbeatable team.

2. Be still and know that I am God.

Another method of charging up your power is to visualize a symbol that denotes your full power — maybe a sword, a crown, the Rod of Moses, a baseball bat. If you combine this kind of imagery with your affirmations, you will feel even more power.

Psychological Disidentification and Identification Exercise

Suggested instructions: Every morning and every night for twenty-one days these affirmations should be repeated out loud three times until they fully sink into your conscious and subconscious minds.

Disidentification Exercise

I have a body, but I am not my body. My body may find itself in different conditions of health or sickness. This has nothing to do with my real self, or the real "I."

I have behavior, but I am not my behavior. All my behavior comes from my thoughts. If I have not developed self-mastery and I am operating on automatic pilot, I sometimes behave inappropriately. Even though I behave well or poorly, I am not my behavior. This has nothing to do with my real self, my real "I."

I have emotions, but I am not my emotions. If I have not yet developed self-mastery, my emotions are sometimes negative and sometimes positive. As I become more of a master of my life, this will change. Though a wave of emotions may overtake me, I know I am not my emotions. My true nature will not change. "I" remain the same.

I have a mind, but I am not my mind. My mind is my tool for creating my emotions, behavior, and body, as well as what I attract into my life. If I have not developed self-mastery, my mind sometimes runs me, instead of letting me control my mind. My mind is my most valuable tool, but it is not what "I" am.

Identification Exercise

What am "I"?

After disidentifying myself (the "I") from the contents of consciousness, I affirm that I am a center of pure self-consciousness. I am a center of will and personal power, capable of being the cause and creator of every aspect of my life. I am capable of directing, choosing, and creating all my thoughts and emotions, my behavior, the health of my body, and the kinds of things I magnetize into my life. This is who "I" am.

Affirmations

Personal Power and Becoming a Creative Cause

I am the power, the master, and the cause of my attitudes, emotions, and behavior.

I am 100% powerful, loving, and balanced at all times.

I am powerful, whole, and complete within myself. I have preferences but not attachments.

I am 100% powerful and decisive in everything I do.

I have perfect control over all my energies in service of a loving spiritual purpose.

I am the master of my life, and my subconscious mind is my friend and servant.

I am a center of pure self-consciousness and will, with the ability to direct my energies wherever I would have them go.

I am powerful, centered, and loving at all times.

I am powerful and centered at all times and I allow nothing in the external universe to knock me off balance.

I have 100% personal power and I vow never again to give that power to my subconscious mind or to other people.

I have perfect self-control and self-mastery in everything I do.

Emotional Invulnerability

I am 100% invulnerable to other people's negative energy. Other people's negative energy slides off me like water off a duck's back.

I am the cause of my emotions, not other people. I will not give them this power over me ever again.

Other people's negative energy bounces off me as though I were a rubber pillow.

I hear what other people say to me. However, I internalize only that which "I" choose to internalize.

The only effect other people's negative energy has is the effect I let it have. I choose not to be affected ever again.

2

Unconditional Self-Love and the Inner Child

If there is a panacea, or cure-all,
for life, it is self-love

Paul Solomon,
Spiritual Teacher and
Universal Mind Channel

If the development of personal power is the first golden key to psychological and spiritual health, then unconditional self-love is definitely the second golden key.

Personal power and self-love are the building blocks of a healthy self-image. The most important relationship in your life is your relationship with yourself. If you are off center within yourself, how can you be on center with others?

Self-love begins with the understanding that there are two types of love in the world: conditional love and unconditional love. Conditional love is egotistical love. Unconditional love is spiritual love.

The first question to ask yourself is whether you love yourself conditionally or unconditionally. Unconditional self-love is based on the understanding that you have worth and are lovable because God created you. You are sons and daughters of God, and God doesn't make junk. Of course you have worth! If you don't have worth then God doesn't have worth. In other words, your value and lovableness are a spiritual inheritance.

But the ego says your worth and lovableness are based on meeting certain conditions. You have to have a certain kind of physical body. You have to go to college, have money, have a high-paying job, be of a certain social status, be spiritual, meditate, exercise, have a relationship, get good grades, be successful, be perfect, and so on.

Now a lot of these things are very noble things to strive for. *However, they have nothing to do with your self-love and self-worth!*

Your self-love and self-worth come from who you are, not what you do. There are no conditions you have to meet. You can do everything in your life well or everything in your life badly and your worth and lovableness are the same. I cannot emphasize this strongly enough.

A good metaphor for understanding this important point is to imagine having just had a baby. Does this baby have to do anything to have worth? Does he or she have to look a certain way? Isn't there an inherent value in the spark of life? Of course, a baby is of value and lovable. Don't parents continue to love that child as he or she grows older, even if he or she gets into trouble or fails the first grade spelling test?

The point is that there is a difference between the soul that is that child and the child's behavior. The soul is always lovable and worthy. The behavior may not always be so. This is an extremely important discrimination to make with others and with yourself.

To take this analogy a step further: you are God's child. He gave birth to you. He loves you as you would love your child. He continues to love you even though you make mistakes in the spiritual school called Earth life.

You need to love yourself as God loves you – unconditionally! Jesus said, "You shall love your neighbor *as* yourself." He didn't say you should love your neighbor and hate yourself.

You can determine where you are on the spiritual path by seeing how much you love your neighbors and how much you are loving yourself.

You also need to learn to allow yourself to feel God's love. God's love is like the sun; it is always shining. It is just a matter of giving yourself permission to receive it.

One of my favorite metaphors is the idea that you are a diamond splattered with mud. God created you, so you are a diamond. Your faulty, egotistical, negative thinking has put mud on you. I am trying, in this book, to get out the hose and wash off the mud of faulty thinking so you can see your true self. Your true identity is the Christ, the perfect creation of God. It is only the ego's false, negative, pessimistic interpretations that make you feel unworthy or unlovable.

Earth is a school. Your mistakes are not held against you. There are no sins, only mistakes. Some believe that a sin is like a stain on your character that cannot be removed. This is absurd. Mistakes are positive. *Mistakes are positive!* You don't go out of your way to make them, but if they happen, they are opportunities to learn from.

Every mistake is a blessing in disguise because there is always a golden nugget of wisdom to be learned. You learn the easy way or in the school of hard knocks, but you are in this school to know yourself and, hence, know God. God's universe is governed by laws: physical laws, psychological laws, and spiritual laws. You learn by making mistakes and then making adjustments.

The spiritual path up the mountain consists of five steps forward and four backward, seven forward, then six backward. Don't buy into the ego's game of creating an impossible perfectionistic standard in which mistakes are unacceptable. The spirit believes in striving for perfection but looks at mistakes as positive and unavoidable.

Thoughts Create Reality

When you go to sleep at night and have a nightmare, you wake up and say to yourself, "Boy, am I glad that was just a dream; it seemed so real while I was sleeping!" Well, that is what I am saying right now: Wake up from that bad dream, that negative hypnosis you have been experiencing.

It is time to wake up! Let the mud fall off the diamond and look at who you really are. You are the most precious thing in all creation. Do you think God loves a rock or tree more than His own children who are made in His image?

Now comes the key to the whole process: Your thoughts create your reality. Thoughts don't create truth. They just create the reality of the people who are thinking them. In other words, if you think you are unworthy, then you are going to live in the nightmare and self-created hell of your own thoughts' creation.

You will live in your own nightmares, even though they aren't true. You are what you think, so you need to push false attitudes of unworthiness and unlovableness out of your mind and start affirming the truth about yourself. By doing this you will record a new message into your subconscious tape recorder.

Selfish-Selfless Balance

Another aspect of self-love is what I call the selfish-selfless balance. This means there is a time to be selfish and there is a time to be selfless. To be selfless is to direct your energies to helping others; to be selfish is to take care of yourself. The spiritual path is the path of balance. You are not here to be a martyr, but you must learn to be spiritually selfish.

Many very sincere and good spiritual people misunderstand this. I am not saying you shouldn't help others; the greatest among you are the servants of all. I am just saying that you have to take care of yourself, also. You are a part of God, a son or daughter of God.

Not to be spiritually selfish at times is to reject a part of God. If you are too selfless, you will probably become resentful. The great lesson is that when you are selfish, you shouldn't feel guilty, and when you are selfless, you should give without resentment. Whichever you are doing, you should be doing it completely.

Developing an Understanding of the Inner Child

The second major understanding necessary for feeling unconditional self-love deals with the understanding of the inner child.

You have a relationship to yourself. What is this self I am talking about? Another name for this self is the inner child or the inner self. In other words, you parent yourself.

In the following diagram, I am suggesting that there are two ways of parenting either yourself or an external child. There is a spiritual way of parenting and an egotistical way of parenting. The spiritual way of parenting is to be firm but loving, so that yin and yang are balanced. The wrong way to parent is to be either too firm or too permissive. A parent who is too firm is critical. As the diagram indicates, when a parent is too critical, the child tends to feel unworthy and unloved. When a parent is too lenient, the child can become spoiled or rebellious. A firm and loving parent helps the child to become a balanced, well-adjusted child.

The first step in understanding this whole process is to look at the way you were raised, determining whether your parents were critical or loving. It is very likely that you treat yourself exactly the way your parents treated you. Now look at how you have raised your children. And lastly, look at how you are currently raising your own inner child.

The inner child is a psychic reality. Learning to raise your inner child properly is one of the most important skills you can possibly learn. Also, you will be a much better parent to your real children once you have learned to parent yourself properly.

How to Improve Parenting Skills

When you are being too critical of yourself, what is really happening is "child abuse." If you were to see child abuse occurring you would step in and say something to stop it. Well, that is what you need to start doing with your own inner child, who needs the same protection.

The critical parent is like a mean baby sitter with whom you have unwittingly left your child. Now you are returning (waking up) to reclaim the child as your own. You need to start by giving your child the protection he or she needs.

What this means psychologically is that when you become aware that the inner critical parent has started beating your inner child, you must stop him! It doesn't matter how. You can put up your protective bubble and say, "I am not going to let my little child get beaten or abused any longer. I am

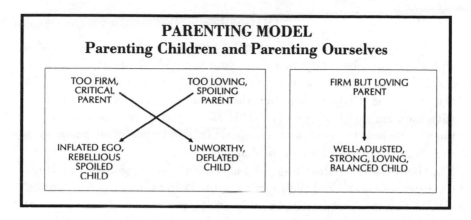

PARENTING MODEL
Parenting Children and Parenting Ourselves

TOO FIRM, CRITICAL PARENT	TOO LOVING, SPOILING PARENT	FIRM BUT LOVING PARENT
INFLATED EGO, REBELLIOUS SPOILED CHILD	UNWORTHY, DEFLATED CHILD	WELL-ADJUSTED, STRONG, LOVING, BALANCED CHILD

going to protect him (her). I love my inner child and will not let that child continue to be hurt.

When the overindulgent parent steps in and wants to be permissive, you can say, "No. I give up this extremism. I don't want to be too yin or too yang. I want balance. Get out!" Push the permissive-parent thought out of your mind.

The second step, after pushing the critical or permissive parent out, is to affirm that you are going to be firm and loving toward yourself from then on. Continually doing this will allow the critical or permissive parent to fade from lack of attention, and the firm and loving parent will strengthen. It will take practice and vigilance. Just remember that if you choose to forget to pay attention, you are allowing child abuse to take place in your own mental home.

What also must be considered here is that if improper parenting has taken place, then the inner child is going to be in need of healing just as a real child would be after being abused. The inner child who has had a critical parent is going to need a lot of extra love and nurturing.

The inner child who has had a permissive parent is going to need "tough love." A child who is acting-out in real life needs to be sat on a little bit, not in a critical way but in a tough-love way. This child has had more power than the parent, but the parent is in charge, and the inner child needs to be told this. You might have to get very tough in the beginning to get the point across, just as you would with a real child. The inner child will get the message if he sees that you mean business. The inner child doesn't really like being out of control anyway.

Your inner child desperately wants your unconditional love just as a real child does. Down deep, your inner child wants firm limits just as a real child does. If you are firm and loving, then both inner and outer children will develop self-control, personal power, and self-love within.

Dialoguing

A very helpful tool in developing the proper relationships is to dialogue with these parts in a journal. Talk to your inner child and see how he or she is feeling; then let the inner child talk back as you imagine he or she would respond. Dialogue with the critical and permissive parents and then with the firm and loving parent. This allows you to get more deeply in touch with how the dynamics are operating within you. You might even introduce the higher self into the dialogue.

There is a very interesting point about that last suggestion. The Huna teachings of Hawaii call the higher self the "utterly trustworthy parental self." I find that fascinating. In other words, you need to learn to parent yourself as your higher self parents you. Doesn't your higher self parent you with firmness and love, tough love?

Victory Log

This suggestion is essential for fully stabilizing self-love and worth. So far I have talked about self-love on the essence level, the level on which you have worth and love because you are a son or daughter of God.

There is also the form level, and you need to feel good about what you are doing and creating in your outer life, too. The critical parent spends all its time being a perfectionist in a negative sense, looking for what you are doing wrong. In a given day you may be doing things 98% well, but the critical parent focuses on the 2% you are doing wrong. This doesn't make sense. You should be able to be 98% happy that day and 2% depressed, seeing the glass of water as being half full rather than half empty.

The purpose of the victory log is to look at what you are doing well, not at what you are doing poorly. There are two steps in developing a proper victory log. First, go over your entire life with a fine-toothed comb, listing all the things that you have done well in your life. List all your fine attributes and qualities, everything, no matter how minute. Doing this allows you automatically to feel good about yourself. Your perspective changes, and you begin to see things the way your higher self sees them.

The second step in the victory log is this: Every night before bed and every morning, add to the list and review the victories of that day and week. By doing this, you are giving strokes, positive reinforcement, psychological hugs and kisses, and love to your inner child. You are telling the inner child how much you appreciate his or her cooperation. You might tell your higher self the same thing. Together, you are an unbeatable team.

What to Do When You Make Big Mistakes

When you do make mistakes, it is important to keep the critical parent out. It is okay to make *observations* about yourself or others; this is also called spiritual discernment because it is done in unconditional love.

Whatever the mistake is, gain the golden nugget of wisdom from the experience and it then becomes a positive experience. If you truly learn from a "mistake," you will never have to go through a similar suffering again. Tell yourself that you are worthy and lovable even though you have made a mistake or made an error in judgment. Mistakes are positive and unavoidable. Pick yourself up and get on with it.

A crucial part of self-love is forgiveness. You have a choice of subscribing to a philosophy of forgiveness or holding grudges. This applies to yourself also. Remember that if you hold grudges, you are holding them against the inner child. Would you hold the same kind of grudge against a real child? If you want to be forgiven by God, it is reasonable to give the same energy back, both to yourself and to others.

This chapter has been focused on internal parenting; I have added a short chapter at the end of this book about external parenting from a spiritual perspective. Even if you don't have children at home it might be worthwhile to read these key points, as there is a direct similarity between inner and outer parenting.

What Happens to You If You Don't Have Self-Love?

If you don't have unconditional self-love within yourself, then you automatically end up seeking it outside of yourself. Love is a survival need; children have actually been known to die in institutions from lack of love.

The ideal is to give love to yourself and to allow yourself to receive God's unconditional love. If you don't do this, then you end up seeking love and acceptance from other people. This puts you in a compromised position. Other people become your computer programmers and the cause of your reality. Your worth is in their hands. Do you really want other people to hold this power over you? Not having self-love puts a hole in your protective bubble so that when people criticize you, you can't protect yourself.

The ideal is to give yourself so much love and to allow yourself to feel so much of God's love that you go into the day feeling totally powerful and totally loved before you encounter another human being. Ideally, you are feeling full and complete within yourself and feeling your oneness with God. Ideally, you are so filled with love that you can give love to others even if others don't love you. In essence, you can *want* love but you don't *need* love from a particular person. You prefer loving relationships but are not attached to getting love. When you are a self-actualized person, you first form a right relationship with God; you then form a right relationship with yourself.

These are the two most important relationships in your life. You then can move into life as a whole, masterful, independent person who is in the world to give rather than trying to get, to fill an empty void within the self. This is the work of the spiritual path.

You actually have it all right now. The only problem is that often, you think you don't. You live in the nightmare of self-inflicted limitation that isn't even real. You can get rid of those limitations any time you want to by owning your power and taking command over your mind.

Self-Love Affirmations

The following are self-love affirmations for reprogramming both conscious and subconscious thinking:

1. I love and forgive myself totally for all my mistakes, for I now recognize that mistakes are positive, not negative.

2. I now fully recognize that I have worth because God created me, and I do not have to do anything to earn it.

3. I now recognize that I am a diamond, not the mud on the diamond.

4. My worth is unchangingly positive because it is a spiritual inheritance. It is not increased by my success nor decreased by my mistakes.

5. I realize now that I have total worth and value as a person, whether I learn my lessons in life or not.

6. I now recognize that everything that has ever happened in my life has been positive, because it all contained lessons I needed to learn.

7. I choose to live in the now and not hold the past against myself.

8. I hereby choose to approve of myself so I do not have to go around seeking approval from others.

9. I deserve love because God created me; I know my mistakes are not held against me.

10. I realize that everything that happens in life is a lesson, a challenge, and an opportunity to grow.

11. I now realize that I am the "I" person, the chooser, the consciousness, and the spiritual being and that this part of me deserves unconditional love at all times.

12. I am the light and not the lampshade over the light.

13. I deserve love because my true identity is not what I do in life. I am the chooser of what I do.

14. I now understand that I am here in life to learn lessons and grow, but if I make mistakes I am still totally lovable and unchangingly worthy.

15. I hereby choose to be very firm and unconditionally loving with myself.

16. I am the master of my life. I choose to be my own best friend instead of my own worst enemy.

17. I choose to love myself as God loves me — unconditionally.

18. I now choose to understand that I want to be perfect, but mistakes are positive and part of the growing process.

19. I now realize on the level of my true identity, the "I," the chooser, the soul, that I am a perfect equal with every other person in the world.

20. I now choose to awaken and recognize that it was only the faulty thinking of my ego that caused me not to love myself.

21. I now choose to undo all the faulty thinking society has programmed into me and replace it with self-love.

22. I now choose to recognize that I deserve love and so do other people.

23. I now choose to recognize that I am guiltless and sinless because all mistakes are just lessons and opportunities to grow.

24. I now realize that God does not hold my misuse of free choice against me, so why should I?

25. I love me. I forgive me. I approve of me, and I commit myself from this moment onward to treating myself in a spiritual manner rather than in an egotistical manner. I now fully realize that the way I think is the reality in which I live. I now choose to release faulty thinking and to live in my self-created heavenly state of consciousness.

26. I love me unconditionally because I am a son/daughter of God, and my misuse of free choice, or faulty thinking, is not held against me.

27. Could what God created not be lovable and worthy?

28. I love me because I am innocent and not guilty.

29. The only thing in this universe that says I do not deserve love is my "ego." I hereby reject my ego and its false attitude. I allow myself to get back in tune with my true spiritual self.

30. I now, once and for all, release the ego's game of "having to do" in order to deserve love and worth. I now fully recognize I have always been lovable and worthy and will always be so.

Self-Love Visualization

Begin by imagining a beautiful scene in nature. Visualize yourself as smiling, happy, joyous, loving, and at peace with yourself and the world. Look around and enjoy the colors, smells, and sounds and the feeling of being in harmony with nature.

Next, imagine one of your favorite animals being with you in your natural setting. See the animal come to you and give you love and affection. Then imagine that your best friend is walking toward you from a distance. Your friend is carrying a six-month-old infant. See yourself greeting your friend, giving him or her a hug and talking a little bit.

Your friend asks you to baby-sit this infant for a couple of hours. He carefully and gently hands you the infant. See your friend leaving and promising to return within two hours. See yourself holding, rocking, and giving love to this beautiful baby.

Next, realize that this infant is really the inner child within you. You are now the parent who has a choice as to how you are going to raise this infant that is you.

The ideal is to give firmness and unconditional love. The other options are to be the critical and overly-firm parent or the permissive and spoiling parent to yourself. If you are too critical, this inner child will grow up feeling unworthy, incapable and unloved. If you are too permissive, this child will grow up spoiled and inflated. How do you want "you" to grow up? Make this choice now and give firmness and unconditional love to this infant that is you as a baby.

Now imagine that five years have gone by and this little child that is you is playing in your natural setting. Again practice being an ideal parent. Talk to the child. Say how you feel. Let the child respond.

Now imagine that ten more years have passed and this child that is you is an adolescent of fifteen. Be the parent you want to be to this teenager.

Now imagine that this adolescent has grown to your present age. See yourself as you look and are now. Recognize that you are still parenting this adult person within you. Now that this child has grown to be the adult you, have you thrown unconditional love and firmness out the window?

Make a choice right now to communicate with yourself, to get back to having a right relationship with yourself. Go up to yourself and give yourself a big hug, recognizing that this is, in truth, your best friend. Apologize to yourself for being so hard on yourself in the past. Forgive your parental self for its mistakes and forgive the adult-child self for its mistakes.

Let the inner adult-child tell you what kind of relationship he or she wants to have from now on. Make a choice to live in the now and make a fresh start from this moment forward. Make a choice to look at the past as being filled with positive experiences because you now choose to look at everything that has happened as opportunities to grow. You can give yourself approval and acceptance because you now recognize that mistakes are positive, not negative.

Tell your adult-child that you will love him or her unconditionally from now on. Tell him or her that you are not going to base your love on what he does but rather on the fact that he was created by God, so of course he has value and worth, regardless of mistakes or successes.

See the "I," the person, the spiritual being as differentiated from behavior, mistakes, successes, personality, physical body, thoughts, or emotions. Make a commitment to yourself from this moment forward to form a right relationship with yourself.

Take time now to have a heart-to-heart talk with yourself, treating yourself with love. Take the time now to talk out all unfinished business and faulty thinking, so that when this meditation is over, there is a fresh start, a rebirth in your relationship with yourself.

Your True Self: the Causal Consciousness

Even though you have both a child and a parent self within you, it is important to realize that the real you is neither the parent nor the child. The real you is "consciousness" or the "I" that is choosing what kind of parent-child dynamic you are creating within yourself.

The real you is the observer self, who is the controller and director, the chooser and causer. The key to being the director is understanding the need to be disidentified from the content of consciousness. You are not your thoughts, emotions, body, behavior, actions, personality, mistakes, successes, abilities, past, future, or beliefs. You are the essence and not the form. You are the consciousness, not the creation. You can direct and control only that from which you are disidentified. In other words, that with which you, as the consciousness, or "I," are identified will be your master. Living in this world, you must deal with form. This is why it is essential that you choose the form of parenting you are going to provide for yourself.

You can now do a visualization in which you put all the things you have thought were you (the contents of your consciousness) into a big metal pot that is in the middle of your natural setting. Put everything in it until you are naked of all mental, emotional and physical form. All that is left is a center of pure awareness with nothing in it.

Then practice taking out qualities, attitudes, feelings, beliefs, abilities, and non-abilities, trying them on and then throwing them back into the pot. Practice identifying, then disidentifying. Practice being the controller, causer and creator of your life, as you would in a role in a play. Always remember what your real self is and who and what you truly are.

3

Integrating the Three Minds and the Four Bodies

Be moderate in all things
The Buddha

One of the key points in becoming a self-realized or God-realized being is learning to balance and integrate the three minds and four bodies. Now, in actuality, you have more than three minds and more than four bodies, because at the fourth initiation the soul, or higher self, merges back into spirit, or the monad, and the spirit and monad become the consciousness that is your guide. This happens in stages, however, so for the purpose of this discussion I am putting the soul and the monad into the same category since they serve similar functions.

With respect to the discussion of the four bodies, I am doing a similar thing, calling the four bodies the physical, emotional, mental, and spiritual bodies. In actuality, the spiritual body can be divided into the causal, the Buddhic, the atmic, the monadic, the logoic, the Light, and on and on into cosmic levels of consciousness.

You work with these higher spiritual bodies in stages as you go through the initiation process in a way similar to the way you work with the three minds, so for the purpose of this discussion, I am also lumping all these higher spiritual bodies into what I am now calling the spiritual body.

First, I want to focus on the three minds. Each mind is a level of mentation, each one being a higher-level mind than the previous one. The ideal is for the subconscious to become subservient to the conscious mind as the conscious mind becomes subservient to the superconscious mind, or soul.

Another way to say this is that your conscious self is meant to become the master of your subconscious mind, and your soul, or higher self, is your master teacher or guide. The kahunas of Hawaii had a very eloquent way of explaining this. They call the higher self, or soul, the aumakua, which is defined as the "utterly trustworthy parental self." As the higher self is the utterly trustworthy parental self, so the conscious mind is the utterly trustworthy parental self for the subconscious mind and inner child. You learn how to raise yourself properly by following the example set by the higher self.

The Bible states that you are made in God's image. It says that God is a trinity: the Father, the Son, and the Holy Spirit. In Hinduism they call this trinity Brahma, Vishnu, and Shiva. In the Huna teachings of Hawaii the trinity is termed Ku, Kane, and Kanaloa.

Since you are made in God's image, then you must be a trinity also; and you are. Your trinity is that of the superconscious, conscious, and subconscious minds.

God, Christ, and the Holy Spirit are different levels of divinity; however, they function as one consciousness. The same is true for you. The ideal is that your three minds function as one mind. The problem is that for many of you the three minds are imbalanced. You might not even know you have a soul or higher mind guiding you, and many times, you let your subconscious, or lower-level mind, run your conscious mind.

When your subconscious mind runs your life, the negative ego becomes your director, and your emotional body usually ends up running your life. The first step toward becoming balanced and integrated is to recognize that you have three minds.

The second step is to begin the processes of learning to own your personal power and of taking control of your subconscious mind and three lower vehicles. The third step is to begin attuning to your higher self and asking it for help.

The three minds could be looked at as large metal rings. In the early stages of your evolution the rings are very separate. As you evolve and begin to develop self-mastery and attunement to the soul, the rings begin to link up.

At the time of the third initiation, the soul merge, these rings begin to merge and start to function as one mind. This is because self-mastery has been achieved to a great extent over the threefold personality (physical, emotional, and mental vehicles) and because the personality has become at least 51% merged with soul consciousness.

As the stabilization of the soul merge continues, the three minds function in greater and greater harmony and balance. As you continue to evolve, the monad, or spiritual mind (as distinguished from the soul) begins to guide. At the fourth initiation the soul merges back into the monad and the monad becomes the full director from then on in your evolution.

At the fifth initiation a further integration and balancing of the three minds takes place in that as you evolve, you merge completely with the monad. (At the third initiation you have soul merge, and at the fifth initiation you have monadic merge.)

The three rings in my metaphor have come together in an even higher union. At ascension the monad descends completely into you as you evolve on Earth and into the four bodies which are transformed into Light. Even the physical body merges completely with the Light. Then you have achieved perfect integration and balance of the three minds and four bodies.

Balancing the Four Bodies

To achieve the union, integration, and balance of an ascended master, you must learn to balance the four bodies. You have four distinct and separate bodies, each with a unique perspective: a physical body, an emotional body, a mental body, and a spiritual body. The ideal is to respect and listen to all four bodies simultaneously. What happens more often than not is a tendency to over-identify with one or two of the bodies to the detriment of the others. More than half the people in the world respond to life through an emotional-body focus.

Some of you feel life. Others of you think about life and are less concerned with your feelings. Still others of you are so involved with the spiritual body that you don't take care of the physical body, and you might not care about thoughts or feelings, either.

Some of you are so involved with your physical existence that you are completely cut off from the spiritual body and possibly even from intellectual pursuits or thoughts. You are likely to focus on one or two bodies in particular.

It is possible to be over-identified or under-identified with each body. When this is occurring, the energy flowing down from the Creator does not move properly. If such a situation continues, it will ultimately manifest as disease in one of the four bodies.

The physical body usually ends up being the mirror of these psychological imbalances. This is based on the Hermetic law: "As within, so without; as above, so below." You can correlate the mental, emotional, or spiritual causation with the location of health problems in the physical body.

You might not think about your four bodies until you feel uncomfortable, but the goal is to integrate the four bodies and to align their differing points of view so as to use them all to be fully creative and to fulfill your potential and divine purpose for being here. You are a cell in the body of God. When you don't work in harmony with God's divine plan, then, in a sense, God has cancer. Part of the lesson of the four-body system is to get all the cells working for the same purpose — ideally, spiritual growth and God-realization.

When the four bodies are balanced and integrated there is no restriction and you are freely flowing. When the four bodies are balanced you are fully able to realize God. Many of you understand this with the mental body but haven't yet aligned the other bodies with this truth.

The same thing happens in the balancing of the three minds. For example, the conscious mind might not want to worry or be depressed anymore, yet the subconscious mind might not be cooperating. The mental body might understand the ideal, but experiencing it fully in all four bodies to make the ideal a living reality might take a little more work.

Each of the four bodies and three minds has a unique gift of information and guidance to give you. The soul, or monad, can give you intuitive perceptions and be the voice of your conscience. The conscious mind gives you logic and deductive reasoning. The subconscious mind gives you emotional reactions. The physical body gives you instinctive reactions and sensations. The emotional body, which is connected to the subconscious mind, focuses on how you feel at any given moment and might produce psychic impressions. The mental body gives you a perspective regarding the logic of what is going on. The spiritual body, which is intimately connected with the monad, gives you intuition, conscience, and God's guidance.

When you over- or under-identify with one body or mind you are losing invaluable information. It is the nature of the ego to tell you that the way that it processes reality is the best. I am here to say that God's understanding of the best way to process reality is that you should use all levels of guidance.

If, in doing business, you were to tune in to your three-mind and four-body systems when making major decisions, I am sure that your business would be much more successful and you would make fewer costly mistakes. Your spiritual vehicle might tell you one thing, your mind another, your feelings something else, and your physical body and instincts yet another thing. You limit yourself by focusing on just one kind of input. Why not access all levels of information and guidance that God has provided?

As you become more and more balanced you will find your three minds and four bodies working in harmony toward the three-faceted goal of success on all levels, God-realization, and the fulfillment of your part of the divine plan on Earth.

The Emotional Body

An emotional focus upon life can be wonderful in its positive aspects. It makes you very sensitive to beauty, the arts, nature, music, and dance. An emotional-body focus in its negative aspects often causes you to be on an emotional roller coaster, constantly tossed around by the instability of the emotional body.

You can learn to use your personal power and will to pull yourself out of the focus because it is your thoughts that are creating your feelings. This can be difficult to do if you have an emotional focus because you are so habituated to accessing just the emotional body. So you must learn to analyze and logically process what you experience. A helpful visualization to use when the emotional body is in crisis is to imagine a red ladder, which is symbolic of the will. Visualize climbing the red ladder to get out of the negative feeling. Another tool is to immediately make some affirmations or to chant the name of God and visualize His form. The point is to use your mental faculties to balance the emotional over-identification occurring at that moment.

You can imagine the golden bubble of protective Light around yourself. This bubble allows in the love and guidance of God and the ascended masters. It protects you from negative feelings in your subconscious mind and from the negative energies in other people and in the outside world. This golden bubble is semipermeable in that it will let in the positive energies but keep out the negative ones. Now, in your mind's eye, open a little hole in the bubble from the inside and push out all negative energy or bad feelings that might possibly still be inside the bubble. Once they have been pushed out, close the hole again and seal it shut.

Now from above, imagine a golden-white Light pouring in from your soul, monad and God, filling the inside of the bubble with positive energy and loving feelings. If you start every day with this image, using it as spiritual and mental armor, you will find yourself much more even-minded, peaceful, and joyous.

Even the Earth has four bodies. What does the feeling body of the Earth look like? It has to do with its relationship to water. You can contrast a torrential rainstorm with a placid lake at sunrise.

Understanding the four-body system can help you greatly to understand both romantic relationships and friendships. If you think about your relationships with those people to whom you are closest, you can determine whether they are emotionally focused, mentally focused, physically focused, spiritually focused, or a combination. By understanding this you can avoid imposing your own focus of identification on them.

Very often in marriages and romantic relationships, the man tends to be more mentally focused and the woman more emotionally focused. A lot of fights occur because each does not appreciate the gift he or she is bringing to the other. It could be said that each is the disowned self of the other.

In my relationship with my wife this is the case. Terri tends to be more focused on her emotional and spiritual bodies. I tend to be more focused on my mental and spiritual bodies. In the beginning of our relationship this caused some clashing because we were trying to impose our way of processing reality on each other. Although we both drink from the same well, we process reality totally differently. We have learned now to really appreciate each other's gifts. Terri is developed in areas I am not. I am developed in areas Terri is not. As we have grown together, we have learned to get along better and to appreciate the gifts that we bring to each other. This understanding of the four-body system has been invaluable to me in understanding and truly appreciating our differences. In reality, together we make a much greater whole.

In reality, it is the soul that is learning when you are working with the four-body system. What I mean by this is that the soul incarnates twelve personalities, or soul extensions, into physical incarnation. Each of these soul extensions is experienced by the soul in simultaneous time, not in sequential time. If in one soul extension it is trying to work out a particular emotional problem and isn't succeeding, then it will work out that lesson through another personality.

The soul might focus on a man in the Mayan civilization, a woman in Lemuria, and another woman living in Los Angeles in the 21st century to work through the same lesson. The soul learns through all twelve soul extensions simultaneously to achieve the soul-realization it is looking for. Finally, through all the experiences of the twelve soul extensions, the four bodies become sufficiently balanced and developed that one soul extension can accept the full expression of the soul. This is called the soul merge or third initiation. This same process occurs at a higher level when one soul extension merges completely with the monad at ascension.

Terri and I are both from the same monad. Therefore, our monad is gaining a wholistic perspective from our being together. Djwhal Khul has termed this the union of the mystic and the occultist. Both of these are totally valid paths back to the Creator. As we learn from each other, I am becoming more and more the master mystic and Terri more and more the master occultist, all for the good of our monad.

To view spiritual growth from the perspective of the soul or the monad rather than from that of the personality is quite an interesting process. From the perspective of the soul, beings on Earth as the soul's extensions are like the fingers on the soul's hand. If one isn't working properly it will just use another finger that is working better. All the fingers belong to the same body so it doesn't really matter which finger it uses to learn its lessons.

The Mental Body

Mass consciousness on Earth is in the process of achieving complete development of the mental body. This is because Earth is currently in the Aryan race cycle whose focus is mental attunement. (Atlantis was focused on emotional attunement, and Lemuria on physical attunement.) Advanced humans have already developed the mental body and are working on the future Aquarian cycle with its development of the spiritual body.

Those of you who identify with a mental focus often get so absorbed in that focus that you pay little attention to your emotions. You can be like the stereotypical college professor who pursues only the intellectual life.

If you pay attention to the mental and spiritual bodies you might become a highly developed occultist, but be insufficiently focused on loving relationships. Very often, if you are mentally focused, you will be less developed psychically and intuitively.

The danger of being over-identified with the mental focus is that you might feel superior to the person who is emotionally focused. It is essential to realize the equality of all four bodies. The same is true of all the chakras. The higher ones are not better than the lower ones. The ideal is for all the chakras to be balanced.

The state of balance and integration is the state of God-realization. Those of you with a mental focus will seek to study everything, finding life interesting and always seeking greater knowledge. This is fine, as long as it is balanced with the other three bodies.

Great scholars often forget their physical needs and become depleted physically because of it. If you are over-identified with the mental focus you need to use your will to shift this focus and balance it with love, the needs of the inner child, and play and recreation time. To climb the ladder of awareness, evolve spiritually, and fulfill your potential, you must use all four bodies. The mental body on its own has a limited perspective.

One helpful exercise might be to let the mental and emotional bodies talk to each other, either out loud or in your journal writing, to help create a better balance. Then you can let the spiritual body guide the two of them, while also giving a voice to the physical body. The four bodies will be happy to cooperate as long as each of them knows that it has its balanced place in service of the divine plan.

When a problem or challenge arises, determine whether it is a physical, emotional, mental, or spiritual problem, or a combination. Determine whether the communication links among the four bodies are operating effectively and try to determine how the four bodies can work together as one team to solve the problem in attunement with the soul's purpose.

In the Earth's four-body system, the mental body might be considered the man-made structures such as the pyramids, skyscrapers, and cathedrals. From a different point of view, the element of air could be considered the mental body of the Earth, as water is the emotional body of the Earth.

The Physical Body

The physical body is the part of self that functions here on Earth. This vehicle, as with other bodies, performs only as well as it is cared for. If you don't give it proper food, exercise, sunshine, fresh air, and recreation, it will have problems.

Another thing the physical body needs is love. Very often the physical body is taken for granted and not recognized as the divine being it is. You might forget to thank it enough for the wonderful service it performs for you.

You might be one of many people who have chosen to experience your spiritual lessons in life through the physical body in the form of illnesses and other types of dysfunctions. When this happens, the body is trying to tell you that you are out of balance in some way. This is a gift and a teaching.

As mentioned earlier, the physical body is a reflector or mirror of the state of functioning of your other bodies. If you have stomach problems, they usually have to do with emotional imbalance. If you have foot problems, they have to do with your understanding. If you have headaches, they have to do with issues of control, either your being too controlling or people controlling you too much.

When you truly learn to be balanced in all four bodies and to be guided and merged with your soul, and later your monad, the physical body literally will live forever. An ascended master can live indefinitely on Earth, as many of the ascended masters have proven.

It is very important to make sure that the energy intake valve at the top of your head is always open. It can be visualized as a funnel. If this valve is closed, tiredness and fatigue result. When the four bodies aren't balanced it takes a toll on the physical body, for the proper flow of energy is not feeding it.

Subconscious patterns often get imbedded into the physical vehicle. Just clearing your thoughts is not enough; physical exercise and bodywork also help to move the pattern. You must work on all levels to clear yourself, not just on the spiritual or mental levels.

The physical body provides a point of focus on the Earth through which the soul can experience. It is a means for the soul to enter school and learn an entirely new set of lessons, which can greatly accelerate spiritual growth. When a soul is not in a physical body, spiritual growth is much slower. When you understand what a great demand there is for physical bodies in the spiritual world you will respect the one you have much more.

The physical body also provides a grounding place for the soul from which it can explore and integrate what is learned on other levels. You cannot go through the initiation process without being in a physical body.

You must learn to treat the physical body as the divine being and partner that it is. It has intelligence and can communicate. It desires to be of service to you and to the divine plan as long as you give it the respect of an equal partner.

The four bodies are like musical instruments, each with a different vibration and tone. You must learn to weave these bodies together in a beautiful symphony. To play just one instrument would be boring and monotonous. To play them all together in perfect balance and harmony, in service of the soul and God's divine plan, is something to listen to. It is what the masters have referred to as the music of the spheres.

It is okay to emphasize one of your four bodies in a more focused manner for a short period of time, such as when writing a book, taking a vacation, going to a meditation retreat, or training to run in a marathon. This is fine as long as the overall context of your life is one of balance and integration.

The Spiritual Body

The spiritual vehicle, or body, is the means by which you experience yourself as an individualized portion of the Creator. It is the vehicle in which you begin your experience and in which you are destined to complete your experience.

As you grow and evolve, you ultimately drop the physical vehicle, then the emotional vehicle, then the mental vehicle, eventually returning to your spiritual vehicle. You drop them one by one until you return to the essence of your self, your soul, and then to your monad.

The other vehicles are your means of achieving this ultimate goal of ascension. In order to achieve this goal the four bodies must be balanced and integrated properly in daily life on the Earth plane in service to God's divine plan.

To become a master mechanic you must know how to take a car apart and put it back together almost blindfolded. As a future cocreator with God at the highest level, you must know how to take your four bodies apart and put them back together in perfect harmony and balance before you can ascend and become a master. As you learn these lessons, the knowledge is absorbed back into the spiritual body. You are then thrust forward into a higher level of awareness and spiritual expansion.

The spiritual vehicle, on whatever level of awareness you perceive it, is forever attuned to God. When you reach that level there is no more pain because there is never a point when you lose focus on God. You suffer in your four bodies whenever you are out of harmony with God and God's laws.

As long as you stay in harmony with God's laws on this plane you will not suffer. When you do suffer, it is just a sign that you need to seek truth and that you have broken one of God's laws. This is not a punishment, but a gift. If you didn't suffer, I don't think you would be very likely to seek God. The small amount of joy that the personality can obtain through Earth life is infinitesimally small compared to the joy and love found in God and the spiritual path. Suffering is like a gentle kick from God to keep you on the straight and narrow path toward the realization of God and service to humankind. This is what you really want anyway. The suffering is just a safeguard keeping you moving in the right direction.

The spiritual body encompasses all of the potential you are not yet able to use. The spiritual body is like a ladder you climb by interacting with the other bodies. Another way to put it is to say that you use your other bodies to climb the ladder of awareness to your full spiritual potential.

Each time you achieve a realization, you lighten up your spiritual body, or Lightbody. A person who is clairvoyant can tell what point you have reached in your evolution by looking at the amount of Light you are allowing into your physical, mental, emotional, and spiritual bodies.

Ideally, the three bodies work toward the goal of the spiritual body, and the soul, or monad. As the soul merges into the four-body system it brings even more balance. The soul (and later the monad) are incapable of any other response. It is only the negative ego that causes you to be out of balance. That is why the soul merge, or third initiation, is such a significant achievement in your evolution. It means you have balanced your four bodies enough to achieve this merger, which helps to create even greater stabilization in the four-body relationship. After the soul merge there is more energy and life force present on the physical level.

4

The Christ Consciousness and How to Achieve It

Forgiveness is the key to happiness

A Course in Miracles

About forty years ago, a woman by the name of Helen Schucman channeled a set of books called *A Course in Miracles*. These books were written by Jesus Christ and telepathically channeled to Helen much like the Alice A. Bailey books were channeled to her from Master Djwhal Khul.

I can honestly say that in the past twenty-two years these books have had a more profound effect on me than anything else I have ever studied. *A Course in Miracles* is basically a set of teachings about attitudinal healing. The basic premise of these books is that there are two ways of thinking, two philosophies of life, and only two. Every person in the world follows one or the other. There is the voice of the Spirit, or of the Christ, and there is the voice of the ego. They could also be called the voices of your higher self and of your lower self; the voices of the big "I" and of the little "i"; the voices of the Holy Spirit and of glamour, illusion, and maya; the voices of the Holy Spirit and of the negative ego.

As children you are conditioned by society to perceive and interpret life from the negative ego's perspective. That is why so many people are so filled with negative feelings and lack of inner peace. *A Course in Miracles* teaches a very systematic way to undo the negative ego's thinking and begin to think, henceforward, with the Christ mind. The Bible does say, "Let this mind be in you that was in Christ Jesus." Jesus, as we know, was a human being just like you and me who became the embodiment of the Christ by becoming one with the Christ consciousness.

The Christ consciousness is not just for Christians. The Christ consciousness, the Buddha consciousness, the Krishna consciousness, God consciousness — the consciousness of all religions is the same thing. You might have had a lot of negative programming behind your religious upbringing, and it is important here not to get caught up in semantics; all religious or spiritual paths are fine. The new religion of the future is the one that honors and recognizes all religions and all spiritual paths, for they all lead to the same place. The introduction to *A Course in Miracles* states,

> This is a course in miracles. It is a required course. Only the time you take it is voluntary. Free will does not mean that you can establish the curriculum. It means only that you can elect what you want to take at a given time. The course does not aim at teaching the meaning of love, for that is beyond what can be taught. It does aim, however, at removing the blocks to the awareness of love's presence, which is your natural inheritance. The opposite of love is fear, but what is all-encompassing can have no opposite.
>
> This course can therefore be summed up in this way:
>
> Nothing real can be threatened.
> Nothing unreal exists.
>
> Herein lies the peace of God.

A Course in Miracles is for most people a very difficult book to read and understand. One of my main purposes in writing this particular chapter is to take the essence of the Course's teaching and make it easy to understand. I know during my personal spiritual evolution, a chapter explaining and summarizing the Course in simple language would have been very beneficial. I have also expanded on the Course's teachings to make them more universal and applicable to all religions and all spiritual paths. And I have added many of my own ideas so that you can reach a complete understanding of what "Christ consciousness" really means.

A course in miracles is a required course, the introduction says. What this means is not that everyone has to study these books but rather that all must learn to think with their Christ or God mind. The Lord Sai Baba has said that "God equals man minus ego."

You cannot pass your spiritual initiations and realize God without transcending the selfish, separative, fear-based mind of your ego. The curriculum is set, and *A Course in Miracles* is just one way of learning the lessons.

The core of *A Course in Miracles* is that God created you, and your true identity is the Christ. In other words, you are all sons and daughters of God, made in God's image. God is love, so you are love. You don't have to become love; love is what you are. It is only the negative ego programming and conditioning that hides this awareness from you. It is only the mud on the diamond. Even Jesus said, "Everything that I can do, you can do, and more."

The Christian church has misinterpreted the message of Jesus. Sure, Jesus was the son of God, but so are you. Or you could say you are the Buddha, the Hindu Atma, or Eternal Self. In the Old Testament the Jewish prophets said, "Ye are gods and know it not." They also said, "Ye are gods and children of the Most High." David, in the Psalms, said, "Be still and know, I am God."

This is why the introduction to the Course says, "Nothing real can be threatened. Nothing unreal exists. Herein lies the Peace of God." Your true identity as the Christ or Buddha or Atma or Eternal Self cannot be changed. That is how God created you. You can think you are something other than this but that does not change reality. You are the Christ, the Buddha, the Atma, the Eternal Self, whether you believe it or not.

The reason you have no choice is that you didn't create yourself; God created you. The spiritual path is really not about trying to get anyplace. It is just the reawakening to who you are. The second step is the practice of being the true Self in daily life.

Where Did the Negative Ego Come From?

The negative ego did not come from God, it came from humanity's misuse of free choice. Man is the only creature who has the ability to think out of harmony with God. The fall, to which the Bible refers, occurred when humans, in the form of monads, or individualized sparks of God, chose to come into matter. It wasn't the coming into matter that caused the fall; it was the over-identification with matter. It was that moment when they thought they were physical bodies rather than God-beings inhabiting or using physical bodies.

In thinking they were only physical bodies, there came the illusion of separation from God and separation from their brothers and sisters. Then came the perception of selfishness, fear, and death as "real." From these faulty premises a whole thought system developed that was based on glamour, illusion, and maya.

Humanity has spent hundreds of incarnations caught up in this illusion. The amazing thing is that what *A Course in Miracles* teaches is that the fall never really happened. You just think it did. The basic law of the mind is that it is your thoughts that create your reality. Your feelings, your behavior, and what you attract and magnetize into your life all come from your thoughts.

Is the glass of water half empty or half full? Are you optimistic or pessimistic? Do you look at what happens in life as teachings, lessons, challenges and opportunities to grow? Or do you look at things as bummers, problems, aggravations, irritations, and upsets? It is how you think, interpret, and perceive that will determine how you feel in any given situation.

You have always been the Christ, the Buddha, the Atma, the Eternal Self, and you have always been one with God. All of your negative egotistical thinking has not changed this one single bit.

A good metaphor for this is the dream. When you wake up from a nightmare you are relieved that it was just a dream. When you were dreaming, however, it seemed real. Well, I say now, in this holy instant, wake up! Wake up from the negative hypnosis you have been living in, thinking you are unworthy, unlovable, inferior, separate from God, powerless. In this holy instant, wake up and realize that you are the Christ, the Buddha, the Atma, the Eternal Self. You always have been and always will be.

The great saint from India, Ramana Maharshi, said that the spiritual path is like a person who comes to him asking his help in finding a necklace lost for forty years. Ramana Maharshi says, well, what's that you are wearing around your neck? The woman, all of a sudden, realizes that she has been wearing the necklace all along. Well, that is how the spiritual path is. You don't have to find God; you already *are* God and have been all along. It is the insane voice of the ego, or separative mind, that keeps you lost in glamour, illusion and maya.

Sai Baba says, "The mind creates bondage, or the mind creates liberation." A lot of people downplay the mind as though it were not important, but as Sai Baba says, it is the mind and how you manage it that will determine whether you achieve liberation or remain in bondage.

Heaven and Hell are places, but first they are states of mind. When the ego is your guide and teacher, you are in Hell. When soul consciousness is your teacher, you are in Heaven. Buddha, in his four noble truths, said that all suffering comes from wrong points of view.

You can interpret life from the negative ego's viewpoint or from that of the Buddha or the Christ. It is important to understand that you don't see only with your eyes; you see with your mind, through your belief systems.

The major work of the spiritual path is to clear out all the negative egotistical beliefs from the conscious and subconscious minds, and to replace them with the spiritual pattern of the Christ and the Buddha. The rest of this chapter will go into more specific detail on how to do this.

The Authority Problem

The authority problem has to do with the core issue of who is the ultimate authority in life. The Course teaches that the ultimate authority is God, and that it is God that created you. The ego tells you, however, that God doesn't exist because you can't see Him with your physical eyes;

hence, He or She or It is not the ultimate authority. The ego tells you that you are just a physical body, not the Christ living in a physical body.

The absurdity of the ego is quite obvious: God created you, and you created the ego; however, you have been letting the ego be the ultimate authority. It is time to recognize and own your personal power and authority over yourself. It is time to gain mastery over your mind, emotions, physical body, and ego.

It is not God's job to get rid of your ego, it is your job. You created it, so you can get rid of it. God could do it but that would be like giving birth and then doing everything for the child. If you did that, the child would grow up to be completely incapable. Similarly, if God did everything for you, then you would be incapable and there would be no reason to incarnate into this school called Earth life. God doesn't need to learn these lessons — you do. One of the lessons of *A Course in Miracles* is "my salvation is up to me."

God has already given you everything. You have separated yourself from God by listening to the voice of the ego. In reality, you have never been separated; however, in your consciousness, or your perception of reality, you are separate. This situation can be easily remedied just by changing your thoughts. The Bible says, "Be ye transformed by the renewal of your mind" and "As a man thinketh so is he." Lincoln said, "A man is as happy as he makes up his mind to be." I think it was Emerson who said, "A man is what he thinks about all day long."

It is time to wake up and snap out of this self-created hell of your own negative thinking. It is time to take control of the subconscious mind and stop letting it push you around. It is meant to be your servant, not your master.

How is Attitudinal Healing Accomplished?

The process of accomplishing this attitudinal healing is, in actuality, very simple. What I would recommend is this: imagine that you are surrounded by a golden bubble that protects you from the outside world and other people and also protects you from your own subconscious mind. In other words, you can imagine that all of your thoughts, feelings, impulses, desires, and images are outside of your golden bubble; all of what is termed the content of consciousness is outside of the bubble.

The idea, then, is that every time a thought, feeling, or impulse arises from your subconscious mind, you make it stop at the gate of the bubble, almost as if there were a guard there checking its passport. If the thought or feeling or impulse is positive, loving, spiritual, balanced, Christ-like, of God, then you can let it through the bubble and into your mind. If the thought, feeling, impulse, or desire is negative, egotistical, separative, selfish, fear-based, imbalanced, and not of God, then push it out of your mind. *A Course in Miracles* states, "Deny any thought that is not of God to enter your mind."

You must understand that the mind works like the physical body. If you want to be physically healthy you must eat good food. If you eat bad food or spoiled food you will get physically sick. The same thing applies to the mind. If you want to be mentally, emotionally, and spiritually healthy, you must let only positive God-like thoughts into your mind. If you let negative, egotistical thoughts into your mind, you will become mentally, emotionally, or spiritually sick.

It is not God or the ascended masters' job to control your mind; that is your job. One of the most important principles of *A Course in Miracles* is to be "vigilant for God and His kingdom." It is likely that you are not vigilant enough over your mental and emotional diet. You probably live on what I call automatic pilot, not conscious of, aware of, or alert to the thoughts and feelings you allow into your mind from your subconscious mind and from the outside world. You probably do not have enough detachment, spiritual discernment and spiritual discrimination.

When you push a thought out of your mind, it can be likened to a plant that is not being watered. It withers and dies from lack of attention. After pushing the negative thought out of your mind, the idea is to then switch your mind, like a TV set, to the opposite, positive, spiritual, or Christ-like thought, feeling, and image. This is like a new seed that sinks into the soil of the subconscious mind and sprouts.

The law of the mind is that it takes twenty-one days to cement any new habit into the subconscious mind. After twenty-one days it will be automatic to think with your Christ mind. It will not even be difficult. It will be a habit. You might think that habits are always bad. Not necessarily. The idea is to fill the subconscious mind with positive, Christ-like habits and to get rid of the egotistical ones.

Jesus, in the New Testament, applied these principles when he was walking with his disciples and one of his disciples started to complain. Jesus whirled around and exclaimed, "Get thee behind me, Satan!" He was saying no to the ego, which the fundamentalist church refers to as Satan or the Devil.

I cannot emphasize enough the importance of being vigilant. When people in the outside world are negative, the idea is to keep your golden bubble intact and let their energies slide off like water off a duck's back.

You Can Be a Master or a Victim

Spirit guides you to be a master; the ego guides you to be a victim. When you are in your master consciousness you fully recognize that you create your own reality. You create everything. You create your thoughts, feelings, behaviors, physical health – all that you attract and magnetize into your life. This is based on Hermetic law: "As within, so without; as above, so below."

That which you think and image within your conscious and subconscious minds will manifest its mirror likeness in your external circumstances. The outer world is a mirror of your inner world. Remember that you are a cocreator with God, made in His image. God is not a victim and neither are you.

The microcosm is like the macrocosm. As you learn to control your mind, you then learn to control your emotions. Feelings and emotions do not just happen; they are created by how you think.

There are particular beliefs that cause specific emotions. When you learn to think with your Christ mind all of your negative feelings begin to disappear. It is a way of thinking that will bring you inner peace, unconditional love, joy, and happiness all the time.

Nothing outside of yourself causes you to think or feel anything. It is your interpretation, your belief, your perception of the situation that cause you to feel the way you do. For example, in the 1929 stock market crash, one person might have jumped out of the window of a building to commit suicide. Another person who lost a million dollars might have said, "Easy come, easy go."

Two people come to work; the elevator is broken and they have to walk up ten flights of stairs. One person curses and swears. The other says, "Oh great, an opportunity to get some physical exercise."

When you walk down the street you can see other people as just other physical bodies or as brothers and sisters in a much larger spiritual family. You see with your mind, not just with your physical eyes.

Your behavior is also caused by your thoughts and feelings. You never do anything that does not have an antecedent in some thought or feeling in either your conscious or subconscious mind. The idea is to completely clean out the subconscious mind of all negative programming. Later in this book I will dedicate an entire chapter to tools and methods for achieving that.

As you achieve mastery over what Djwhal Khul has called the three lower vehicles (mental, emotional, and physical bodies) and control over your negative ego, you become in tune with the soul and eventually merge with the soul at the third initiation.

The soul merge brings you a Midas touch; everything you do turns to gold because you are in harmony with God's laws. As you continue to evolve, your attunement moves from the soul up to the spirit, or monad. You become fully merged with the monad at the fifth initiation and you ascend at the sixth initiation.

As this mastery is achieved, you become able to program the subconscious mind to attract to you anything you need. The subconscious mind works according to the law of attraction, magnetism, and repulsion. The idea is to consciously program your subconscious mind with only positive, Christlike thoughts which will attract to you only positive things from the outside world. It is probable that you are not fully using the incredible power of your subconscious mind. The reprogramming that will allow you to do so can be achieved through the process of denial and affirmation. The idea is to deny the negative thoughts and to be constantly affirming the positive spiritual thoughts. In the chapter on how to reprogram the subconscious mind I provide all kinds of positive affirmations and visualizations you can work with in order to achieve whatever it is you want to create in your life.

Sickness Is a Defense against the Truth

You cause the sickness or health of your physical body. The subconscious mind runs the physical body. This can be clearly proved through the use of hypnosis. If your true identity is the Christ, then how can you get sick? If God isn't sick, then, in reality, you can't be sick either.

You get sick because of your belief in sickness and your indulgence in negative, egotistical thoughts. Sickness is a defense against the truth because the truth is that you are the Christ and he can't be sick. If you hold this thought, then the subconscious mind, which does whatever you order it to do, will keep you healthy.

This applies to the aging process also. If you didn't believe you had to age, you wouldn't. Ascended masters prove this; they can live in the same physical body indefinitely. Saint Germain did it for three hundred and fifty years in Europe. Thoth did it for two thousand years in Atlantis and Egypt. Physical immortality is totally achievable because, remember, you are God.

It is still important to eat well, exercise, and follow God's physical laws until you reach that ascended state of consciousness at the sixth initiation. Many younger souls try to defy God's physical laws at a stage in their spiritual evolution when they are not yet able to walk on water. They will get to this point; however, until they do, it is wise to respect God's laws on the physical, emotional, mental, and spiritual levels in a balanced fashion.

The spiritual path is a process. It does not happen in one instant. In one holy instant you can fully realize that you are the Christ and that you are God; however, this illumination must be demonstrated and grounded on the Earthly plane, and shared with others.

The spiritual path does not go straight up to God. It is, rather, a process of attuning upward and then bringing that consciousness downward, back to Earth. God's divine plan is to create Heaven on Earth. You are here as a bridge between spirit and matter. You are here to spiritualize the material plane.

The Holy Encounter

The holy encounter is an exquisite idea presented in *A Course in Miracles*. It is the understanding that every time you meet another person in the world, it is a holy encounter. Each encounter with another person is, in reality, Christ meeting Christ, God meeting God. Every person you meet, whether you know him or not, is God visiting you in physical form.

This concept applies to animals, plants, and minerals, also. There is only one Being in the infinite universe, and that is God. God has incarnated into infinite numbers of forms. He has incarnated as you and as me, as the animals, plants, and minerals, as everything. Everything has a soul.

Sai Baba has said that the fastest way to realize God is to see Him in everything and everyone, to see Him in your brother and sister because He *is* your brother and sister. This can be clearly demonstrated by the language. When you speak, you often say, "I feel this way," or, "I am going to the market." Have you ever thought about what the "I" is? The "I" is the God-self or the Christ or the Buddha or the Atma or the Eternal Self. No matter what words you speak in any given sentence, the "I" is the same for everybody. The "I" underlies the mental, emotional, and physical vehicles. God is incarnated as the Eternal I in everything and everyone.

When you see a person on the street as just a stranger, you are seeing him or her through the negative ego's eyes. The truth is, whether you believe it or not, that he is the Christ. If you don't see him that way, you are removing the possibility of finding God for yourself.

You are not just doing that person a service by seeing him in his true form, you are doing yourself the greatest service, for the world is a mirror of your own state of consciousness. By seeing your brothers as strangers you have lost contact with God in yourself.

The Lord Maitreya has called this having right human relations. Jesus Christ said the whole law could be summed up in this statement: "Love the Lord thy God with all thy heart and soul and mind and might, and love thy neighbor as thyself." I would go so far as to say your neighbor *is* yourself. For God has only one son, and everyone is part of that one sonship. All share the same "I." How you see your brothers and sisters is literally how you are treating God and yourself.

Imagine that you are walking down the street and suddenly, there before you, is your favorite spiritual master. It could be Jesus Christ, Sai Baba, Djwhal Khul, the Lord Maitreya, Saint Germain, Kuthumi, El Morya, the Virgin Mary, Moses, the Buddha, Quan Yin, whoever. Now consider how you would treat that master as you approach him on the street, walking toward him. Well, if you treat every person you meet in your life, be they beggars, grocery clerks, gas station attendants, mothers-in-law, husbands or wives, any differently, you are missing the mark. There is absolutely no difference between these masters and so-called ordinary people.

Jesus made this point when he said, "Everything I can do, you can do, and more." Our identity is exactly the same. The only difference is that the masters are doing a little better than you are at demonstrating it. But you must never give up, for as the great Paramahansa Yogananda said, "A saint is a sinner that never gave up." The ascended masters had to battle through exactly the same lessons you are struggling with now. *A Course in Miracles* calls this type of perception "innocent perception."

The Outcome is Inevitable

It is inevitable that all of God's sons and daughters will eventually return home. Can God and the Christ lose against illusion and maya? If ever you get discouraged, ask yourself this: Can God and the Christ lose this battle? It is impossible!

You must never forget that the ego doesn't really even exist. It is ridiculous to get angry at it, for in reality it is not even there. It is nothing more than a bad dream, from which you can awaken at any time you choose to do so. "Nothing real can be threatened. Nothing unreal exists. Herein lies the peace of God."

The outcome for all souls in this journey is to return back to the Godhead. It is just a matter of time. Even Hitler will eventually return home. He will have to balance his karma first, but he will return home also. The purpose of *A Course in Miracles* and the purpose of my book is to shorten the time needed.

You are living in a period of history in which what formerly took fourteen years can be done in fourteen months. Never in the history of this planet has there been a greater opportunity for spiritual growth. The key is to commit yourself to your spiritual path 100%, with all your personal power and concentration. The transformation that will take place will be amazing. Why delay until a future incarnation that which you can do now?

Sins versus Mistakes

There are no such things as sins, only mistakes. The true definition of sin is "missing the mark." You should understand that mistakes are positive, not negative. You shouldn't go out of your way to make them, but when they happen, you learn from them. When you make a mistake, you can stop and gain the golden nugget of wisdom, learn the lesson, forgive yourself and go forward. On the spiritual path you can move three steps down for every four steps you go up; that is the normal way to grow.

Some religions look at sin as a stain on your character, or they attribute to you some kind of original sin. This is ludicrous. You have no sin, for each of you is the Christ, the Eternal Self.

All mistakes are forgiven. *A Course in Miracles* states that "Forgiveness is the key to happiness." God has already forgiven everything. You need to learn to forgive yourself and your brothers and sisters. It is important remember that no one has ever done anything to you; you have allowed it all to be done to you, and if it happened, you attracted it or needed it for soul growth.

Unconditional Love versus Conditional Love

God would have you always practice unconditional love. The rationale for this is that each person, in reality, is the Christ even if his thoughts, feelings, and behavior are not demonstrating that. Jesus said, in the New Testament, "Love your enemies." This is one of the true tests and initiations of the spiritual path. It is your lesson to learn to be bigger than others, to practice innocent perception, and to practice forgiveness, for what you give is what you get back. If you want God, you must give God, otherwise you will not realize Him.

Everyone is God; however, everyone is not realizing God in his or her thoughts, feelings, and actions. Earth is a school to practice realizing God in daily life. Much of the spiritual path consists of the small things such as how you treat your neighbors. Conditional love places some condition on those people that they must meet to deserve your love. Ego tells you that you are hurting them and helping yourself by doing this. In reality, you are hurting both the others and yourself.

One of the basic principles of *A Course in Miracles* is the giving up of attack thoughts. You are either loving or attacking; there are no neutral thoughts. When you are demonstrating conditional love, you are unconsciously attacking, and the other person, on an energetic level, is experiencing that attack. It is like an arrow that is piercing his aura. If he is weak or acting like a victim, it can affect him quite adversely, for you must remember that all minds are joined. Your thoughts are not contained in your physical body as though behind a fence. In reality, it is quite the opposite. The second you think about another person, whether in a positive or negative way, that thought or feeling hits his energy field.

Conditional love also separates you from God. You are not separated in reality. You are separated only within your own state of consciousness. In every situation of life there is an appropriate response and an inappropriate response. How you respond determines whether you will realize God or not realize God in that moment. If you make a mistake, you can stop, gain the golden nugget of wisdom, learn the lesson, forgive, and choose once again.

By staying vigilant and focused, over time you will begin to develop a habit of being unconditionally loving. In every situation of life you can ask yourself, "Do I want God or my ego in this situation?" If you sincerely ask yourself this, you will find it impossible to choose the ego. Practice makes perfect!

Top Dog/Underdog versus Equality

The ego will tell you that you are superior to everyone else or that you are inferior to everyone else or both. This is truly a hellish state of mind to exist in and it is amazing how many people are unconsciously trapped in the ego's game. Spirit says that you are all equals because you all are the Christ, in truth. People may be at different levels of demonstrating this truth; however, the "I" in you is the same as the "I" in me.

Whenever you find yourself comparing yourself with any other person, the ego is gripping you. You need never compare yourself with other people; you need only compare yourself with yourself. If you look at the progress you have made within yourself only, it is easy to feel good about yourself.

Whenever the top dog or underdog dynamic comes up, you can do what Fritz Perls, who coined these terms, said to do: "Laugh it off the stage." The Course calls this owning your grandeur, but not your grandiosity.

The Meaning of the Crucifixion

In the text of *A Course in Miracles* Jesus gives a fascinating account of the true meaning of the crucifixion. What he says is that the crucifixion was nothing more than an extreme lesson of love and forgiveness. He was not dying for your sins because you do not have any sins.

What he was demonstrating was that even in the most extreme lessons, in which a person is being whipped, beaten, tortured, and crucified, it is possible to remain loving and forgiving. "Forgive them, Father, they know not what they do," he said. He went through this most extreme challenge to prove to humanity that forgiveness is possible even under the most extreme circumstances. If Jesus, the Christ, could do it under those circumstances, then certainly you can forgive a mother-in-law, boss, parent, friend, or business partner.

Love-Finder or Fault-Finder

Spirit would have you see the positive, the good, and the innocent in people. Ego as guide and teacher has you seek and see the negative. The ego does this to put other persons down in order to make itself feel good.

Spirit's philosophy is a win/win philosophy, not a win/lose philosophy. Why can't everyone win? Isn't that a better way to live?

You will see what you look for; you will see what you put your attention upon. When you see fault and judgment, you are, in reality, faulting and judging yourself, for what you see in another is just a mirror of your own state of mind. When you see God and love and blessings, that is what you give to yourself. Whether you see it or not, that is what is there, for that is what God created.

Faulty perception doesn't create truth; it just creates the reality you will live in. You can see the glory of what God would have you see. If you see fault, then you are creating separation from yourself, God, and your brothers and sisters. Spirit would guide you to remain in a state of oneness at all times, for all is God.

In the New Testament Jesus said, "Judge not, that ye be not judged"; "He that hath no sin, cast the first stone"; "Don't try to take the speck out of your brother's eye when you have a log in your own eye." The log that Jesus speaks of is the log of ego and the lower self.

Perception versus Knowledge

All forms of perception, according to *A Course in Miracles,* are a type of dream. God would guide us, however, to live and experience the happy dream of the Christ consciousness which is a perfect mirror of that state which Jesus calls knowledge. By living the Christ dream or perception, Jesus says, there is a translation into pure knowledge that will inevitably take place.

Atonement

Atonement, or at-one-ment, is the process of undoing the ego's grip and returning to the at-one-ment of spirit. The Holy Spirit and/or soul serves as your guide, along with the ascended masters.

Teachings and Lessons versus Bummers and Problems

It is important to realize that everything that happens in life is a teaching, lesson, challenge, and opportunity to grow. Edgar Cayce referred to this when he said that everything that happens is a stepping stone for soul growth.

Paul Solomon, who channels the Universal Mind, has said that the proper attitude toward everything that happens in life is "Not my will, but thine. Thank you for the lesson." Everything that happens in life is a gift. It wouldn't be coming to you if you didn't have something to learn. Everything that comes to you is your own personal karma and is something that you have set in motion either in this lifetime or in a past lifetime. Your lesson is to welcome it, own your personal power, and deal with it appropriately.

Personal Power versus Powerlessness

A spiritual master and God-realized being remains in a state of personal power all the time. Maybe you own your power only in an emergency or when you have to go to work. If you don't own your power, it becomes projected. You give it to other people or to your subconscious mind.

In my opinion there are two keys to psychological health. One is to own your personal power and the second is to have self-love. If you don't own your power you can be run by almost anything in the universe. This includes discarnate spirits, other people, weather, biorhythms, the Dark Brotherhood, your ego, thoughts, feelings, desires, impulses, the physical body, past-life karma, and mass consciousness.

It is clear that there is danger in not owning your personal power. Edgar Cayce has said that your will or power is the strongest force in this universe. You have heard the saying, "An idle mind is the devil's workshop." Most people have consciousness but don't have personal power. The extended use of personal power is self-discipline which a lot of people don't have, either. You will never progress on the spiritual path without personal power and self-discipline.

Power is an attitude or state of mind that you need to cultivate every morning to start the day. Part of owning your power is being decisive in whatever you do, even if you make the wrong decision. At least then you are not stuck in indecision. As the old saying goes, "Fish or cut bait."

Cayce occasionally referred to personal power as positive anger. Anger is ego; however, there is enormous power in anger which can be channeled into positive anger, or positive personal power. Earth is a difficult school, and it is necessary to be very tough in life or you can easily become overwhelmed. You must be a spiritual warrior. The best attitude to have in life is one of tough love.

In the *Bhagavad-Gita*, which is the story of Krishna (the Lord Maitreya), Arjuna, Krishna's disciple, is on the battlefield about to fight the evil enemy's army when he completely loses his balance psychologically and falls into his ego. Arjuna is the head of the righteous army and they are all depending on him.

Krishna, Arjuna's charioteer and spiritual master, begins to lecture Arjuna on the folly of his ways in giving into his ego, thereby losing his power and control over his energies. Krishna is guiding Arjuna into the spiritual mysteries, much as I am attempting to do in this book, when he says, after his long speech to Arjuna, "Get up now, and give up your unmanliness. Get up and fight. This self-pity and self-indulgence are unbecoming of the great soul that you are." This is my favorite statement in the *Bhagavad-Gita*.

Arjuna is awakened by Krishna's spiritual discourse, including this statement, and he reclaims his personal power, leading his men to victory in the battle. Krishna's statement applies to each and every one of you in your daily life.

To Have All, Give All to All

To have all, give all to all, is a message of *A Course in Miracles*, for what you have is, in reality, what you give. What you are holding back from your brothers is what you are holding back from God and from yourself. To have all you must give all, for, in reality, you already have and already are everything. You always have and always will. It is only your belief in the ego as your guide and teacher that has made you believe otherwise.

There Are Only Two Emotions

The Course teaches that there are only two emotions — love and fear. All other emotions return to this basic core. Fear is of the ego, and love is of the spirit. When you indulge in attack thoughts it causes you, by the law of karma operating within your own mind, to live in fear. If you attack, you will be fearful because you will expect other people to attack you, which will cause you to be afraid. If you live in love, then by the law of karma you will expect love in return.

The Course teaches that an attack is a call for love. You need to see beyond or through the attack to the fact that the person who is attacking is really living in fear. Fear is an indicator of lack of love, lack of self-love, lack of allowing in the experience God's love. As the Bible says, "Perfect love casteth out fear."

The Past and Future versus the Eternal Now

One of the profound realizations I had when studying *A Course in Miracles* was understanding what the past and the future really are. Think about the past. What is it? It is a memory. What is a memory? A memory is an image in the mind. What is an image? An image is a thought. So what this means is that the past is totally under your control, for it is nothing more than images, or thoughts, in your mind.

The same applies to the future. The future is nothing more than thoughts and images in your mind. They are of a positive or negative nature, which determines whether you are worried or excited about the future. This means that your future is totally under your control.

All that really exists is the now. You do not have to be victimized by the past or by a worrisome future because it is all within your own mind.

The proper attitude toward the past is to take the golden nuggets of wisdom from the mistakes and from what you have done well and then bring forth the positive memories you choose to keep and release the rest.

In terms of the future, the proper perspective is to plan for the future in a creative way that serves you and then leave the rest to God. Edgar Cayce said, "Why worry when you can pray?" I would add to this by saying, "Why worry when you can pray, own your personal power, and do affirmations and visualizations to attract everything you need?"

In this holy instant, I am the Christ, and you are the Christ. We are one with each other and we are one with God. The fall never really happened, you just thought it did. You have and are everything, for you are God. The prodigal son and daughter have returned home, for God never took anything away. You are and always have been as God created you — a perfect Christ. He has just been waiting for you to reclaim your inheritance, which has always been yours.

The Two Most Important Relationships

The two most important relationships in your life are your relationship to self and your relationship to God. In actuality, your relationship to self is even more important than your relationship to God, for if you are "wrong" with yourself and allow yourself to be run by your ego, then you will project this wrong relationship to self onto everything in your life, including your relationship to God.

This is the cause of the angry Old Testament God. It is also the cause of concepts like original sin, the idea that you are a lowly, sinful worm, and the judgmental nature and self-righteousness of the fundamentalist religions.

This projection has also occurred in the Islamic religions to a certain extent. It is what happens when the ego is allowed to interpret scripture. It is like the game of telephone, played for two thousand years. The masters like Jesus, Mohammed, and Moses said one thing and the disciples, who were not at their level, completely distorted what they had actually said. There is no judgment in this, it is just a simple statement of fact.

Attachment versus Preference

The ego is drawn to attachment but, as Buddha said, "All suffering comes from our attachments." What he is saying is that if you give up all your attachments, you no longer have to experience suffering at all. It isn't the outside thing that causes the suffering, it is your attachment and addiction to outside things that causes your suffering.

Spirit guides you to have preferences rather than attachments. An attachment is an attitude that causes you to get depressed or angry or upset if your expectations aren't met. A preference is an attitude that lets you be happy either way. You might prefer to go to the movies but if that doesn't work out, you can still be happy at home. This is a profound concept. If you were to release all your attachments, you would find instantaneous peace of mind.

Some spiritual people believe that they are not allowed even to have preferences. I would say that this is a faulty belief on their part. It is very important in life to have your preferences and to go after them with all your heart and soul and mind and might. However, if they don't come about, it is important to be prepared to be happy anyway. That way, happiness becomes a state of mind rather than a condition outside of self.

The happiness that so many of you are seeking lies in a certain perspective toward life. You are born with it but the negative ego's programming blocks the awareness of your natural state, which is joy.

The Transcendence of Duality

One of the basic teachings of all Eastern religions is the transcendence of duality. Duality could be another word for ego. The ideal is to learn to be even-minded and in a state of equanimity all the time, regardless of the ups and downs of life.

The ideal is to maintain this even-mindedness regardless of profit or loss, pleasure or pain, sickness or health, victory or defeat, praise or criticism, good weather or bad weather. It is okay to have a preference, but if it doesn't happen your baseline can be joy and inner peace.

The Job Initiation

The Job initiation is a test all seekers go through at some point in their spiritual journeys. It is really the ultimate test of your spiritual faith and righteousness in God.

Job was a righteous man of God who had a family and children, a big ranch, and material wealth. One day Satan came to God and said, "Sure, Job is a righteous man. You have given him everything. Take away his wealth and let's see if he remains so righteous." God said, "I have confidence in Job. Take away his wealth." Satan did so and to Satan's consternation, Job remained righteous.

Then Satan sheepishly came back to God and said, "I am impressed! However, let's take away his wife and children and see if he remains so righteous." God said, "So be it." Job's wife left him, took the kids, and got a divorce. Amazingly enough, Job remained righteous. Satan was really shocked now. He returned to God and said, "Let me try one more test, and if he passes this, I give up, and I will declare you were right all along."

Satan said, "For this final test let me take away his physical health."

God said, "Okay, you can take away his physical health, but you can't kill him." Satan agreed and Job's health was taken away. He had terrible boils and was tired. He didn't feel well at all. This was the straw that broke the camel's back. Job completely lost his righteousness. He became angry and bitter and depressed. His friends tried to cheer him up but he would have nothing of it. Job's attitude was that he was a righteous man of God and a good person, and look at the trials and tribulations he was going through. This state of affairs lasted for a number of years.

Finally one day, in a quiet moment, a whirlwind of Light came to Job and entered his crown chakra. God spoke to Job. God shared with Job that this had all been a test of character, virtue and righteousness in God. He explained that anyone can believe and worship God when things are going well, but how about when things are not going well and all outer supports have been stripped away?

Job heard the truth of what God was saying, just as Arjuna had been awakened by Krishna. Job made one of the most moving statements in the entire Bible then:

> Naked I came from my mother's womb,
> Naked shall I leave.
> The Lord giveth and the Lord taketh away,
> Blessed be the name of the Lord!

Job had regained his righteousness. His health returned. His wife and children returned. His wealth returned by one-hundredfold. Job went on to say, "Even if I should die, I will remain righteous in the Lord."

I think the meaning of this story is obvious. I would venture to guess that a good many people reading this book have gone through some form of the Job initiation. Never forget that what happens to you in life is a spiritual test of your character and your righteousness in the Lord.

Look at what Jesus went through. No matter what your situation, you can challenge yourself to keep your faith and righteousness, whether those challenges be in terms of health, finances, death, relationships, or mental or emotional problems. You can hold on to your personal power and your ideals and your faith, for did not Jesus say, "Be ye faithful unto death and I will give thee a crown of life."

Optimism versus Pessimism

The spiritual attitude toward life is to remain optimistic at all times. If you have a good attitude you can be put in the worst situation and you might be bummed out for a little while, but you are going to become happy again. On the other side of the coin, if you have a bad attitude, you can be put in the best situation possible and you will be happy for a little while, but then you will feel bummed out again.

Part of the purpose of life is to spread joy and happiness. Sickness can be contagious if you feel like a victim and have low resistance. Since so many people live in a victim consciousness, why not lift them into joy and happiness? The purpose of life is to spread this joy, happiness, love, goodwill, and blessings everywhere you go, so that when you leave this place the world will be better for your having been here.

The Ego's Purpose versus the Spirit's Purpose

The ego's purpose in life is basically hedonistic — pleasure-seeking, gratification of carnal desires, power in a top-dog sense, material wealth, and control over others rather than control over self. The spirit's answer is this Biblical statement: "What is a man profited, if he shall gain the whole world, and lose his own soul?" (Mt 16:26)

The spiritual purpose of life is to achieve liberation from the wheel of rebirth, to realize God, to become an ascended master, to be of service to humankind. Did not Jesus say, "The greatest among you is the servant of all." The spiritual purpose in life is also to be happy and to enjoy yourself, in a way that is balanced with spiritual growth.

A Course in Miracles states that true pleasure is serving God. I know that this is true for me. As long as I am serving God, I am happy. To me, everything is serving God, as long as whatever I do is done with that intent.

Poverty Consciousness versus Prosperity Consciousness

The ego's interpretation of life is that of lack, that there is never enough. The ego teaches that money is the root of all evil or that it is the answer to all problems. The ego is quite hateful by nature, and it sends a message of total lack of self-worth, guilt, and undeservingness of prosperity. The spirit sees the universe as abundant, with plenty for everybody and no need for negative competition.

The spirit's attitude is that you can be the richest person in the world and lead a most spiritual life simultaneously. Money, in and of itself, is divine. It is how you use it that determines whether it is good or bad. The spirit guides you to love money and to make as much as possible so that it can be used to make physical changes in the Earthly world for spiritual purposes.

The more money you have, the more you can give to charities, or use to start spiritual centers and institutions. If you have prosperity consciousness you know you can make money, get a job, manifest a business, or create opportunities whenever they are needed. There are many people in this world who are millionaires but have a total poverty consciousness, and they will probably eventually lose the prosperity they have because of it.

Who is more prosperous, a woman living in the ghetto with seven children who has total faith in God to provide her with everything she truly needs or a multimillionaire who is stingy and worries about money, constantly backstabbing clients and competitors? Millionaires who have prosperity consciousness might talk about losing all their wealth but without worrying, because they know that they can earn it all back again.

You are prosperous when you truly know that God, your personal power, and the power of your subconscious mind are your true stocks and bonds and financial security. You can find a job or make money even during a recession when God, the creator of the infinite universe, is helping you and when you, with your full personal power and the power of your subconscious mind, are helping yourself.

Can God and the Christ, who you are, not win every battle? As the Bible says, "If God be for you, who [or what] can be against you?"; "I can do all things with God and Christ who strengthen me." With this power and faith you can manifest whatever it is you need. You are prosperous because your power is in God and in the application of God's laws for your own benefit.

Death versus Eternal Life

The ego believes in death because the ego believes you are your physical body rather than the soul which is inhabiting the physical body. The ego is right about one thing, and that is that the physical body will die. The only problem is, you are not that physical body. You are the Christ and the Eternal Self living in the physical body.

The physical body is your temple and the instrument through which you communicate on this Earthly plane. When you are finished with it, you will immediately translate into another dimension of reality. What dimension you translate to will be determined by how much soul growth you have achieved in this lifetime. Death is an illusion, as everything the ego says is an illusion.

Anger and Depression versus Peace of Mind

The feeling of anger stems from the ego's interpretation of life and is usually caused by one of four attitudes. The first faulty attitude that causes anger and depression is attachment and addiction. When your attachments aren't met, it causes upset and anger. Secondly, anger and depression are caused by not seeing that what is happening is a lesson, a gift, a spiritual test. Thirdly, if you don't have your bubble of protection up, you are allowing yourself to be victimized by another person's negative energy. The fourth cause of anger and depression is based on a definition of anger I learned from Paul Solomon. He defined anger as a loss of control and an attempt to retain it. Whenever you lose your personal power, mastery, and control over yourself and fall into what I call an underdog, or victimized, state of consciousness because of listening to the voice of your ego, then the ego will flip from playing the underdog back into playing the top dog (or anger) to get back in control. This kind of anger is really a loss of control that lets you feel as though you are getting back in control.

There is a lot of power in anger and ideally this angry energy, instead of being blocked, is channeled into personal power and beneficial activities. When this is done properly, it is called positive anger.

Depression is the state of consciousness of just giving up. Whenever you give up in life you get depressed. Of all the negative attitudes of the ego, giving up is probably the worst and most dangerous. If you give in to this evil game of the ego, all the defenses of the conscious mind against the ego are laid down and the ego is able to gain total control.

The most important thing in life is never to give up. As the I Ching constantly says, "Perseverance furthers success." You must have spiritual tenacity and what Cayce called "long-suffering," if need be.

There is no need to suffer in life; however, if you do find that you are suffering, you can just keep praying and affirming and visualizing what you want. Keep powering it out and seeking an answer. For doesn't the Bible say, "Seek and ye shall find. Knock and the door shall be opened." God helps those who help themselves. God will do His part, but you must do your part. Together, God, your personal power, and the power of the subconscious mind are an unbeatable team.

Gratitude versus Taking Life for Granted

The ego's attitude is one of taking people and life for granted. The spiritual attitude is one of constant gratefulness and thanksgiving, humbleness and humility. It can be summed up in the Biblical statement, "By the grace of God go I."

The Bible also says, "After pride cometh the fall." There is so much to be grateful for every day. All you have to do is watch the news to see all the terrible things that are going on around the world and to feel how incredibly blessed you are.

If you have handicaps and limitations for the moment, the best spiritual attitude is to focus on what you can do instead of what you can't do. I have always been moved by Saint Francis who was the ascended master Kuthumi in a past life. He apparently faced terrible health problems he had to live with his whole life, and yet he became one of the most revered Christian saints.

Mother Teresa has terrible heart problems and yet she spends her life in service, helping others. Everyone on the planet has a weak spot. For some it is physical, for some emotional, for some mental, spiritual, environmental, or financial. You are here to try valiantly to overcome those dragons and be grateful for the grace God has bestowed upon you. Remember, even the bad things that happen are really gifts and spiritual tests, blessings in disguise.

God never gives you more than you can handle. You can change your attitude and welcome your lessons and challenges with a smile and with strength. When a challenge comes, you can make yourself bigger than it is instead of allowing yourself to be overwhelmed by it. Thank God for the lesson and pray for His help in learning it.

Feeling Rejected versus Acceptance

The ego would have you interpret the end of a friendship or relationship as one person winning and one person losing; hence, there is a rejecter and a rejectee. This is not the spiritual interpretation. There are no winners and losers, only winners. If a relationship ends, the spiritual attitude is that it is just not meant to be any longer; then you can both leave as winners. I'm okay and you're okay, in forgiveness and unconditional love.

Guilt versus Innocence

The ego tries to make you feel guilty for your mistakes, or sins, as it tries to call them. The spiritual attitude is that you are instantly forgiven. There is no need to hold the past against yourself in punishment. There is no need to punish yourself. The idea is to recognize that you have made a mistake and to learn from it. The spiritual attitude states that you are always innocent. The Course suggests that when you make a mistake of some consequence, you should pray to the Holy Spirit and/or your soul or God to undo the consequences and results of that mistake. The Holy Spirit will be happy to do this for you, and then you don't have to worry about it.

Personal Surrender versus Personal Power and Surrender Simultaneously

The ego's attitude is either to own the power and control and never surrender to God, or to surrender to God totally, avoiding all responsibility and owning of power. The spiritual attitude is to own your power and to surrender simultaneously. It is imperative to own your power, otherwise you will be overwhelmed by the subconscious mind. It is also essential to surrender to God and the soul, or monad, as your teacher.

In doing both simultaneously, the three minds begin to function as one mind in perfect integration, balance, and harmony.

Ego Sensitivity versus a Centered Spiritual Attitude

Ego sensitivity is that tendency to feel hurt, rejected, put down, or inferior at times when there is no discernible reason to be feeling that way. It occurs because of a lack of personal power and self-love, the absence of a bubble of protection, or not having right relationship with self and right relationship with God.

When you are run by your ego, there is a tendency to project onto others motives that are not, in reality, there. A good example of this can be seen in the life of Jesus Christ. All he did was love and heal people, yet many wanted to crucify him. Their egos interpreted Jesus as attacking them when, in reality, that was not the case, as he was the embodiment of love. Because they interpreted attack, their victim consciousness caused them to feel put down or defensive and they attacked back.

You know people like this who get defensive or hurt even when you have not attacked them. Such a person needs to be treated with extra love and tact until his self-concept can be rebuilt into a sturdier form.

It is important to realize that when you are centered you can't be hurt because you let any attack slide off your bubble. You respond instead of reacting. You are more detached. You don't let other people cause your emotions. You don't take mental or emotional poison into your system just as you don't take physical poison into your body.

You still might communicate your feelings but you do it as an observation and as a preference rather than feeling victimized and lashing back in attack. You don't want to let other people be the computer programmers of your emotions; you want to program your own emotions.

No one can make you think, feel, or behave in any way you choose not to. You are not an effect, you are a cause. You are not a victim, you are a master and a cocreator with God. You can simply decide to feel good, and since your thoughts create your feelings, you immediately feel good.

Since it is your thoughts that create your reality, why would you want to create anything but joy, happiness, unconditional love, and inner peace? When you think with your Christ mind rather than your ego mind, that is exactly what happens.

Security versus Insecurity

The ego creates insecurity because it teaches you to find your security outside of self in people, possessions, houses, money, family, and so on, whereas the only true security, the only security that cannot be taken away from you, is security that is grounded in your personal power, God, the power of your subconscious mind, and God's laws.

Loneliness versus Being Alone

The ego causes you to feel loneliness because it has you seek your wholeness in another person instead of finding it first within yourself and in your relationship to God. You are never really lonely when you are in your spiritual attitude because you are whole within self and one with God.

This is also when you are in proper relationship to your inner child. Under these circumstances the inner child is given the proper ratio of firmness and love. The inner child, hence, feels loved and protected. Loneliness is a sign you have fallen into the underdog, or inferior, state of consciousness and are seeking to fill this space with another person instead of with self and God, which is what is really needed.

The same thing is true of the feeling of abandonment. If you are whole within self and one with God, and the inner child has been taken care of before you have bonded with another person, then the feeling of abandonment won't occur when the person leaves.

Jealousy occurs when you bond out of a feeling of lack of wholeness and right relationship to self and God, and then compete with a known or unknown competitor. The spiritual attitude is to state your preferences in your relationships and surrender them to God. If the relationship is meant to be, it will happen; if it does not happen, it was not meant to be.

Additionally, when you bond with another person from the state of consciousness of being right with self and right with God, issues of cheating, infidelity, and commitment cannot arise in the same way because of the integrity of the individuals involved. If they do arise, and if one partner is not experiencing the sanctity of the bond, it probably means you are not meant to be together.

A Course in Miracles

A Course in Miracles is made up of a workbook, a teacher's manual, and a textbook. The workbook has one lesson a day every day for an entire year. The idea is to do only one lesson a day. You can go slower but not faster with these lessons. The beginning lessons are designed to break down the old negative ego belief system, and the later lessons are designed to build in the Christ pattern of consciousness. I recommend starting the lessons and reading the teacher's manual, which is very easy to read, whereas the textbook is rather difficult. Most people, I find, don't have the patience or fortitude to get through it. However, it is well worth reading. If you do get bogged down you can just focus on the lessons and they will provide a very good theoretical base. Reading the lessons first will actually make reading the text a lot easier.

Other Suggestions

There is more to be learned about egotistical versus spiritual thinking. I have several suggestions. The first is to read Gerald Jampolsky's books. He has written some easy-to-understand books about the teachings of *A Course in Miracles*: *Love is Letting Go of Fear*, *Teach Only Love*, and *Say Good-bye to Guilt*.

Also, Marianne Williamson has written two books and made many very good tapes about *A Course in Miracles* and I recommend them.

I do not consider myself an orthodox "Course in Miracles person" because I am involved with so many practices. Also, I attempt to bring it into more of a psychological context than a spiritual one. There are many people who are now involved with *A Course in Miracles*, and each teacher organizes and presents the material in a different way. In some areas I try to integrate the Course rather than identify with it. *A Course in Miracles* is like the light at the end of the tunnel, but 98% of the people on the planet are not yet at the end of the tunnel in their evolution, so I feel a little bridging help is needed, and that is what I have attempted to do in this chapter.

On the following page is a chart I have created called the Psychological Centering Model. In the center of the chart is what I call the centered spiritual self. Radiating out from the spiritual self, like the rays of the sun, are the Christ or spiritual or Buddhic qualities.

Above the centered spiritual self are the top-dog, superiority qualities of the ego. Below the spiritual self are the underdog, inferiority, egotistical qualities. This is a helpful model to meditate upon and refer to in daily life.

On the subsequent pages is an in-depth list of spiritual attitudes and qualities counterposed to negative egotistical attitudes and qualities. This list is also useful to refer to when your ego has been triggered.

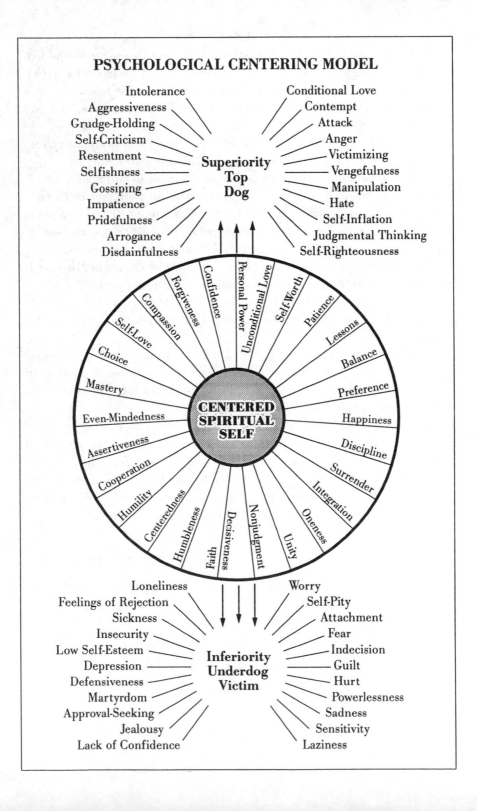

PSYCHOLOGICAL CENTERING MODEL

Superiority Top Dog

Intolerance
Aggressiveness
Grudge-Holding
Self-Criticism
Resentment
Selfishness
Gossiping
Impatience
Pridefulness
Arrogance
Disdainfulness

Conditional Love
Contempt
Attack
Anger
Victimizing
Vengefulness
Manipulation
Hate
Self-Inflation
Judgmental Thinking
Self-Righteousness

CENTERED SPIRITUAL SELF

Forgiveness
Confidence
Personal Power
Unconditional Love
Self-Worth
Compassion
Self-Love
Patience
Choice
Lessons
Mastery
Balance
Even-Mindedness
Preference
Assertiveness
Happiness
Cooperation
Discipline
Humility
Surrender
Centeredness
Integration
Humbleness
Oneness
Faith
Unity
Decisiveness
Nonjudgment

Inferiority Underdog Victim

Loneliness
Feelings of Rejection
Sickness
Insecurity
Low Self-Esteem
Depression
Defensiveness
Martyrdom
Approval-Seeking
Jealousy
Lack of Confidence

Worry
Self-Pity
Attachment
Fear
Indecision
Guilt
Hurt
Powerlessness
Sadness
Sensitivity
Laziness

Ego's Attitude	Spirit's Attitude
Attack, Fear	Love!
Selfishness	Selfish-selfless balance
Grudge-holding	Forgiveness
Top dog/Underdog	Equality
Competition	Cooperation
Judgment	Spiritual discernment
Guilt	Innocence
Self-righteousness	Detached personal opinions
Fights universe	Accepts challenges
Bummers, problems	Lessons, challenges
Pessimism	Optimism
Insecurity, self-doubt	Self-confidence
Powerlessness, lack of control	Personal power, self-mastery
Anger, depression	Lessons, emotional invulnerability
Defensiveness, hurt	Love
Neediness, dependency	Preference, want
Victim; effect	Master; cause, chooser, creator
Feels self-pity	Takes responsibility
War	School
Learns by karma, school of hard knocks	Grows by state of grace the easy way!
Subconscious control	Conscious control
Impatience	Patience
Suffering	Joy and happiness
Reactive	Responsive
Vulnerability	Invulnerability
Sin	Mistakes
Attachment	Involved detachment
Laziness/Procrastination	Discipline
Jealousy	Whole and complete, non-attached
Law of the jungle	What you sow, you reap
Demanding	Requesting
Moodiness/bad moods	Good mood all the time
Self-punishment	Self love and forgiveness
Mistakes/negative	Mistakes/positive
Lampshade over light	Light!
Ego sensitivity	Unchanging self-worth
Must prove self to obtain worth	Worth/spiritual inheritance
Mud on diamond	Diamond!
Giving is losing	Giving is winning
Stealing is gaining	Stealing is losing
Rejection	Remaining centered/whole; knowing it was not meant to be
Self-centered	One team
Intimidation	Uses power appropriately
Automatic pilot	Consciously creates life
Overindulgence & under-indulgence	Balance, integration, moderation
Run by past thoughts & future fears	Now/present-centered
Loneliness	Finds wholeness in self
Stranger	Brothers and sisters
Embarrassment	No judgment
Selflessness (martyrdom)	Selfish-selfless balance

Ego's Attitude	Spirit's Attitude
Gossips	Remains quiet if judging
Seeks approval or control	States preference and accepts
Worry about others' opinions	Inner-directedness, non-conformism
Worry, anxiety	Faith, trust in self, higher power and laws of universe
Indecisiveness	Decisiveness
Envy	Joy in another's abundance
Attachment to other people's lessons	Responsibility only for own lessons
Comparisons	Inner-directed/secure
Undeserving	Deserving
Sickness	Perfect health
Sexuality (without love)	Sexuality (with love, caring, intimacy and pleasure)
Poverty consciousness	Prosperity consciousness
Arrogance and pride	Humility, humbleness, gratitude
Sullen, serious, over-involved	Humor, objectivity, perspective
Fault-finder	Lifter of others
Rebel or conformist	Inner-directed
Curses	Blesses
Scattered	Focused, purposeful
Fear of failure or success	Successful
Aggressiveness	Assertiveness
Harshness	Gentleness
Emotional roller coaster	Emotional stability
Disorganization	Organization
Boredom	Enthusiasm
Abandonment	Whole, complete within self
Sadness and grief	Even-mindedness; joy; acceptance
Disappointment	Involved detachment
Rationales and excuses	Self honesty, tough love
Immature honesty	Spiritual honesty
Folds up under tension or lesson	Withstands tension or lesson
Needs center stage or hides in fear	Takes center stage, neutral, back stage at appropriate times
Conditional love	Unconditional love
Inappropriate response	Appropriate response
Rejecting	Accepting
Lessons as punishment	Lessons as gifts
War zone, dog-eat-dog world	School for spiritual evolution
Total power, no surrender or total surrender, no power	Power plus surrender
Limited	Unlimited or limitless
Intolerant	Tolerant
Conflict	Peace
Illusions	Truth
Hypocritical	Honest, consistent
Despair	Hope
Closed-minded	Open-minded
Distrustful	Trust and faith in self and others
Defensive	Defenseless, nothing to defend

5

Soul Psychology as Compared to Traditional Psychology

Matter is the vehicle for the manifestation of soul on this plane of existence, and soul is the vehicle on a higher plane for the manifestation of spirit

Djwhal Khul
through Alice A. Bailey

I went through traditional psychology training while immersing myself in my spiritual studies. Both my parents, my stepmother, and my sister are also in the field of psychology. I grew up with it and have lived it, breathed it, made my living at it, and been surrounded by it my entire life. Because of this, I have a lot of very strong opinions about the entire field.

Even though I practice soul psychology, which also might be called spiritual or transpersonal psychology, I have a lot of respect for traditional psychology. I learned a lot in my traditional training and am glad I have the foundation it provided. The problem is that the field of traditional psychology is very limiting. The way I look at it, it is like a horizontal graph that goes from one to one hundred. Zero might be considered the lowest level of consciousness and one hundred that of an ascended master. Traditional psychology might take you up to level thirty; however, it will never take you any further, even with five sessions a week for the next fifty years. The reason for this is that traditional psychology is 98% devoid of spirituality.

When I went through my B.A., M.A., and Ph.D. programs, the way psychology was taught was that they presented you with hundreds of different psychology theories with absolutely no guidance as to which ones were correct and which ones false. That was because no one teaching the classes knew. Every professor had his or her favorite. Your job as a student was to develop some understanding of all of them and independently choose the one you happened to like best. That is how you ended up practicing therapy.

The problem lies in the fact that none of them is true, really. They are all what I would call slivers of truth. Maybe if you put them all together, you would have a half-truth. The problem is compounded because each theorist thinks he or she has the whole truth.

In my first book, I spoke of the three levels of self-actualization. There is the personality level, the soul level, and the monadic level. Psychology, at its absolute best (and even this is debatable) will help you to achieve personality-level self-actualization. That is the 30% I spoke of. Traditional psychology cannot help you to gain soul self-actualization or monadic (spiritual) self-actualization because it doesn't even recognize the existence of soul or spirit.

Of the hundreds of different theories I studied in school, I can think of only three that had a spiritual orientation. Those three were the theories of Carl Jung, Abraham Maslow, and Robert Assagioli. I will start with the last one first.

Robert Assagioli was an Italian psychologist who developed psychosynthesis. This is one of the few forms of traditional psychology I think is really worth studying, yet he was never mentioned in all the books I studied throughout my formal education. He is basically unheard of in the field of psychology in terms of college and postgraduate education, except in the transpersonal schools.

Abraham Maslow, although mentioning the value of a spiritual life, wrote very little on the subject. He was well-known for studying healthy people instead of sick people – which was a major breakthrough in the field.

Carl Jung was the only famous traditional psychologist who integrated a spiritual aspect. He was truly a great catalyst in the field. He recognized the ideal of the self, and he broke away from Freud's fixation on sexuality. He was a master of dreams and believed in reincarnation, although he didn't really advertise the fact.

I greatly respect his work and recommend reading it. The problem is that although Jung was a great catalyst for the field, even his work was quite limited when you compare it to the fuller understanding of spiritual psychology that we know of today.

One of the basics of soul psychology is that there are two ways of thinking in the world. You can think from your negative ego mind or you can think from your soul or spiritual mind. Traditional psychology tries to heal within the web of the negative ego. However, true healing cannot occur unless the negative ego is fully transcended. Was it not Sai Baba who said, "God equals man minus ego."

Traditional theories of psychology include absolutely no reference to the idea that thought creates reality. They do not see that there are two diametrically opposed ways of interpreting reality. By definition, it is impossible for this to be seen because there is no integration of the soul aspect. Thus, traditional psychology sees life through a set of glasses worn by the negative ego.

Traditional psychology might be able to help you see better through those glasses; however, you will never truly be able to see unless you take off those glasses and put on your Christ consciousness glasses. The negative ego has infiltrated every aspect of society — religion, traditional medicine, the prison system, and all institutions on the planet — including psychology.

Now here comes the major problem. There are tens of thousands of people graduating from college and doing postgraduate work, getting degrees and licenses, who are ill-qualified to be doing therapy or teaching psychology in our schools. They have, for the most part, not even stepped onto the path of initiation, and you can't truly understand psychology unless you have integrated the soul.

Traditional psychology believes that negative emotions are unavoidable and a normal part of living. It teaches victim consciousness. It has no understanding of the chakras, the soul, the spirit, the negative ego, intuition, higher mind, abstract mind, or the real purpose of life. It doesn't, for the most part, even understand how the subconscious mind really works or how to reprogram it.

I am not saying that traditional psychology has no value. It does have some initial value. If it can lead a person to personality-level self-actualization, that is a great thing and nothing to shrug off. The problem is that very few forms of traditional psychology lead even to this point.

The real problem arises because many people seeking help stay stuck in traditional psychology for endless years and don't really move that far beyond their first year's work. They can't because it is not within the theory they are working with or within the consciousness of the therapist to take them any further. How can a therapist lead a person to enlightenment and self-realization when he or she hasn't even taken the first initiation?

The problem for the average person is that there are not that many spiritual counselors around. The average person who has a religious orientation might consider going to his church or temple to receive counseling. That would probably be even worse than traditional counseling, as traditional religion is as filled with the contamination of negative ego as is the field of psychology.

The truth of the matter is that we need more New Age spiritual counselors. A lot of them are unlicensed; in other words, they haven't gone through the traditional schooling. The average person finds this unacceptable and, in fact, is often warned against such therapists. However, I think they are, for the most part, better qualified to do counseling than traditional professional psychologists who have no relationship to soul. This goes completely counter to the views of the average materialistic person who cannot imagine such a possibility. Spiritual people who take the traditional route are, in my opinion, extremely contaminated intellectually by the time they get out.

There are very few people who do not become overwhelmed and confused by all the theories of psychology that are thrown at them. I will briefly go through some of the main ones and compare them to soul psychology.

In summary, there is nothing wrong with going to a traditional therapist for a time. It can be of great value in getting your personality under your control, if you find the right therapist. But at some point you need to get out and find a spiritual teacher to take you the rest of the way or you will never get beyond that 30%.

Traditional psychology, ideally, can be looked at as a pie, each form of psychology being a slice of the pie carrying some small morsel of truth. I suggest being eclectic and integrating all of them. Add to that soul psychology, which is the other 70%, and then you will have a truer understanding of what Djwhal Khul has called esoteric psychology.

This is the true future of psychology. Psychology, as it is now being practiced, is still in its infantile stages, or what might be called the dark ages. Twenty to thirty years from now there will be a complete revolution in the field.

Just as the soul is not integrated into the study of psychology in college and postgraduate work, the same is the case in all forms of education — politics, sociology, sports — and in every aspect of society. Humankind has sought to create a world that separates the spiritual realities of life and holds them apart from the everyday world. A good example of this was Communism. It was a political theory devoid of God; that is why it had to fail.

In truth, our political system is only a little bit better than that. Politicians speak of God; however, politics is completely run by the negative ego. Look at the corruption, the negative campaigning, the legalized bribery, the total and complete bipartisanship of the members of the Democratic and Republican parties. Their God is what is right for the party, not what is right for the world and all people.

The extraction of soul from the field of psychology is not unique.

There is not one field of study or one institution on the planet in which this has not been done in the exact same way, including religion. The human kingdom has separated itself from the kingdom of God. There will never be any true sense of happiness, inner peace, enlightenment, or understanding until these two kingdoms merge.

This chapter is an attempt to combine the psychology of the kingdom of God with the psychology of humanity. When this is achieved, people can heal themselves completely in months, rather than the years required by traditional psychology.

The Limitations of Traditional Forms of Therapy

Most readers of this book are fairly advanced, so I don't see any need to go into each form of traditional therapy in depth and explain its position. What I am going to do here is go into the different forms of therapy with what I would call the "sword of discernment," from the perspective of the soul, and attempt to elucidate each method's strengths and limitations. I will try to go right to the core of the essential teaching and not waste time with nonessential information.

Psychiatry

Let us begin our discussion with the different modes of therapy now available and contrast them with soul psychology. Psychiatry is a nightmare. I hate to be so blunt and don't mean to be critical; however, if I am going to wield the sword of discernment, I must speak the truth.

The psychiatrist is a medical doctor who receives, in fact, very little training in psychology. The average psychiatrist's form of therapy is a Valium: "Take two of these and see me three times a week for $200 a session." The ordinary psychiatrist has been trained in Freudian therapy, which will take three to five sessions a week for the next twenty years. It might sound as if I am being humorous, and I am, but there is much truth to what I am saying.

The only form of therapy worse than this is when the medical doctors get hold of someone and give him electroshock therapy to snap him out of his depression. To say this is barbaric is the understatement of the universe, and it is still being done, my friends.

In the average psychiatric ward, the patients are so filled with drugs that it would take years just to cleanse their physical bodies, let alone their minds. Their care is custodial at best. Many of these patients are having valid spiritual experiences which the doctors interpret as hallucinations. In truth, it is the doctors who are having hallucinations, while the patients are often tuning into genuine spiritual realities. The care of the mentally ill in our society is a travesty of the highest order. Medical sense is so unclear that doctors actually think they are going to heal the mind, psyche, and soul with a drug. They have no concept of the inner realities of life.

Behaviorism

Behaviorism is the second worst form of therapy. It represents the complete worship of material science. It sees people as nothing more than laboratory rats. There is no such thing as free choice. It states that you are totally shaped by your environment. Positive and negative reinforcement govern all. Of all the slivers of the pie, behaviorism holds only the faintest taste of truth.

It is true that the environment affects people, especially in early stages of evolution. To fail to see any aspect of inner reality and to say humans are no different from the animal kingdom is quite disturbing, to say the least. I am sorry to say, this is the main form of psychology in all the schools in the United States.

It is only the clinical departments, those that deal with counseling, that break away from this mold. All the research departments are governed by behaviorism. The psychologist who invented it, B. F. Skinner, actually kept his child in a box and tried to raise him like that. Can you imagine!

Humanistic Psychology

I would intuitively guess that 70% of the clinicians practice this form of therapy. Humanistic psychology is the "worship" of feelings. You go to therapy to "get out your feelings." You get out the batacas and smash the pillow which represents a spouse or parent, express your anger, and have a good cry.

The therapist is so proud of you for letting your emotions out! The key word is "catharsis." If you will excuse my coarse metaphor, it is like emotional throwing up. Now, the amazing thing about this form of therapy is that you do feel better when you leave the session; this is a fact. The only problem is that since there is no understanding that it is your thoughts that create your reality, your mind builds it all back the next day. It is a feminine type of psychological theory which ultimately makes you a victim of your subconscious mind and emotional body. I speak from personal experience on this one.

There is nothing wrong with having a catharsis, and I am the first to admit the value of such a process. You cannot, however, base your entire therapy on it, as Humanistic psychology does. You also need training as to how your thoughts are creating your feelings and emotions and there must be an integration of the spiritual aspect of life.

One extreme example of this type of therapy, to really bring this point home, has to do with a former client of mine. I saw her for about six months and when she "graduated," she was doing very well and feeling very good. This continued for about a year, until one day I received an emergency phone call from her. She was in terrible shape. She came in to see me right away and I asked what was wrong. She told me that she had been doing fantastically well for the past year, until about a week earlier when a friend had asked if she wanted to go to a workshop called a "rage weekend." She decided to go and found that the idea of the weekend was for every person to have a catharsis and express rage.

People were swearing and cursing up a storm when it was finally my client's turn. The "problem" was that she was not feeling any anger or rage; she was feeling very joyful and peaceful. I had trained her to own her power and to cause her own reality. I had trained her in the science of attitudinal healing and in seeing life from her Christ consciousness rather than from her negative ego consciousness. Not being run by her ego, she didn't have a lot of anger. She was happy and even-minded. The people in the group thought this was impossible, so they all kept attacking her until finally she broke down and started to cry. They did not let up until she did get angry.

By the time she got to me, she was a mess. I explained to her what had happened and why it had happened, and I also explained to her that she had to be a little more discriminating about the kinds of workshops she attended in the future, given her spiritual orientation. She quickly got the lesson and we patched her up better than ever, and a little wiser.

The encounter groups of the sixties, which are still going on, are also a product of this type of psychology. The idea here is to share your feelings at any cost. It does not matter if you are unloving or if you are attacking or hurting someone. As long as you are getting out your feelings, everything is wonderful. It is most definitely an Atlantean (emotionally based) form of therapy. It might be good for a short period of time for those who are controlled by and polarized in the mental body, if the right person or group is found. Otherwise, its value is quite limited.

Cognitive Psychology

If Humanistic psychology is Atlantean, then Cognitive psychology is based in the Aryan root race because of its mental attunement. Cognitive psychology is unique in that it is the *only* form of traditional psychology that teaches that it is your thoughts that create your reality. There are many very good ideas and tools in this form of therapy, and it definitely gets some results. The limitation is that the soul is missing from the system; nor does it go all the way in understanding that emotions are caused by thoughts. It does say you cause your reality but it does not go to the point of seeing that you don't have to experience negative emotions if you don't choose to.

This form of psychology is definitely a step in the right direction. It might be especially good for those who are too emotionally polarized and need to develop the mental body. Nevertheless, I would not choose any of the forms of traditional counseling over a spiritual counselor who has a good overall understanding.

In a sense, I make these recommendations for people who might not be open to seeing a spiritual counselor because they are not yet at that level of evolution in life, so must see someone who works only on the personality level and not on the spiritual level.

For a person who is spiritually based but who is feeling victimized by the emotional body, reading some books on Cognitive psychology might be very appropriate. Unfortunately, this is a system that is not often taught in traditional colleges and universities.

Freudian Psychology

Freudian psychology is getting less and less attention as time goes on, although in the past it was very important. A lot of psychiatrists seem to gravitate to it. Sigmund Freud definitely has his place in history, and he came up with some important concepts; however, he was very fixated at the second chakra level.

His theories were also totally cut off from spirit. A person who goes to see a Freudian analyst, in my opinion, is going to get very screwed up. A strong codependence is created between the therapist and patient, and the therapist will place all his Freudian philosophy on the patient's reality. If he didn't go in with sexual problems and problems with his outer and inner parents, he will have them by the time he gets out. He will also have a lot less money in his bank account.

Freudian psychology is not worthless, but in my opinion, it can take a person only from level one to level ten on a scale of one to one hundred. If a person goes five times a week for fifty years, he will never get beyond level ten because it is not within the theory to take him any further.

Jungian Therapy

Jungian therapy, of course, was started by the famous Swiss psychologist, Carl Gustav Jung. He was a contemporary of Freud and a student of his for a while but he broke away because of Freud's fixation on sexuality as the cause of everything.

Of all the forms of traditional psychology I would give this form the highest marks. It can take you higher than the 30% I spoke of earlier because it is spiritually based. Jung had a vague understanding of the Eternal Self, although not as complete an understanding as someone like

Djwhal Khul has. But Jung was in the ballpark.

He had an excellent understanding of dreams. He intimated a belief in reincarnation in his autobiography, although he didn't advertise this. He strongly believed in God, which was refreshing when I was having to study all the traditional therapies in school.

The best way to describe his contribution is to say that he was a fantastic catalyst for the field. It is very easy to get stuck in Jungian psychology, for the people who are really into it operate a bit like a cult, although I am sure Jung would turn over in his grave at the idea. I speak from experience because my parents were Jungian therapists and I saw what they had to go through in dealing with the Jung Society in Los Angeles.

We all know what happens when people form organizations around a certain set of teachings. This is not a criticism of Jung, but rather a commentary on what has been done with his teachings. This happens to all spiritual teachers, including Jesus and Buddha.

The limitations of Jungian psychology are that even though it is moving in the right direction and is most definitely spiritual in orientation, it is not complete. For example, there is no understanding of the difference between negative ego thinking and spiritual thinking. There is, in fact, the erroneous concept of having to own your shadow. Many people are caught up in this false teaching.

If God created you, then you are made in His image which is Light and love. If you have a negative, or shadow, side it comes from misuse of free choice or from thinking with the ego mind instead of with the Christ mind. The ideal is to not own your shadow, or negative ego, but rather to die to it. As Sai Baba says, God equals man minus ego.

You experience negativity because you think negatively. If you think with your Christ mind you will experience joy, happiness, unconditional love, and inner peace. When you feel negative, you can always trace it back to a negative thought coming from your negative ego. If you die to your negative ego, you die to the creation of a negative reality for yourself.

Other limitations of Jungian psychology are that it doesn't teach affirmations, visualizations, or how to reprogram the subconscious mind. There is no real inner child work and no focus on prayer or meditation. Jung did not teach unconditional love. You will not realize God if you do not realize unconditional love. Again, I do not mean to be critical of Jung, for I have the highest regard for the contributions he made to the field. A person who stays focused in Jungian psychology will progress but will not go all the way. I see many people getting stuck in the school of Jungian teachings and limiting themselves. I would recommend to anyone the reading of his books. I am even supportive of being in Jungian therapy as long as you also study and work with other theories and practices.

If you compare Jung's teachings with the teachings of Paramahansa Yogananda, Sai Baba, or Djwal Khul, you can see they are not in the same league. Jung was not a self-realized spiritual master. If your goal is self-realization and ascension, then you must have a teacher who is self-realized or ascended. What I am saying is that you can integrate Jung into your eclectic stew of studies, but you shouldn't totally identify with him.

I see a great many people who are totally identified with him and, in my opinion, they are holding themselves back. On the other side of the coin, this might be what they need for a while at this point in their evolution to take them to the next step. I am just suggesting that when they reach that point they acknowledge it and not hold on to the old form, but take the next step, for it will lead to that which Jung couldn't teach — the state of bliss, unceasing joy, unconditional love, enlightenment, and ascension.

Gestalt Psychology

Gestalt is another school of traditional psychology that is quite interesting. I speak from experience because I was in Gestalt therapy for a number of years when I was younger. Fritz Perls, the founder, was quite dynamic and many brilliant minds have built upon his theories. It is a more feminine type of psychology as opposed to a masculine type such as Cognitive psychology. Gestalt psychology sees no inherent structure in the mind. Gestalt therapy is very much into *experiencing* everything first before dealing with the mind. It tends to be a little bit anti-mind.

This school of thought was probably a needed backlash against the overemphasis on mind in some other theories. My favorite thing about Gestalt psychology is what Fritz Perls said: "When the top dog or underdog come up within your mind, laugh them off the stage." This was quite an astute statement, for without completely understanding what he was saying, he was talking about transcending the negative ego, and no other form of traditional psychology has ever addressed that.

Gestalt therapy uses a lot of roleplaying which can be a very effective tool. When dealing with a dream, instead of talking about it, you are asked to act it out. I once had a dream about a tarantula and made the mistake of telling my Gestalt therapist. He had me climbing around his office like a spider!

I am being funny here, but in truth, I got a lot out of Gestalt therapy, compared to other forms I tried. It is definitely a good methodology for those who are very intellectual and uptight.

The limitations are quite evident, also. It is, in my opinion, too feminine in its approach and needs to find a male/female balance. An example of this is its anti-mind attitude that sees absolutely no structure to the psyche. It has gone to the opposite extreme from the position of other therapies. Maybe it was an appropriate pendulum swing, but ultimately, to achieve self-realization, you need to be fully balanced. Gestalt psychology also does not integrate the spiritual aspect of self.

People have said Perls himself was quite ordinary and even nasty at times. He definitely did not believe in unconditional love; it probably would have been too constricting for his theory. Perls made a great contribution though, and if this type of therapy is used scientifically for the adjustments needed to find personality-level self-actualization, it can be of great value.

All these different therapies lead toward personality-level self-actualization. My complaint is that they don't lead to soul-level self-actualization and then to spiritual-level self-actualization.

Carl Rogers

Carl Rogers was considered one of the great Humanistic psychologists. His form of therapy is called client-centered therapy; it is very nondirective. He believed the client had all the answers and one had simply to give the client unconditional positive regard and practice "active listening."

I like his idea of unconditional positive regard. He was basically practicing and teaching unconditional love, and he should be commended, for that was a major breakthrough in the field of psychology.

His idea that the client had all the answers and his letting the client run the sessions, in my opinion, was a serious mistake. Most clients, by definition, are totally run by their emotional bodies, negative egos, and subconscious minds. I believe a therapist is a teacher, and there are definite things that a client needs to learn in order to get his or her life together.

Rogers' practice of active listening meant that he would repeat back whatever the client said. If he said, "I am pissed off at my wife," then Rogers would say, "So you are angry at your wife." It wouldn't be bad if he did this a couple of times in a session, but therapists are taught to do this constantly, which would drive me nuts.

This type of therapy is a pendulum swing away from the other types of therapies in which the therapist talks too much, gives too much advice, and doesn't listen enough. In my opinion, Rogers' original theories went too far to the other extreme. An interesting side note, of which many people are not aware, is the fact that in Rogers' later years he moved into Transpersonal psychology, which is the traditional name for spiritual psychology.

Alfred Adler

Adlerian psychology is practiced by those who consider themselves social psychologists. Adler had some good ideas. He saw the purpose of life as being the striving toward mastery and perfection, which is right on. He also saw the purpose of life as moving from the self-centered viewpoint to a more socially useful viewpoint. He felt strongly that you need to own your power and extricate yourself from inferiority and superiority complexes.

Adler was clearly moving out of the negative ego thought system whose core is selfishness and separativeness. I commend him for this. The only problem is that he didn't go quite far enough. In a complete spiritual understanding, the purpose of life is to move from a self-centered viewpoint to a soul-centered viewpoint, not just to a social viewpoint. This is where the theory stays on the humanistic plane and doesn't take the step to the soul level.

Adlerian psychology is not very often taught in schools, and this is unfortunate, for he had a lot of good ideas. All the good theorists don't seem to be taught in schools. In my estimation, traditional school is 90% behaviorism and humanistic psychology — although, in recent times this may be changing.

Family Systems Psychology

Family Systems is a form of psychology that many marriage, family and child counselors are trained in. It is an interesting theory in that the family is viewed as though it were a functioning personality in and of itself. Any change of behavior on the part of a family member causes a repercussion in the entire family system.

Instead of dealing with the individual psyches of each individual, a Family Systems therapist seeks to make adjustments in the family system as a whole. If a child, for example, is having a problem, this kind of therapist might not even deal with the child, but might make adjustments in the parent's marriage. That adjustment might then heal the child.

There is some validity in this. The problem is that it has gone too far to the other extreme again, in not dealing enough with the individual psyches of the people involved.

Each theory brings a sliver of truth from the entire pie, but each one goes too far in one extreme or the other. My suggestion is that you stay in the center of the pie and not go to any extreme, that you integrate all the different points of view. Then you have a more balanced understanding.

Transactional Analysis

Transactional Analysis was developed by Eric Berne, M.D. It divides the personality into parent, adult, and child. It is a very simplistic model, but if you are just starting off on the path of personality-level self-actualization it can be a very helpful model for beginning to integrate the personality. I do like this model better than Freud's id, ego, and super-ego, as it is a much clearer understanding.

The False Holistic Theory

The False Holistic theory of psychology is one that I myself have named. I think it is unknown to most people either because they are caught in it or because they have a whole bunch of unintegrated theories in their minds. The False Holistic theory, as I define it, is the belief that you need to balance the light and dark aspects of yourself.

Many of you might be nodding your heads saying, "This sounds all right. I think we are supposed to do that." Well, I am here to say that you are *not* here to do that. Yes, you are here to balance the feminine and masculine parts of yourself. Yes, are here to balance the Heavenly and Earthly aspects of yourself. You are also here to balance your chakras and four bodies as well as all other aspects of yourself. It is certainly true that you need to balance and integrate the ego and the spirit.

But there is one thing that you are not here to balance, and this is a key point that few people in this world understand: You are not here to balance negative ego consciousness and the Christ consciousness. You are here to get rid of and die to the negative ego. That is why Sai Baba says "God equals man minus [the negative] ego." This is also the essence of *A Course in Miracles*, Buddha's teachings, and, in truth, all the teachings of all the self-realized masters.

People who are caught in the False Holistic theory think that they have to balance everything and that if they disown anything, it will come back and bite them on some level. This is not true. Remember, it is your thoughts that create your reality, and the negative ego is, in essence, fear, selfishness, and separation.

You are not here to balance fear and love. Does not the Bible say, "Perfect love casts out fear." You are not here to balance separation and oneness. You are here to live in the oneness. You are not here to balance feelings of inferiority with high self-esteem. It is the negative ego that creates hatred, revenge, jealousy, lack of self-worth, false pride, depression, and low self-esteem. God created you, and your true identity is the monad, the Eternal Self, the I Am Presence. Does not the Bible say, "Ye are gods and know it not."

Does God experience hatred, revenge, jealousy, lack of self-worth, false pride or depression? Of course not. Where do these qualities come from if God created you? They come from misthinking on humanity's part. They come from thinking with the separative, fear-based mind instead of with the love-based Christ mind. Does not the Bible say, "Let this mind be in you that was in Christ Jesus."

To realize the Christ consciousness, you have to get rid of the negative ego consciousness. As *A Course in Miracles* says, "There are no neutral thoughts." You are either egotistical in your thinking or spiritual in your thinking, or a mixture of both. The ideal is, obviously, to be spiritual.

When you achieve this state of thinking you are loving, joyous, happy, even-minded, and peaceful all the time. Did not Buddha say, "All suffering comes from your attachments." God does not suffer so why should you if you are made in His image and likeness? You are here to become the Light, to become the love, to realize God.

As Sai Baba says, you will not achieve God-realization unless you die to the negative ego, which is fearful, separative, and selfish. When you die to the lower self's way of thinking and are reborn to your higher self's way of thinking, then you will realize God.

This is the main curriculum of the spiritual path, regardless of which particular route or teacher you choose to follow. Contrary to what other people might say, you do not need negative emotions. They are created by the mind. They do not come from outside of yourself or from your instincts. They come from your interpretations, perceptions, and beliefs about reality.

Each of you is seeing your own movie. Did not Buddha say, in the four noble truths, that all suffering comes from "wrong points of view." You are to think with your God mind which is Light. That is why it is called en-light-enment. It is not called en-dark-enment. We are not here to balance happiness and suffering. We are here to live in happiness and the Light all the time. This is the mastery over what Djwhal Khul has called "the dweller on the threshold," which is the embodiment of glamour, illusion, maya and the negative ego.

I hope I have provided a glimpse into the future. Transpersonal psychology is the new wave. In the coming years it will completely revolutionize the field of psychology.

6

Pitfalls and Traps on the Path of Ascension

*Glamour is not dispelled by paying close
attention to it. It disappears by the power of
clear and steadfast meditation, and the
freeing of one's self from self-attention.*

Djwhal Khul
through Alice A. Bailey

In my travels through life as a spiritual teacher, spiritual psychologist, and disciple on the path, I have become aware of many of the pitfalls and traps on the spiritual path. I consider myself something of an expert on this subject for I have fallen into most of them.

I highly recommend meditation upon the following list. Although short on words, it is profound in insight. My purpose in sharing these potential problems is to save as many as possible from the suffering, bad karma, and delay on the path of ascension that result from not learning these lessons. The spiritual path is very easy on one level and incredibly complicated on another.

There are glamours and snares that the negative ego and the dark forces provide every step of the way. Making mistakes and falling into them is okay. My concern is preventing seekers from staying stuck in them for extensive periods, or even lifetimes.

1. Giving your personal power away. This applies to giving it to other people, the subconscious mind, the negative ego, the five senses, the physical body, the emotional body, the mental body, the inner child, a guru, the ascended masters, God. You would do well to ponder on this for there is much wisdom in this short sentence.

2. Loving others but not loving yourself.

3. Not recognizing the negative ego as the source of all your problems.

4. Focusing on God, but not properly integrating and parenting your inner child.

5. Not eating properly and not getting enough physical exercise, which result in physical illness, which then limits all other levels.

6. Being deeply into the spiritual life but not recognizing the psychological level that needs to be understood and mastered also.

7. Material desire.

8. Holding power over others once you become successful.

9. Becoming too ungrounded which then has a deleterious affect on the physical body.

10. Trying to escape Earth, instead of creating Heaven on Earth.

11. Seeing appearances instead of seeing the true reality behind all appearances.

12. Trying to become God, instead of realizing you already are the Eternal Self, as is everyone else.

13. Not realizing that you cause everything.

14. Serving others totally before you have become self-actualized within yourself.

15. Thinking that there is such a thing as righteous anger. Anger is a big trap.

16. Becoming an extremist and not being moderate in all things.

17. Thinking you have to be ascetic to be spiritual.

18. Becoming too serious and not having enough joy, happiness, and fun in your life.

19. Being undisciplined and not continuing your spiritual practices unceasingly.

20. Stopping your spiritual practices and studies when you get involved in a relationship.

21. Putting a relationship before self and God. This is a major trap.

22. Letting your inner child run your life.

23. Being too critical of and too hard on yourself.

24. Getting caught up in the glamour and illusion of psychic powers.

25. Owning your power but not learning to surrender to God simultaneously; or surrendering to God, but not learning to own your power simultaneously.

26. Losing your personal power when you get physically tired.

27. Expecting God and the ascended masters to solve all your problems.

28. Allowing yourself to go into automatic pilot and losing your

vigilance.

29. Giving your power to channeled entities.

30. Reading too much and not meditating enough.

31. Letting your sexuality run you instead of mastering it.

32. Overidentifying with your mental or emotional body and not achieving balance.

33. Thinking you need to be a voice channel or see or experience all kinds of psychic phenomena to be spiritual or to ascend.

34. Forcing the raising of the kundalini.

35. Forcing the opening of the chakras.

36. Thinking your own personal spiritual path is the best.

37. Judging people because of the initiation level they have reached.

38. Sharing your "advanced" initiation level with other people.

39. Telling people about the "good spiritual work" you are doing, instead of just having humility.

40. Thinking that negative emotions are something you have to have.

41. Isolating yourself from people and thinking that that is spiritual.

42. Thinking the Earth is a terrible place.

43. Giving your power to astrology and the influence of the stars.

44. Being too attached to things.

45. Being too nonattached to life; not striving for involved detachment.

46. Being too preoccupied with self and not being concerned enough about being of service to others.

47. Getting stuck in the numerous faulty theories of traditional psychology, each of which is only a sliver of the whole pie.

48. Being too much the mystic or too much the occultist and not striving to integrate the two sides.

49. Giving up amidst great adversity. This is one of the biggest traps of all. You must never give up! You must never give up! You must never give up!

50. Believing that the suffering you are going through — whatever its level — will not pass.

51. Focusing too much on what initiation level you have reached or when you are going to ascend instead of focusing on the work that needs to be done.

52. Getting caught up in spiritual powers and the achievement of siddhas instead of recognizing that love is the most important spiritual power of all.

53. Badmouthing other spiritual or metaphysical groups rather than unifying and networking with other groups even though they may be not in total alignment with all of your beliefs.

54. Getting caught up in the dogma of traditional religion.

55. Thinking you need a priest to act as an intermediary between yourself and God.

56. Using your spiritual beliefs to create separatism or elitism or undue specialness.

57. Becoming too fanatical in your beliefs.

58. Believing you can achieve enlightenment through drugs or some kind of pill; this is the worst form of illusion.

59. Believing that other people don't have to work at their spiritual path as you do.

60. Putting your relationship with your kids before your relationships with yourself and with God.

61. Getting caught up in all the attractions of this most fascinating material world.

62. Becoming too caught up in loving one person instead of spreading your love out to encompass many people and all people in an unconditional sense.

63. Getting caught up in duality instead of achieving even-mindedness, inner peace, and equanimity at all times; when you haven't transcended duality you are on an emotional roller coaster, flipping back and forth between the ups and downs of life. The soul and spirit think with a transcendent consciousness that is detached from the merry-go-round.

64. Being a father or son, a mother or daughter in your relationships instead of being an adult.

65. Thinking you need to suffer in life.

66. Being a martyr on the spiritual path.

67. Needing to control others.

68. Having spiritual ambition.

69. Needing to be liked, loved or approved of.

70. Needing to be the teacher.

71. Being hypersensitive or, on the other side of the coin, being too shielded.

72. Taking responsibility for other people.

73. Being the savior.

74. Serving for selfish reasons and thinking you are being spiritual.

75. Thinking you are more advanced spiritually than you really are; on the other side of the coin, thinking you are less advanced than you really are.

76. Being famous.

77. Placing undue importance on finding your twin flame and soulmate and not realizing that soul and monad are, in truth, who you are really looking for most of all.

78. Thinking you need a romantic relationship to be happy.

79. Needing to be center stage; or, on the other side of the coin, always choosing to be a wallflower.

80. Working too hard and becoming driven, running yourself down physically; or, on the other side of the coin, playing too much and not being about the Father's business.

81. Going to psychics and channels for guidance and not trusting your own intuition.

82. Working with teachers on this plane or on the inner plane who are not ascended masters and are limited in their understanding and conception of reality.

83. Making the spiritual path an interest rather than an "all-consuming fire."

84. Wasting too much time watching TV, reading trashy novels, seeing violent movies.

85. Wasting enormous amounts of time and energy because of lack of organization and proper time management.

86. Thinking that arguing with others is serving you or the other person.

87. Trying to win or be right instead of striving for love.

88. Putting too much emphasis on intuition, intellect, feeling, and instinct, instead of realizing that they all need to be balanced and integrated in their proper proportion; the trap here is becoming overly identified with one of them.

89. Devotion to a guru who makes you smaller instead of devotion to the Eternal Self that you are.

90. Trying to be open all the time, instead of knowing how to open and close your field as the need arises.

91. Not knowing how to say no to other people, the inner child, or the negative ego when the need arises.

92. Thinking violence or attacking others in any form will get you what you want or is serving God in any capacity.

93. Blaming God or being angry at God or the ascended masters for your problems.

94. Thinking that if your prayers aren't answered, God and the ascended masters aren't answering your prayers.

95. Comparing yourself with other people instead of comparing self with self.

96. Thinking that being poor is being spiritual.

97. Comparing and competing with others over your initiation level and ascension.

98. Allowing yourself to be a victim of other people or of your own

physical body, emotional body, mental body, desires, five senses, negative ego, or lower self.

99. Studying too much and not demonstrating in the real world enough.

100. Thinking your moodiness is a true reality of God.

101. Thinking your worth comes from doing and achieving things.

102. Thinking you don't need to protect yourself spiritually, psychologically, and physically.

103. Thinking that glamour, illusion, maya, negative ego, fear, and separation are real.

104. Using sugar, artificial stimulants, coffee, and soft drinks for physical energy.

105. Trying to do everything yourself and not calling on God for help; the other side of the coin, calling on God for help and not helping yourself.

106. Loving people a little less because they are treating you badly or setting a negative ego example; not differentiating the person from the behavior.

107. Losing faith in the living reality of your soul, your monad, God, and the ascended masters, and their ability to help you if you will persevere and do your part.

108. Thinking that other people can achieve ascension but you can't, at least not in this lifetime.

109. Trying to achieve ascension to escape your problems.

110. Thinking that Earth is a prison instead of recognizing it as one of God's seven heavens.

Summation

I think this list should provide a lot of food for thought. The lower self, the powers of glamour, illusion, and maya, and the negative ego are incredibly tricky and elusive in nature. As Master Yoda said in the *Star Wars* movies, "Don't underestimate the power of the dark side of the force." Once you get caught up in it, it can be very difficult to see your way out. Staying clear takes enormous vigilance, self-discipline, commitment, and devastating honesty. If your ego can't make you feel like an underdog it will make you feel like a top dog, which is even more seductive.

Everything in God's universe is governed by laws – physical, emotional, mental and spiritual laws. By learning to understand these laws and become obedient to them you follow the path of ascension. I know these insights can be helpful in avoiding suffering and in learning by grace.

7

Romantic Relationships
from the Soul's Perspective

*Communication is to a relationship
what breathing is to living*

Virginia Satir

It is very important to understand that romantic relationships and relationships in general are very different when looked at from the soul's
perspective. To begin with, I would like to define some of the common
terms that are used in metaphysical circles such as twin flames, monadic
mates, and soulmates. There is great confusion about what these terms
really mean.

Twin Flames

According to Djwhal Khul, a twin flame relationship is a romantic
relationship with a soul extension from your own soul group. Each monad
creates twelve souls, and each soul then creates twelve soul extensions who
incarnate in the material universe. Each of you is one of the twelve
extensions from your soul. A relationship with another of those extensions
does not happen very often; in fact, it is a very rare occurrence. The soul
does not usually like it to happen because the relationship tends to be such
a powerful attraction that the two people tend to get lost in each other. It
does happen occasionally, but not as often as most people fantasize it
happening.

Monadic Mates

Monadic mates are a more common occurrence. A monadic mate is a
relationship with another of the one hundred forty-four soul extensions

from your monad. The monad creates twelve souls, and each soul then creates twelve soul extensions, or personalities who incarnate into the material world. The total number of soul extensions from your monad's twelve souls is one hundred forty-four.

I was told by Djwhal Khul in a dream that my wife, Terri, and I are from the same monad. (We are not from the same soul.) We were also told that we are the only two soul extensions from our monad who are on the Earth at this time.

This brings up an important point. Just because the monad has one hundred forty-four soul extensions, it doesn't mean that they are all incarnated on Planet Earth. There are millions of other planets in our galaxy and in other galaxies upon which they could be incarnated. You must enlarge your perspective here.

It is also important to understand that when you pass the third initiation, the soul begins to call its soul extensions back into the spiritual world so it can focus on the more spiritually advanced soul extensions.

Terri and I were told that three-quarters of our soul extensions were already back in the spiritual world. This does not mean that they are very highly evolved, but rather that they are probably not the more advanced ones, in a spiritual sense. If three-quarters are not in incarnation, approximately thirty-six are still in incarnation, and many of them are in the Pleiades and on other planets unknown to me. So even meeting a monadic mate happens infrequently.

It is also important to realize that if you do meet a twin flame or monadic mate, it doesn't mean an intense romantic relationship will ensue. Two such "mates" might be entirely opposite in all ways. It only means you are going to have a powerful connection with each other. The connection is a spiritual one, not necessarily one that works on a psychological or physical level.

So you need not worry about trying to find your twin flame or monadic mate. If it happens it happens, but it is not something you should look for. What you could look for is the right person; the occult information about that person will take care of itself. Too many people are caught up in trying to find their twin flames. They might be missing wonderful people who are there right in front of them.

Soulmates

A soulmate relationship is one in which you are involved with someone with whom you have a soul connection. This connection might have to do with past lives that you have spent together and it might not. What matters most is that you are both soul-connected. It is possible to have a soulmate connection with someone you are not involved with romantically. I have a soulmate connection with my sister and even with my mother.

It is very important to have these types of friendships, especially if you are not involved romantically. Many of you have very beautiful soulmate types of connections with your cats or dogs. The pets serve as a type of pole or balance. When you are not in a relationship it is good for you to have a pet for this purpose. The pet can serve also as an intermediate step in the process of manifesting a relationship.

Other Kinds of Relationships

The fourth category of relationships includes relationships with people with whom you share many beautiful things but are not connected on a soul level. Those of you in this type of relationship who are being guided to stay in it even though it is not a soulmate type of relationship should know that it is absolutely fine to do so. It will be important, however, for you to have soulmate friendships.

The Two Most Important Relationships

The most important relationship in your life is not your relationship with your partner. The most important relationships in your life are those with yourself and with God. The first and most important relationship is your relationship with yourself. If you are not right with yourself, you will project that wrong relationship with self onto everything else in your life, including God. In reality, the self and God are the same thing. However, before you can fully and truly realize this you must be right with self.

A relationship partner is third on the list. If this isn't clear, you are headed for some suffering. The danger here is trying to find your wholeness in another person, rather than finding your wholeness within yourself and God. If you don't do this, your relationship turns into a type of addictive love.

The Abrahamic Initiation

The Abrahamic initiation is an initiation you must go through if you are going to evolve in this lifetime. The Abrahamic initiation has to do with the Old Testament story of Abraham (El Morya), who wanted desperately to have a son. He and his wife were something like eighty or ninety years old when God blessed them with a son who was named Isaac.

On the birth of his son, Abraham started spending all his time with Isaac and began to forget about God. This went on for a very long time until finally, in a quiet moment, God spoke to Abraham in a forceful voice and told him that he would have to sacrifice his son, Isaac, as a burnt offering. Abraham said, "What? My only son?" God said, "You heard my commandment. Follow it."

Abraham was in total conflict for three days. Finally, he decided that God came before his son. He took Isaac to the altar on the mountain, got out his knife and was about to swing a deathblow to his son when an angel appeared, grabbed his arm and said, "You don't have to do that, Abraham. Now I know that you fear God because you have not withheld from me your son, your only son" (Gen 22).

What is the spiritual meaning of this story? What is it that you need to put on God's altar? What is it that you put before God and your spiritual path? Some of the possibilities are a child, a relationship, drugs, alcohol, sugar, cigarettes, food, sex, power, fame, money, material things, security, and so on. Didn't the Ten Commandments say to worship no idols and to have no false gods? Whatever you put first in life is the God you worship.

To be able to pass the fourth initiation you must renounce all that is not of the soul's purpose; this means the complete letting go of all attachments and addictions. Are you worshiping any false gods? If you wish to accelerate your spiritual growth, you must place them on God's altar. Many of these things will still be in your life but will be in their proper perspective. Walking the spiritual path means living in this world but not being of this world. This can also be described as "involved detachment."

The Soul's Perspective on Self-Love

If you don't love your self it is not possible to have a healthy love relationship with another person. The ideal is for you to love your inner child and to allow yourself to feel and receive God's love. If these aren't established first, then you end up seeking love, worth, approval, and acceptance from another person, instead.

The Soul's Perspective on Happiness in Relationships

Happiness is a state of mind, not the state of a romantic relationship. Happiness should be understood as something you have all the time, regardless of what your partner is doing. You must not put the responsibility for your happiness on your partner. It is your own responsibility.

This lesson has a lot to do with whether you have preferences or attachments regarding what your partner does. If you have preferences, you can be happy no matter what. If you have attachments, you will sometimes feel like a loser.

The Soul's Perspective on Love

For the soul there is only one kind of love and that is unconditional love. From the soul's perspective it is never acceptable to attack your partner. You must never forget that your partner is, in reality, God visiting you in physical form. To attack your partner, or any person for that matter, is to attack God and, hence, attack yourself. You can be honest and share your feelings if you share them in a loving and respectful way. A partner deserves respect even if his or her behavior does not merit it.

The Soul's Perspective on Communication

The soul's perspective on communication can be summed up by a quote from the well known family therapist, Virginia Satir. She said, "Communication is to a relationship what breathing is to living." You must communicate with your partner about what you are feeling, or the relationship can't possibly work.

The Soul's Perspective on Gay and Lesbian Relationships

From the soul's perspective there is absolutely no judgment of gay or lesbian relationships. They are not sins as some traditional religious teachings would have you believe. There is no one explanation of why homosexuals feel as they do and, in truth, it does not matter. All that matters is following the motto that says, "Above all else, to thine own self be true." It is perfectly acceptable and normal in God's eyes to choose this path. To those who have a problem with this I would say meditate carefully on Jesus' statement, "Judge not, that ye be not judged."

The Soul's Perspective on Abortion

I will go right to the core on the controversial subject of abortion. From the soul's perspective, having an abortion is *not* a sin. The reason is that the soul and the physical body are two completely different things. When a woman has an abortion the doctor is not killing a soul but a physical body. That same soul can come back a year later to the same woman if the time is more appropriate. The fundamentalist religions have confused this point, thinking the body and the soul are one and the same. They are not.

However, abortion is not an acceptable form of birth control. If people practiced birth control more responsibly, then the need for abortions would be much less. Also, if people were more responsible in using their sexual energies as the sacred form of communication they are, they would not be as inclined to indulge the carnal lower self as much as some people are.

The Soul's Perspective on Sexuality

From the soul's perspective, sexuality is beautiful and divine. It can be used in service of the ego and the lower self, or it can be used in service of the soul and God.

The ego uses sexuality to treat other people like a piece of beef, not recognizing the soul inside the body. The ego uses it for selfishness and self-gratification. The soul would have you use sexuality as a means of communicating love and intimacy on the physical level. It would have you use it for mutual pleasuring, not just self-pleasuring. The soul would also have you use your sexuality in moderation, recognizing it is just one form of the energy that relates to the second chakra. This same energy can be raised to the other chakras for love, creativity, communication, spiritual insight, and God-realization.

Tantric practices are a path for spiritual use of sexuality, the art of lovemaking while simultaneously raising the energy in a kind of meditation. You must not let the lustful lower self run your life in this regard, but be the master of your sexuality in the service of love and soul-melding.

The Soul's Perspective on the Ideal Relationship

The ideal relationship is one in which both individuals are in right relationships with themselves and with God. Both people are whole and complete within themselves. They are both causers of their own realities, not victims. Both individuals put their spiritual paths first. The reason they are together is that they can grow faster and experience more love and joy by sharing the path together. They can be of great service to God's divine plan for humanity.

The Soul's Perspective on Partners As Teachers

Your partners are master teachers in everything they do. Even when they are misbehaving, they are giving you the opportunity to practice Christ consciousness and to demonstrate qualities your soul would have you develop. You are constantly being taught to stay in your power, to be loving, to forgive, to practice humility, to turn the other cheek, to remain the cause of your own emotions. Lessons in patience, emotional protection, honesty, communication skills, nonattachment, egolessness, unconditional love, seeing experiences as lessons, staying centered, and so on are continually offered in relationships.

Never forget that it is in how you respond at every moment of your life in all situations that you realize God or lose your realization of God. You can easily remain in Christ consciousness living in a cave. But can you remain in Christ consciousness in a relationship, in a big city — in the market place, as Jesus would say?

The Soul's Perspective on Divorce

Divorce is not a sin. Sometimes divorce is the best thing in the world; it depends on the situation. Many times my services as a spiritual psychologist have been utilized to help people break up, although they didn't realize that when they came to me. However, you should never leave a relationship until you have learned the lessons of the experience. Otherwise, you are likely to have to repeat the lessons in a new relationship. It will be a different physical body, soul extension, and personality, but the same psychodynamics will occur.

The Soul and Balancing the Four Bodies in a Relationship

It is essential when living within the four-body system – physical, emotional, mental, and spiritual – to be aware of what your predominant body identification is and what your partner's is, also. A lot of potential problems can be worked out by understanding this perspective. It is critically important to avoid becoming self-righteous about your particular body's modality.

The common psychodynamic is that the woman tends to identify with her emotional body and the man with his mental body, though there are exceptions. Having a spiritual body identification will temper this. However, the man must learn to accept the woman's feelings and the woman must learn to accept the man's thinking modality. A relationship is a great device for teaching us to become more whole.

The Soul's Perspective on Judgment and Protection in a Romantic Relationship

It is essential that both partners learn to be as nonjudgmental as possible. It is okay to make loving observations, but no judgments or putdowns! When your partner does judge you, you need to learn to keep your bubble of protection up and let the other's negativity slide off.

You need to learn not to let your partner be (or think that your partner is) the cause of your reality. You need to learn to cause your own feelings and not let your partner be the cause of your feelings. You create your own reality, and you are the computer programmer of your own subconscious mind, even if you are married or in a committed romantic relationship. Your relationships to self and God come first.

The Soul's Perspective on Father-Daughter/Mother-Son Relationships

When you don't do your inner work and achieve right relationship to self and God, you form father-daughter, mother-son relationships. The ideal is to form mutually independent adult-adult relationships, not dependent relationships.

If you do not first find your wholeness within and oneness with God, then you will end up seeking it within a partner. This will lead to two halves joining together, instead of two whole people uniting. There is no judgment in this, it is just a lesson you must learn.

If you are a daughter or son psychologically, then by the laws of energy you will attract people who want to be mothers or fathers within the relationship. If you are a father or mother psychologically, the only type of people you can possibly attract are psychological sons or daughters.

If you are whole and complete within yourself and one with God, then you will attract a whole person who realizes his/her oneness with God. Many people are desperately seeking a relationship. The problem is that in many cases, an external relationship is the last thing they need; what they really need is a better relationship with self and God.

You Don't Need a Relationship

You don't need a relationship in your life to be successful and happy and to realize God. The proper attitude is to make it a want, not a need, a super-strong preference, not an attachment. Then if it doesn't happen you can still be happy.

If your happiness depends on finding a relationship and not on your inner self and God, then you are worshiping a false god. Whatever you put first in life is that which you worship. Does not the Bible say to not worship false gods?

It is okay to seek a relationship and even to pray for God's help in finding one; however, if it doesn't happen, you can be happy anyway. The paradox of life is that when you truly let go and accept your full happiness, with or without a relationship, then that is when you usually find one.

The key to finding your true mate, in my opinion, is to focus completely on your spiritual path and on service to humanity. Total commitment to God and your spiritual path will attract the ideal spiritual mate.

Honesty, Trust, Commitment

It is of the highest importance to maintain honesty at all times in your relationships. Part of being honest is being honest with yourself. A relationship is like a garden of beautiful flowers that also has weeds. If the weeds aren't constantly pulled out, they can overrun the garden and destroy the flowers.

Lack of honesty can lead to a breakdown in trust and communication. Lack of honesty is a breech of the commitment you have made to your partner. True commitment is not just being monogamous, but also being committed to dealing with issues as they come up. It is being committed to communicating your feelings about the things that are bothering you, instead of pulling away and withdrawing, judging, or leaving the relationship. A true commitment involves being honest about what is going on inside yourself. You owe this to your partner, yourself and God.

The Soul's Perspective on Ego Battles

In all relationships there are times when your ego or lower self is triggered and ego battles can develop. The soul's perspective on this (and this may be a surprise) is to not talk. When you are caught in your ego, all that happens is that you hurt each other emotionally. You say things you don't really mean in a vain attempt to get back at the other person.

The negative ego's game is not love, but who is "right." You must ask yourself whether you want to be right or to have love. You can't have both. If you want love, then you must get out of your ego. When both partners are caught, sometimes the best thing to do is take time alone to calm down, get re-centered, and attune to self and God. Then you can start communicating again.

One of the things my wife and I do that has been extraordinarily helpful is to hold hands, look into each other's eyes, and bring in our soul and our monad before we start communicating. Just imagine a large tube that extends upward from the top of your head into the spiritual world. Call down your soul or monad (or a particular saint or ascended master) into the top of your head, into your third eye or even into your heart chakra. Once you feel this connection within, then connect with each other from this state of consciousness, which is obviously completely antithetical to the negative ego.

This simple technique has been the single most important tool my wife and I have used to stabilize our relationship into a soul- and monad-oriented pattern.

The Soul on Learning Lessons

One of the key lessons of relationships is to be focused on your own lessons and not the lessons you think your partner needs to learn. Many of you are so concerned about all the lessons your partner isn't learning, that you are actually missing your own. I think my favorite saying of Jesus in the entire Bible on this point is, "Why do you look at the speck of sawdust in your brother's eye, and pay no attention to the plank in your own eye?" (Mt 7:3). You are not responsible for your partner's lessons, only for your own lessons.

The Soul on Psychological Disease

If your partner is physically sick, you obviously do not want to catch the disease. You do everything you can to build up your resistance. You take vitamin C, get enough sleep, exercise, and sunshine, keep a positive mental attitude, and don't catch it. There is no such thing as a contagious disease. There are only people with low resistance.

The same lesson applies to the psychological level. If a partner has a psychological "disease" such as judgmentalness, anger, depression, worry, lack of self-worth, lack of faith, self-doubt, the ideal is that you not catch the disease, but maintain a strong psychological resistance. This is achieved by staying in a place of personal power and self-love, using a protective bubble, a positive attitude, meditation, prayer, spiritual reading, journal writing, physical fitness, and good diet. If you maintain this psychological resistance, negative energy does not hook into your subconscious programming. You are setting an example and hence helping the other to come out of his or her off-centeredness.

Otherwise, you can catch the psychological disease. The world is like a hospital that is run by the patients: the purpose of life is to be a healer and a teacher of God so you can set a good example.

The Soul on Differing Perspectives

No two people see things the same way all the time. Remember that you see with your mind, not just with your eyes. You see through your belief systems, since it is your thoughts that create your reality. When you and your partner disagree about the perception of a given situation, the ideal is to not let that create separation but to agree to disagree and stay in love and in oneness. This is possible as long as you don't let the ego in. What a wonderful testing ground relationships are for helping you to get out of your ego!

The Soul on Relationships with Parents

It is of the greatest importance to resolve your relationships with your parents. If you don't you will project unresolved issues onto your partner. This resolution has to do with reclaiming your power, finding your love of self and of God, and forgiving your parents and unconditionally loving them, rather than blaming them or judging them for how they raised you. They provided you with the exact lessons you needed to learn. It is good to remember that as a soul, you chose your parents.

The Soul and the "Differing Elevator Phenomenon"

There is a phenomenon in relationships that I call the "differing elevator phenomenon." It occurs when one person grows at a much faster rate spiritually and psychologically than the other person. That can be okay up to a point but if the difference in the speed of the elevators becomes too great, there is a danger to the relationship.

Most often in relationships one person is developed in one area, and the other in opposite areas. This is good as long as there is some kind of balance. If this schism becomes too great, however, the relationship may not be meant to be, especially if it is holding one person back.

The Spiritual Relationship Contract

Sometimes, when a lot of water has gone under the bridge in a relationship, it can be very helpful to write a spiritual relationship contract together for the renewal of the relationship. This can be done with the help of a trained counselor, a friend, or alone.

The idea here is to make a list of the lessons being worked on both individually and collectively in the relationship, examining how they are affecting the romantic bond. List the principles, tools, and ideas you are committed to working on. Writing them down has a marked effect on the subconscious and conscious minds.

Upon completing this contract, both partners sign it and perform some kind of spiritual ritual, perhaps burning a copy or placing it on an altar. You can be creative here. I would suggest going on a second honeymoon and re-establishing the romance. It is essential then that both people live up to the commitments stated in the contract.

8

The White Brotherhood
Medical Assistance Program

Ask and you shall receive. Knock and the
door shall be opened.

Jesus Christ

Machaelle Small Wright started the spiritual community called Perelandra. There were some extraordinary stories about her relationships with the devas and nature spirits as demonstrated in the gardens of
Perelandra. Recently, I discovered another book she wrote, called *MAP, the
Co-Creative White Brotherhood Medical Assistance Program.* This is an
incredible book that gives detailed instructions on how you can enlist the
aid of the White Brotherhood and the nature kingdom to help with physical
health challenges and even with mental and emotional problems. MAP
stands for Medical Assistance Program; from now on I will use the abbre-
viation.

MAP can be used in conditions of sickness or perfect health. It is an
ongoing system of support that you can always use. The Great White
Brotherhood has special teams that are specifically trained in working with
physical health problems. When you begin the MAP you are calling to
yourself one of these teams, in conjunction with the support of Pan and the
nature kingdom.

The White Brotherhood, Pan, and the nature kingdom are all happy to
be of service. It is through serving that they, too, continue to evolve, so
don't be hesitant to ask for help, no matter how small the need. The
program is completely under your control, and they will work only on areas
you specifically ask for help with. Under cosmic law they can do no other
than this.

All the information that follows is from Machaelle's book. If it is not available in your local bookstore, I highly recommend that you send for it. The address is:

> Perelandra, Ltd.
> P.O. Box 3603
> Warrenton, VA 22186.

I also recommend her book on the story of Perelandra. It is unfortunate that her books are not always in bookstores for her information is clearly equal to the material from the Findhorn community.

I will attempt here to extract the bare essence of how MAP works so you can at least get started in receiving this most wonderful help with your physical health from the White Brotherhood, Pan, and the angels.

The First MAP Session

The first session is quite enjoyable, as are all the sessions. All you have to do is lie down on your back without crossing your legs or arms. The beginning of the program is called "opening a MAP coning." You will basically be inviting in four beings, or groups. They are:

1. The Overlighting Deva of Healing
2. Pan
3. Your personal White Brotherhood Medical Unit
4. Your higher self and/or your monad

To open a MAP coning, just say out loud, "I would like to open a MAP coning. I would like to be connected with . . ."

1. The Overlighting Deva of Healing. Wait ten seconds for the connection to be made. You might feel an energetic tingling or you might feel nothing. Either way, just know that you have asked, and by divine law you will receive. If you are proficient with a pendulum or with behavioral kinesiology as ways of communicating with your subconscious mind, or higher self, they can be used to check the connection. If you aren't, it does not matter because it is not essential to the program.

2. Pan. Wait ten seconds.

3. The White Brotherhood Medical Unit. Wait ten seconds.

4. Your soul or monad. Wait ten seconds. One suggestion I would add, which is not in Machaelle's book, is to say the "Soul Mantra" before beginning the MAP coning process. It is a good way to attune to your soul. The soul mantra is: "I am the soul. I am the Light divine. I am love. I am will. I am fixed design." Say it three times and you will be absolutely guaranteed to get a response. This mantra, brought forth by Djwhal Khul, is a wakeup call to the soul, telling it that it is needed for service.

The coning process has now officially begun. It is very simple! The first session is for scanning purposes only. Your medical team needs to get familiar with your energy fields and aura. You will have the same medical team from this time forward. The idea is for you to lie down for an hour and let them do their work. During this time, if you want to, you can speak to them, out loud or silently, and tell them what your health concerns are and what you would like to heal.

To close the MAP coning, just focus on each member of the group listed, thank them for their help, and ask to be disconnected. You should wait at least twenty-four hours until your next session to allow the energies to settle in.

Machaelle uses many flower essences to enhance this process. It is not essential to use them; however, they can bring an added dimension to the healing. They can be chosen according to a pendulum or kinesiology (muscle testing). Write to Machaelle for more information on this. I think she makes her own flower essences. With her connection to the nature spirits, I am sure they must be absolutely fabulous. This information is in Appendix B of her book.

MAP Session Schedule

Machaelle recommends holding sessions twice weekly the first month, once a week the second through fourth months, and from the fifth month onward, once every other week. This is the schedule for when you are doing well and just want maintenance work done. If you should have an illness or injury, you can hold sessions as often as three to four times a week. It is suggested that you make a five-month commitment to the program in order to fully experience its effects.

It is important to understand that people have varying degrees of sensation during an actual session. Some people are more sensitive to energy changes than others. Since the MAP team is dealing with subtle energy fields, a lot more is going on than you might realize. Many people feel subtle electrical currents or tingling sensations; others don't feel anything at all. You can have a session next to your spouse as long as you have at least three feet of clear space between you during the session.

In your second session, after the initial scanning session, talk to the MAP team and tell them what you want; if you like, tell them what you are experiencing. If you should ever feel any pain, do tell them, although this is unlikely. The second session, more work-focused, is the same as the first, except the MAP team will actually work on your energy fields to make corrections instead of just scanning to see what you need as they did in the first session.

The Calibration Process

The calibration process is an additional process that was developed by Machaelle. In these sessions the nature beings take a more active role. They help to stabilize the energies in the MAP coning, but in the calibration process they are doing more active work.

The purpose of the calibration process is to help you in times of emotional and mental stress, as opposed to the physical health lessons of the MAP coning process. This calibration process can be done separately from the MAP coning process or in conjunction with it. It takes about half an hour, whereas a MAP coning session takes a full hour. It is designed to help when you are stuck, mentally or emotionally.

The reason the nature beings are able to help is that they see everything in terms of energy. Emotional and mental blocks are seen as certain energy configurations in the auric field, which can be shifted around in a way that allows the energy to flow more cohesively and harmoniously. The exact procedure for opening the calibration process is as follows:

1. Just say, "I would like to open a healing coning for the calibration process. I would like to connect with the Deva of Healing, Pan, the White Brotherhood Medical Unit, and my soul and/or monad." Again, wait ten seconds after requesting your connection with each member of the team.

2. Request, out loud, assistance with a problem or lesson you are dealing with at an emotional or mental level. Talk with them as though you were talking with a therapist. As you talk, they are watching your energy fields to see how they respond. From these observations, the healing team can then work to help the energies within your mental and emotional bodies and in your overall energy system flow more in harmony with your soul and spirit.

3. Once you have completed your explanation and request for help, just lie back and allow them to work on you for a full half hour from the time you stop talking. It might be helpful to set a timer. You might feel some resolution right away, or it may take twenty-four hours for the new energy configuration and pattern to work through your consciousness. Flower essences are recommended at the end of the session but they are not required.

4. Close the coning by thanking each member of your healing team and then requesting to be disconnected. It is possible that you might need more than one calibration process to fully complete the mental and emotional lesson you are dealing with. If the problem you are having persists, do explain this to your team at your next session, so they can make the needed adjustments in their work.

It is possible to do the MAP coning and the calibration process in the same session. The steps are the same. Just ask for both processes to occur simultaneously.

Working with a Pendulum

One of the most helpful tools you can use while living on Earth is a pendulum. A pendulum can be bought in a metaphysical bookstore. You can also make your own. Use a small crystal or gemstone tied or glued to a chain or piece of thread or string. In my opinion, it is worth a small investment to buy one, especially if you are just beginning.

Through the use of a pendulum you can communicate with your subconscious mind and higher self. The pendulum is able to give you a yes or no answer to any question you ask.

The way to begin is to sit in a chair at a table, hold the pendulum, and just ask the pendulum to move in the direction that signifies a yes answer. Let the pendulum move on its own without consciously pushing it in any direction. Then ask the pendulum which swing signifies a no answer. The direction can vary. It might swing in a clockwise circle or a counterclockwise circle. It might move back and forth or side to side. The main thing is to work out a system between your conscious mind and your subconscious and superconscious minds as to what yes and no answers will be. Then begin by asking silly questions that you already know the answers to, to see if you are getting accurate answers.

Using a pendulum, as with any skill, takes a little practice. There are many books on the market that provide a whole course in how to work with a pendulum. If you are just starting, I would recommend buying one and going through the lessons they outline so you can become proficient. It will be one of the most valuable skills you have ever learned. You can check which foods you should eat, which supplements your body actually needs, which homeopathics to take, which doctor you should choose, which flower essences to take after your MAP coning sessions.

You can talk to your higher self and get answers, once you become skilled. You might be eating food or taking supplements or medications that your body doesn't really want. You might need a supplement for one week but take it for a month and be poisoning yourself on a subtle level. A pendulum can tell you, through a sequence of yes or no answers, how long you need to take it, when, how many tablets a day, and so on.

The list of questions it can answer is literally infinite. It can answer questions on psychological and spiritual levels, also. Do take the time to invest your time, energy, and a little money to practice with this incredible tool. I absolutely guarantee that it will be the best investment you have ever made.

9

Tools for Healing the Emotions

There are only two emotions, love and fear.
Choose whom ye shall serve.

A Course in Miracles

Your attitudes create your feelings. With the ego's mind, you create fear-based feelings; with a spiritual attitude, you create love-based feelings. You have the ability to choose the way you feel because your thoughts and attitudes cause your emotions.

I have developed a six-step process to help focus this choice clearly. The process is especially helpful when you feel your buttons being pushed in a relationship or other circumstance in life and you are having difficulty figuring out the reason.

Six-Step Process for Spiritualizing the Emotional Self

Step 1: Write down the incident. It might be a traffic jam on the freeway or your mate's becoming angry with you. The first step is just to write down objectively what has happened.

Step 2: Write down objectively your response to the incident or to the person. For example, your response to the traffic jam might have been impatience and aggravation. Your response to your mate might have been defensiveness and anger. Just write down objectively how you responded, whether it was appropriate or not.

Step 3: This is the key step. Choose to look at the incident as if it were your master teacher. It is teaching you a lesson that you need to learn; it is an instrument that God is using to give you an opportunity to grow spiritually. Your negative response always stems from the fact that you are not looking at the situation as a teaching, an opportunity to grow. The traffic jam is your master teacher. Your mate's anger is your master teacher.

Step 4:   Make a list of all the psychological and spiritual qualities that you are being given the opportunity to learn. In the example of the traffic jam, perhaps you are being taught patience; or preference rather than attachment; or how to look at things as lessons; or surrender.

Perhaps the first thing you are being taught is how not to be. Some people set good examples and some set bad examples; you can learn from both. You know how it feels to be on the other end of someone's anger, so your mate is teaching you not to be that way. Other possible lessons are to stay centered; to own your own personal power; to have your bubble of protection up so your mates's top dog response slides off your bubble; to be the cause of your own emotions and not let your mate cause your emotions; to avoid letting your mate put you into the underdog position; to communicate with your mate in a powerful, loving way instead of in a defensive, attacking way; to discuss instead of argue; to respond instead of reacting; to be a master instead of a victim; to stand up for yourself; to learn to make good choices about when to talk and when to be silent; to seek love and worth in yourself and from God first, rather than seeking it first from your mate; to refrain from catching the psychological disease of your mate and to be the healer instead of becoming a patient; to be spiritual instead of egoistical; to view circumstances as lessons; detachment, objectivity; forgiveness, unconditional love; preferences, nonattachment; invulnerability; transcendence of ego; patience; how to set a good example.

Maintaining right relationships to self and God is of primary importance and should come before even your relationship with your mate.

I recommend that you use this list of qualities in examining future lessons. So many of the lessons are really those in that list, repeated over and over again.

Step 5:   After listing all the wonderful lessons you have learned, then bless or thank the other person, in your mind or in person, for giving you the opportunity to learn those lessons. Make a firm resolution that, when you are tested during the following day, week, or month, you are going to be mentally strong and prepared to respond appropriately. Please do realize that you will be tested again, either with the same person or incident or with a new incident, but it will be a similar lesson.

Step 6:   If you have truly learned from the experience, you will never again have to experience those negative feelings.

Use the six-step process for mastering your feelings any time you get into a sticky emotional situation. Putting it on paper will help you see more clearly what is happening.

Catharsis and Identification with Negative Emotions

The six-step process for mastering emotions and the previous discussion of attitudinal healing can be referred to as masculine, yang, or disidentification methods for dealing with emotions. They are the opposite of the feminine, yin, identification methods, which follow.

Certainly you want to identify with your spiritualized emotions of love, joy, and happiness on a continual basis, but I believe that there are appropriate times to identify with and express negative feelings as well.

The Release Method

Dealing with emotions can be compared with the potential of being able to walk on water: Even though you know you have no limits, putting it into practice is a different story. The same thing is true for handling feelings. You know the ideal way to think, but putting it into practice in all areas of life takes a lot of work, just as getting the physical body fit and cleared of toxins takes work and self-discipline.

Especially during crisis periods, fear-based, egotistical emotions arise. What do you do with all these feelings? The first thing to do is try to heal yourself attitudinally, as discussed above in the six steps to mastering emotions. This will definitely help.

What happens if a lot of negative emotions are still coming up? There are two choices: You can push them down or you can allow yourself to identify with them and express them. The first alternative is sometimes extremely important to use. Sometimes you are, for instance, at work or in the grocery store or the bank and it is just not appropriate to burst out crying or screaming. This is the time to own your own power, use self-control, and put your emotions on the shelf temporarily until you can arrange a more appropriate moment to deal with them.

Then it is time for the second alternative. When you get home or to the car or another safe place, you can allow yourself to have a catharsis. In other words, you can express whatever you are feeling, good or bad. Sometimes when you feel overwhelmed and just not on top of things, mentally or attitudinally, you definitely need to allow yourself this kind of release.

From a spiritual perspective, it is important to find an appropriate time and place for the catharsis so as to avoid hurting yourself or other people in the process. For example, let's say you are feeling a lot of anger and you just need to get it out. Instead of taking it out on your children, co-workers, or mate, you might scream while in the car or take a bat and smash a pillow on the bed or hit a punching bag. A good catharsis allows you to release and let go of a lot of negative feelings. Having a catharsis can also bring transformation, insight, and understanding.

The best thing to do after a catharsis, once you are rested, is to write in a journal to effect some attitudinal healing. The dark cloud will have been released so that you will be much clearer and able to do some good attitudinal reprogramming as well as receiving insight and understanding from your journal-writing.

The Indulgence Method

The second yin, or identification, method for dealing with negative emotions is to set a timer and give yourself an allotted period of time to indulge completely. For example, maybe you are really feeling sorry for yourself. You can't seem to break it attitudinally with disidentification and the other masculine methods, so give yourself thirty minutes on the timer to wallow in self-pity. Go for it. Scream, cry, get into a rage and really overindulge. Get it all out! When the timer goes off, stop. Then be about God's business.

You probably already use this method at times. You might do it with food, allowing yourself that dessert, then saying, "Tomorrow morning I am going to bite the bullet and go on a diet." Sometimes you just don't have enough power or energy at that moment, and maybe that option is appropriate. The important thing is not to let a negative mood drag on without doing something about it.

The Acceptance Method

The third method is just to carry the tension of the negative feelings you are experiencing. Maybe you have tried to heal yourself attitudinally but you still haven't been able to break the hold of the negative feelings you are experiencing. With this method you just accept that they are there but you don't give your conscious power to them.

You realize that healing is a process. Just as it takes time to heal physically when you are ill, it takes time for emotional healing, too. If you break a leg, life still goes on and you continue to function. The same is true emotionally. You might be feeling severe emotional pain but have to continue functioning effectively in your daily life. In this state, the conscious and subconscious and superconscious minds are not in accord; the tension must be carried until the minds are all in emotional alignment.

Sometimes, if you are not practicing this philosophy, you just live with emotional pain for an extended period of time. The greater the degree of the attachment, the more severe will be the lesson.

Suppose you are giving a major public speech to two thousand people the next week and you feel nervous and anxious. No matter how hard you try, you can't seem to get rid of the fear. The appropriate method might be just to accept that it is there but to tell the fear you are not going to let it knock you off center and ruin your speech. You carry the tension and give the speech, even though you have stage fright the whole time. This is similar to someone who has to live with physical pain. He gives it acceptance and stops fighting it but does not give away his power and let it ruin his life.

The Secondary Communication Method

The fourth identification method deals with handling negative feelings in relationships. When negative feelings are coming up in your relationship with a partner or mate, the best thing to do is to take some time alone and try to get right with yourself and with God. This means centering yourself and getting things in perspective.

Often, however, there isn't time or, even if there is time, you still are not able to resolve all the negative feelings you are experiencing. What is appropriate here, from a spiritual perspective, is to share in what is called a "secondary communication method."

The primary method is when you are communicating and you are not in your ego. The secondary method of communicating is when you share your negative, egoistical feelings with your partner in a responsible, calm, rational, loving manner. In other words, you share your hurts or resentments in a loving way, telling your partner that you realize you create your own feelings, that you are taking responsibility for your own reality, and that you are communicating in a loving, not an attacking, manner so your partner does not feel threatened.

You tell your partner that you are sharing the negative feelings in the hope that together you can help each other to achieve clarity within yourselves and in the relationship. Sometimes your partner can help you to sort out your attitudes and feelings whereas when you were working alone in your journal, you were stuck. It is imperative to have this method of communication available because it is literally impossible to stay clear every moment of your life.

Your partner will probably be very impressed that you are taking responsibility and not blaming, but communicating in a loving and respectful manner.

If you think your feelings are God's gift to mankind and that the proper way to live is to do whatever your feelings tell you to do, in my opinion, you are being irresponsible. Your feelings stem from your attitudes. If your attitudes are egoistical, then all your emotions are going to be egoistical, based on fear and attack. If you run your life according to your feelings, what happens if you feel like punching someone or stealing something or cursing at someone? Is that a responsible way of living? Is that how God would have humans live on this Earth? Don't be seduced by this false philosophy.

You can trust your feelings once you disidentify from your ego and get your mind under control. Then your feelings will be a perfect guide. It is very important to let your life be directed by your mind and intuition, which are the guidance of the higher self.

Subconscious Mind Letter

A letter can be another helpful tool for dealing with your emotions. The idea is to write a letter to your subconscious mind with the understanding that you are the master of the personality. In a firm but loving manner, often called "tough love," tell your subconscious how things are going to be. In letter form, become the computer programmer. The letter is a method of programming that is more fluid than using specifically designed affirmations. I find this method to be extremely beneficial.

If you want to, you can dialogue with your subconscious mind and see what it has to say in response to your firm and loving commands. This can be done in your journal. The subconscious mind will be a great servant as long as you are in command and you treat your subconscious with love. The idea is to form a team, with you serving the superconscious, and the subconscious serving you. All for one and one for all.

Dialoguing

Another helpful tool for resolving emotional conflicts is dialoguing. This is similar to the previous method except that you do it with the person you are having problems with. Write a letter to the person, and then in your journal let him or her respond to you. Continue this process until your unfinished business is complete. This tool can be extremely helpful.

Dialoguing can also be done intrapsychically with the inner child, critical or permissive parent, firm and loving parent, higher self, physical body, subconscious mind, God, ego, spiritual attitude, and so on. You, the conscious mind, talk in letter form to any one of these aspects of yourself and then let it respond. Create a dialogue and see what evolves. Just remember that you are the commander-in-chief of the personality.

It is possible to dialogue with any subpersonality or thought form within the subconscious mind. Every thought, feeling, impulse, desire, and emotion has a life of its own. It is possible to isolate any particular subpersonality or complex in order to dialogue with it. For example, you can dialogue with the part that wants to stop smoking or the part that wants to travel to Europe. The possibilities are infinite. The important thing to realize is that every part has an opposite. The part that wants to smoke cigarettes has a side that doesn't want to smoke cigarettes. The part that wants to go to Europe has a polarity that doesn't want to go to Europe.

When dialoguing with any specific part, be sure to talk to both sides so you can get a fully balanced perspective on the issue you are exploring.

Negative Emotions Log

Another very helpful tool for refining, purifying, and spiritualizing your emotional self is to keep a negative emotions log. This is a small pad of paper and a pen that you keep with you in your purse or pocket. Any time you have a negative feeling, just make a brief note of the feeling and incident. Then later, when you have free time, you can go back to your journal and work the six-step process to figure out what faulty belief caused you to feel the way you did.

If you don't keep a negative emotions log, you are very likely to forget many of the lessons that occur during the day. If you really want to learn to purify and spiritualize your emotional body, this is the best way to do it.

Carrying this idea a step further, you can go back through your day and relive each of the experiences the way you would have liked it to happen. Since the brain cannot tell the difference between events that happen in imagination and those that happen in actuality, this is a way of programming your subconscious with a positive experience to replace the negative one.

Logging in General

The purpose of a log is to bring more consciousness and discipline into the areas of your life that need it. There are many kinds of logs you can keep. You might keep an exercise log in which you write down the date, how much you exercised, and how you felt about your effort that day. Another type of log is a meditation log in which you write the date, how long you meditated, and any feelings or insights you gained. Doing this is important because it is easy to forget what you receive in an altered state of consciousness, which can be similar to dreaming, and you know how easy it is to forget your dreams.

Another example is a food log in which you write down everything you eat during the day. Having to write it down makes you more aware, which is the reason you are keeping the log. Knowing you are going to write it down is good motivation to eat appropriately. A log can be created for any area of your life in which you are trying to achieve greater mastery and self-control. You score yourself in percentage points based on how you are doing in terms of manifesting that particular attitude or quality. I have listed twenty-one days because that is how long it takes to cement a new habit into the subconscious mind.

These types of logs can help you to focus. Trying to keep it all in your mind is too difficult, and you lose concentration and discipline. Spiritual growth can be compared with keeping track of your finances. If you tried to keep all your finances, tax records, and banking business in your mind, it would be impossible to keep them organized. The same holds true for spiritual life. Trying to keep it together without some form of spiritual bookkeeping is overwhelming, and logging is an excellent tool for such organizing as well as for mastering any area of your life that needs attention.

	Twenty-One Day Psychological Foundation Logging Chart No. 1							
Instructions: Every morning and night write down a percentage, based on a scale of 1 to 100, that indicates where you are in developing and expressing the given qualities. M = Morning N = Night							
Day	Personal Power		Self-Love		Balance		Attunement to Spiritual Attitude	
	M	N	M	N	M	N	M	N
1								
2								
3								
4								
5								
6								
7								
8								
9								
10								
11								
12								
13								
14								
15								
16								
17								
18								
19								
20								
21								

Twenty-One Day Psychological Foundation Logging Chart No. 2								
Instructions: Every morning and night write down a percentage, based on a scale of 1 to 100, that indicates where you are in developing and expressing the given qualities. M = Morning N = Night								
Day	Personal Power Master, Causer		Christ Consciousness (Self and Others)		Balance and Integration		Attunement to Higher Self	
	M	N	M	N	M	N	M	N
1								
2								
3								
4								
5								
6								
7								
8								
9								
10								
11								
12								
13								
14								
15								
16								
17								
18								
19								
20								
21								

Twenty-One Day Psychological Foundation Logging Chart No. 3									
Instructions: Every morning and night write down a percentage, based on a scale of 1 to 100, that indicates where you are in developing and expressing the given qualities. M = Morning N = Night									
Day	Lessons		Preferences		Patience		Forgiveness		Emotional Invulnerability	
	M	N	M	N	M	N	M	N	M	N
1										
2										
3										
4										
5										
6										
7										
8										
9										
10										
11										
12										
13										
14										
15										
16										
17										
18										
19										
20										
21										

Twenty-One Day Psychological Foundation Logging Chart No. 4									
Instructions: Every morning and night write down a percentage, based on a scale of 1 to 100, that indicates where you are in developing and expressing the given qualities. M = Morning N = Night									
Day	Faith and Trust		Unconditional Love		Decisiveness		Being the Cause		Nonjudg-mentalness	
	M	N	M	N	M	N	M	N	M	N
1										
2										
3										
4										
5										
6										
7										
8										
9										
10										
11										
12										
13										
14										
15										
16										
17										
18										
19										
20										
21										

Twenty-One Day Psychological Foundation Logging Chart No. 5									
Instructions: Every morning and night write down a percentage, based on a scale of 1 to 100, that indicates where you are in developing and expressing the given qualities. M = Morning N = Night									
Day	Critical Parent		Overly Permissive Parent		Firm-Love Parent		Conditional Love		Unchanging and Unconditional Self-Love	
	M	N	M	N	M	N	M	N	M	N
1										
2										
3										
4										
5										
6										
7										
8										
9										
10										
11										
12										
13										
14										
15										
16										
17										
18										
19										
20										
21										

Keeping Journals

I recommend keeping two journals. The first is for writing in when you are not thinking clearly or when you just feel like it. By writing in your journal you can empower yourself and achieve attitudinal healing. Since your thoughts create your reality, as you change the way you look at things, your feelings change; attitudinal healing is the process of moving from egoistical thinking to spiritual thinking.

Journal writing is also for reprogramming your conscious and subconscious minds. It is for attunement to your higher self, for gaining insight and understanding, as well as for catharsis.

What you don't want to do is just reinforce the same patterns on paper, without movement or change. It is best to go into your journal writing with the attitude of wanting to move toward self-mastery, personal power, and perfect spiritual attunement.

The second journal is used to store the various tools, logs, and psychological practices on which you are working. The purpose of this journal is to keep all this material together in an organized fashion. Following are some other valuable sections you might keep in your journal.

Major Lessons of the Day

The "Major Lesson of the Day" section of your journal is for use before bed each night or in the morning when you get up. Review your day and write down the golden nuggets of wisdom you have learned that day. The nugget might be something you did well or a lesson you learned from a negative experience. Getting into the regular practice of doing this is very important, and it will be much more effective if you do it in your journal because the act of writing things down has a much greater impact on the conscious and subconscious minds than thinking has.

Many people live their lives without learning from their mistakes, so spiritual progress is slowed and the school of hard knocks is perpetuated. Learn continually from what you have done well and what you have done poorly, and then build upon your strengths each day. No matter how good yesterday was, you want to make today better. Enjoy your victories but never be satisfied until your ultimate divine goal is met.

Goals and Priorities

An essential section to have in your journal is one labeled "Goals and Priorities." You are never going to get anywhere if you don't know where you are going. For this section, make a list of all your goals on the Earthly physical level, the psychological level, and the spiritual level. List all the things you want to accomplish in this lifetime. List the psychological qualities you want to develop, the abilities you want to improve, your ultimate purpose and goal, and the Earthly experiences you want to have.

A helpful mini-meditation you might try in order to help in this process is to imagine that seventy-five years have passed and your soul has passed on to the spirit world. Imagine that you are looking back on this lifetime. From that perspective, what do you want to see? How do you want to see yourself as having lived? What do you want to see yourself as having achieved? What do you want to appear on your tombstone?

This experience is actually going to happen in your future. You have the opportunity now to create a life about which you will feel good then. It is very easy to misuse time and energy. Are you using your time and energy to achieve your God-given potentials? If not, you need to form a clearer focus on exactly what you want to achieve.

Life Plan and Design

The second step, after getting clear on your goals and priorities, is to set up a life plan and design. This is a tentative map for the next fifty years, or however long you think you will be living on this Earthly plane.

The life plan begins with your ultimate goal of self-actualization. From there you break down your goals into a timetable, loosely designating what years you are going to focus on what. Part of this is a process of prioritizing. What do you want to focus on in the next year? Then in the next five years? Ten years? Fifteen years?

For example, you might write down when you want to get married, have a child, go to Europe, study meditation or healing, get a college degree, go to India, read certain books, take certain classes, perform certain services, or make certain contributions. This plan can be tentative so you can constantly change it as you see fit. It begins to give your life a focus that will keep you on the right path.

It is easy to stray from your path. There are many temptations and different energies pulling on you from many directions. Without a psychological and spiritual map, you are likely to be pulled off course.

Cycles

The next step is to refine this process even further. The idea here is to take the goals and priorities of the next year or two and make a timetable for accomplishing them.

For example, you might say to yourself that this spring your goals are to focus on physical fitness, writing a book, and maintaining the status quo. Then your summer goal might be to spend more time with your family, go to Hawaii, and concentrate on making more money. From September to the following Spring, you might want to put energy into practicing meditation and studying healing.

Developing short-term goals for yourself in this way helps you to be more focused, disciplined, and motivated. As your life changes you might have to make adjustments, but you can always set up a new cycle of short-term goals.

It is also extremely helpful, in considering this concept of cycles, to use one of your journal writing sessions to examine the past cycles that led you to your present state of consciousness. Certain initiations, or turning points, have led you to your present position. Understanding your past cycles will help in creating what is appropriate for the present cycle and what is appropriate for future cycles. Examples of past turning points might be graduating from high school, receiving an award, making the basketball team, meeting your first boyfriend or girlfriend, having your first religious experience, or having a baby. Each of these turning points marked the beginning of a new phase of your life. I am suggesting that you become much more conscious of these stages by writing about them. I think you will find it very helpful.

A Weekly Routine

The next step is to refine the process even further by creating a weekly routine. (See the following diagram.) I am not saying you should do all the things suggested in this routine; the diagram is meant to give you an overview of some of the kinds of things you can include in your weekly routine.

It is of the utmost importance, in my opinion, that every person have a routine or regime. You will never develop spiritually or on any other level if you don't. The danger of a routine is in becoming too yang or regimenting your life to the point where there is no spontaneity. On the other side of the coin, you don't want to be too yin.

To be too yin is to be too flowing, too flexible, too laissez faire. There are no hard and fast rules in creating a routine. Some people need more structure than others. Routines can be likened to braces you wear to straighten your teeth; they guide you in the direction in which you need to move. A routine is to be followed whether you feel like it or not. This is not to say that you have to be neurotic and become an absolute slave to the routine.

Again, it is more of a tentative guide to use except when an emergency or a special occasion arises. Its purpose is to help you achieve the goals and priorities that you have clearly set up for yourself. Haphazard exercise is not going to achieve physical fitness any more than haphazard meditation will give you the fruits of the spirit.

Time Management: Weekly Routine

Monday	Tuesday	Wednesday	Thursday	Friday	Saturday	Sunday
Alarm	Alarm	Alarm	Alarm	Alarm	Planning	Sleep In
Dreams	Dreams	Dreams	Dreams	Dreams	Paying Bills	Good Breakfast
Affirmations	Affirmations	Affirmations	Affirmations	Affirmations	Doing Errands	
Meditation	Meditation	Meditation	Meditation	Meditation	Cleaning	Recreation
Prayer	Prayer	Prayer	Prayer	Prayer	Shopping	Fun
Journal Writing	Journal Writing	Journal Writing	Journal Writing	Journal Writing	Studying	
Organizing	Organizing	Organizing	Organizing	Organizing		
Good Breakfast	Good Breakfast	Good Breakfast	Good Breakfast	Good Breakfast		
(Supplements)	(Supplements)	(Supplements)	(Supplements)	(Supplements)	Pleasure	Pleasure
Work (Service)	Work (Service)	Work (Service)	Work (Service)	Work (Service)	Pleasure	Pleasure
Lunch	Lunch	Lunch	Lunch	Lunch	Physical Exercise	
Physical Exercises	Physical Exercises	Physical Exercises	Physical Exercises	Physical Exercises	Good Dinner	Good Dinner
Cat Nap	Cat Nap	Cat Nap	Cat Nap	Cat Nap	Clean Up	Clean Up
Relaxation	Relaxation	Relaxation	Relaxation	Relaxation	Fun	Reading
Good Dinner	Good Dinner	Good Dinner	Good Dinner	Good Dinner	Pleasure	Good Dinner
Reading, Tapes	Reading, Tapes	Reading, Tapes	Reading, Tapes	Fun	Good Dinner	Journal Writing
Journal Writing	Journal Writing	Journal Writing	Journal Writing	Pleasure	Recreation	Meditation
Meditation	Meditation	Meditation	Meditation		Fun	Prayers
Prayers	Prayers	Prayers	Prayers		Fun	Set Alarm
Set Alarm	Set Alarm	Set Alarm	Set Alarm		Good Dinner	
Sleep	Sleep	Sleep	Sleep	Sleep	Sleep	Sleep

Most people do not function well at all without a routine. If you took away their jobs or school, they would be lost and without motivation. Most people look to other people to set up structure and routine for them. Ideally you want to have the personal power and self-discipline to set up and follow a weekly routine with your own goals and priorities.

Don't make the routine too difficult or you won't follow it. On the other hand, don't make it too easy. You will find your routine constantly changing as your life changes, and that is fine. But always keep a routine to help you develop positive habits in your subconscious mind.

After a while you will have positive habits of exercising, eating healthfully, meditating, and so on. Having a routine will also make you much more efficient in your use of time and therefore more productive. By following a routine, you know you are accomplishing your goals, so your free time is much more enjoyable.

A Daily Routine

Now, if you really want to get fancy you can take this one step further and have a daily routine, too. This is something I do and I really enjoy it. Every night before bed I map out the next day, including telephone calls, clients, errands, spiritual disciplines, diet, vitamin and mineral supplements, food planning, physical exercise, thought forms and attitudes I am trying to hold, and so on.

I have memorized my weekly routine so I just write out my mental, emotional, physical, and spiritual life plan on paper the night before. By doing this I feel organized and efficient, so I sleep better. In the morning I can go right into action because my inner and outer day is laid out before me.

As I think of new things, I write them in; and as I finish things, I cross them off. That way, I don't have to hold on to things in my mind, which allows me to be more creative and less worried. Doing this before bed also serves as a type of programming device. I find that to a certain extent I have the energy that I program myself to have; if I plan for a big day the night before I am better able to face the day's challenges.

The Battle Plan

The battle plan is one of the most helpful journal sections of all. I cannot recommend it highly enough. Here, you look closely at whatever area of your life you are currently working on and you make a list of every possible thing you can do to achieve that goal. If you are having health problems, make a list of every action you can take to get better. If you want more clients, business contacts, or money, make a plan listing every possible inner or outer tool you can think of.

For example, let's say you are sick with some kind of systemic infection and your immune system is weak. The following are examples of just a few of the things you might write down on your battle plan:

Own personal power
Pray for healing
Affirm and visualize health
Eat steamed vegetables
Drink lots of water; take vitamin C
Take herbal immune formula; take homeopathic remedies
Get some acupuncture
Lie in the sun
Go for a walk
Do deep-breathing exercises
Get into a jacuzzi
Keep a positive mental attitude
Sleep as much as possible
Write in journal
Have faith.

By creating this list you are attacking the problem instead of letting it attack you. If you are feeling victimized, you are going to be depressed. When you attack the problem, even if you are physically sick, you will feel better. I guarantee it. You feel better because you are assertively doing something to remedy the situation.

The creating of this battle plan inspires lots of good ideas and also serves to attract what you want. It is very likely that you will have battle plans for a number of areas in your life.

Whenever you are feeling off center, unmotivated, indifferent, or uninspired, either review your battle plan or create a new one. You will immediately feel better. I have mine taped onto the wall so it is right in front of me whenever I sit at my desk. The battle plan renews your faith and inspires your personal power. It feeds the part of your consciousness that knows you are a causal master.

Quotations and Good Ideas

Another section of your journal can be reserved for inspiring ideas, essays, poetry, or pictures. You might even keep a separate journal for matters of an aesthetic nature. Since your thoughts create your reality, having a journal like this can serve to awaken you to the joy and beauty of life when you are feeling down. Looking through such a journal will help to rekindle your awareness of the ultimate beauty of reality that you know to exist.

You can experiment with these tools and find out which ones work best for you. You will be pleasantly surprised at their effectiveness.

Prayer versus Meditation

Prayer is the act of talking to God; meditation is the act of listening to God. Prayer is the masculine or yang aspect; meditation is the yin or feminine aspect.

Contacting Your Higher Self

There are a number of methods by which you can develop greater attunement to your higher self.

Letters

This I find to be a very enjoyable and helpful tool. The idea is to write your higher self a letter. I do this every morning and sometimes before bed as well. The higher self is like an older and wiser brother or sister. Talk to him or her as you would to your best friend. Form a relationship in free-flowing letters. You will find that your higher self will respond in subtle thought channeling, in dreams, or in the other ways I have already mentioned. I sometimes use my "Dear higher self" letters as one form of praying.

Affirmations

Affirming certain statements to yourself throughout your day will create instant attunement to your higher self. My favorite ones are these:

a. I can do all things through Christ who strengthens me.
b. God goes with me wherever I go.
c. I trust in the Lord, and He will light the way.
d. If God be for me, who can be against me?
e. I have perfect faith, trust, and patience in God and God's laws.
f. All things are possible with God.
g.. Father, I expect a miracle.
h. God and Christ are now bearing my cross with me.
i. God is my copilot.

Visualizations

Close your eyes and imagine a symbol or image that reminds you that your higher self is with you all through the day. It could be a dove flying above you. It could be a golden-white Light hovering above your head. There are infinite possibilities, so use your imagination.

Shuttle back to these different images and affirmations throughout your day to reattune yourself. The affirmations and images provided in this book will give you comfort, peace of mind, strength, and power in time of need. It might also be helpful to create imagery for the presence of God and Christ and the guides, teachers, and helpers who are also available to assist you.

Altars

A small holy place or shrine in one corner of your bedroom is a lovely way to attune to your higher self. It can be created in many ways. Some people have little statues of Jesus, Buddha, or Moses. Others have pictures of the great masters. I also recommend incense and spiritual music, which help you to align your consciousness.

You can add affirmations, poetry, or pictures from magazines. Some people create a bulletin board or poster. I pin up all my battle plans, centering models, schedules, commitments, and inspiring thoughts. It is really fun to create. Candles can be added, too. It is nice to meditate near your altar, if possible. It serves to remind you of your connection to spirit and your high calling.

10

How to Reprogram
the Subconscious Mind

Be vigilant for God and His kingdom

Jesus Christ
A Course in Miracles

Since I have already mentioned affirmations in the previous chapters, I think it is appropriate now to explain more deeply what affirmations and visualizations are and how you can use them. An affirmation is, in reality, an attitude. Every thought you think, be it positive or negative, is an affirmation. Every word you speak is an affirmation. Every action you take is an affirmation. This is true because everything stems from your thoughts. Your thoughts create your reality.

Affirmations used in a psychological and healing context are statements specifically designed to program a desired feeling or behavior into your subconscious mind, such as the affirmations to develop your personal power and your protective bubble that were mentioned earlier.

Whenever you practice positive thinking you are making affirmations. The affirmations in this chapter are designed to help you develop certain key attitudes that pertain to your self-concept and self-image.

The continued process of pushing the negative attitudes out of your mind with your personal power and then repeating the new, positive affirmations is the main key to reprogramming the subconscious mind.

Pushing negative thoughts out of your mind is like not watering a plant: the negative thought gets no energy, so it withers and dies. The repetitive use of positive thinking and affirmations waters the new seed-thought in the soil of your subconscious mind and it begins to grow. To use another metaphor, it is like a tape recorder that re-records over old information.

Methods of Reprogramming

To reprogram your subconscious mind, try the following ways and see which ones are most effective for you.

1. *Affirmations*

An affirmation is a strong, positive statement that something is already so! The statement is repeated silently until it is fully programmed into your subconscious mind, and the pattern has become a reality in your life.

2. *Decrees*

A decree is a spoken affirmation.

3. *Creative Visualizations*

Creative visualization is the process of imagining that the healing or the finished result has already occurred. It acts as a direct suggestion to the subconscious mind just as an affirmation does; pictures are perhaps even more powerful than words.

4. *Journals*

Write down your affirmations in a journal. This is a very effective way of programming your subconscious mind. The act of physically writing causes the thought pattern to take a more tangible and stable form. Change the wording as better ways of stating your affirmations come to you.

5. *Affirmation Cards*

Write affirmations on cards and place them all over your house and your place of work This is a very effective method. Put these affirmation cards next to your bed, on the mirror, in the bathroom, on the refrigerator, in your car, in your wallet, and on your desk. They will act as reminders to repeat them, which will accelerate the process.

6. *Affirmation Walks*

Go for a walk! An affirmation walk is one of my favorites. I walk for as long as I am in the mood to do so and affirm to my subconscious mind how I want everything to be. The subconscious mind will manifest anything you tell it, good or bad. The value of affirmations and positive visualizations is obvious, for if you are not affirming and visualizing the positive, you are doing the opposite.

7. *Rhythmic Repetitions*

Say your affirmations rhythmically while you are physically exercising. This is an excellent programming technique and it keeps your mind focused while you are exercising.

8. *The Three Voices*

Say your affirmations in first, second, and third person. For example: I, Joshua, am in perfect radiant health; you, Joshua, are in perfect radiant health; he, Joshua, is in perfect radiant health.

This technique is especially useful when taping your affirmations.

9. *Positive-Negative Clearings*

Draw a line down the middle of a piece of paper. Write one affirmation on one side of the page. Then wait and listen for any thoughts that come into your mind to contradict your positive affirmation. Write down the negative thoughts that come up from your subconscious mind.

The next step is to change each negative thought into a positive affirmation. Record any negative thoughts that come up after you have written that new positive affirmation. Change all the negatives into new positive statements. Continue this process until no more negative thoughts come up. You now have a list of the affirmations that deal specifically with your personal lessons in this lifetime. This method is also excellent because it teaches you the process of creating your own affirmations, an essential ability to develop.

10. *Mirrors*

Look in the mirror every day for twenty-one days and say your affirmations aloud. Say them with total personal power and conviction. Look yourself right in the eye! Continue affirming aloud until there is no subconscious resistance.

11. *Endless Tapes*

Record your affirmations onto a cassette tape that plays all night without stopping. Play the tape while you sleep, every night for twenty-one nights.

It is also possible to buy a cassette tape recorder that will play any standard tape all night long. This sleep tape method is 100% effective! Pillow speakers are available. Endless cassette tapes are usually available at Tower Records or Radio Shack and run from three to twelve minutes in length.

12. *Hypnosis*

Find a trustworthy hypnotherapist to hypnotize you and plant positive suggestions into your subconscious mind while you are in the hypersuggestible state.

13. *Reading*

Read and reread good books in the field of psychology and spirituality. This serves as a powerful patterning device.

14. *Pendulums*

Make or buy a pendulum and communicate with your subconscious mind through yes and no answers. This is a process that retrieves information from the subconscious mind and can be used in the programming of the subconscious.

15. *Dialogues*

Another very effective tool is to dialogue with the subconscious mind or with one subpersonality within the subconscious mind. This can be done in a number of ways.

    a.   Voice dialogue: Use chairs to represent the conscious and subconscious minds. Create a dialogue between them. Add chairs to represent your isolated subpersonalities. The idea is to role-play the various parts of your subconscious mind. The conscious mind then dialogues with these various parts. This is a very powerful tool in helping you to become the master of your life rather than a victim.

    b.   Using this same process in a journal can also be exceedingly helpful. Have a dialogue on paper with any thought system within you that you are trying to manifest into your consciousness. For example, you can have a dialogue with your higher self.

    c.   A third way to dialogue is within your mind. When a destructive thought system arises, talk to it. Tell it you are the captain of the ship and you have the power in the personality, not it. Then affirm the opposite to yourself, and tell the opposite you will listen to it.

16. *Acting As If*

Act in your daily life the way you want to be, even if you don't feel it, even if your subconscious is trying to do the opposite. This method takes an act of will power. If the tension can be carried long enough, eventually it will act as a reprogramming procedure.

This is an essential method to develop because sometimes you just don't have the time to prepare properly for everything. For example, you might have a spur-of-the-moment job interview in which you must act confident and qualified, even if you don't feel that way.

17. *Pictures*

Create a physical picture of your desired reality. It serves as a suggestion to your subconscious mind, just as the creative visualization process does, except this is an actual physical reproduction of the imagined result. For example, if you are overweight, find a picture of someone who has the figure you want and attach that picture to a picture of your own face. Your subconscious mind will seek to manifest that image.

18. *Self-Hypnosis*

Suggestions given to your subconscious mind while in a relaxed state can symbolize the meaning of a longer affirmation. The discipline of hypnosis has demonstrated that when the conscious, critical mind is relaxed, suggestions are almost immediately accepted by the subconscious mind. What this indicates is that you can take advantage of these relaxed states to pattern your subconscious mind more quickly.

Affirmations are important but do take more work than this method. Some examples of periods during the day when you can use autosuggestion are as follows:

   a. Just before falling asleep, while you are in the twilight zone between sleep and wakefulness; affirm to yourself a key word or phrase such as perfect health, wealth, success, a good night's sleep.
   b. When you are just relaxing.
   c. After meditation; this is an excellent time for auto-suggestion.
   d. After you've done self-hypnosis.
   e. In the ionized atmosphere of a shower.

19. *Tape Recordings*

Make a tape recording of affirmations and autosuggestions and play it during any of the above-mentioned hypersuggestible states of consciousness.

20. *Subliminal Tapes*

Another method of reprogramming the subconscious mind is the use of subliminal tapes. A subliminal tape is one on which a suggestion or affirmation is given in a barely audible tone, with a background of classical, new age, or environmental music. The suggestion is so quietly given that you can't hear it consciously unless you really strain to do so. Subliminal tapes are excellent as sleep tapes, especially if you find that regular affirmational sleep tapes keep you awake.

21. *Songs*

Make up songs and sing your affirmations to yourself. You don't have to be a professional musician; use the melodies of your favorite music. Create personal power songs, self-love songs, and financial prosperity songs. Allow yourself to be a little crazy and to have fun with this. If you feel hesitant, you can sing while you are driving in your car alone.

22. *Poetry*

Another method along this same line is to write poetry embodying the new ideals you are trying to program into your subconscious mind.

23. *Artwork*

Draw or paint pictures of the new you that you are becoming.

These last three methods are more right-brained or yin methods of programming.

24. *Self-Talk*

A very effective tool is to practice self-talk. The self-talk that arises out of the subconscious mind is usually negative. The idea here is to practice positive self-talk. Just talk to yourself as you would talk to a best friend or loved one. Affirmations are very formal and set, but this method is more informal.

For example, if I were working on self-love, I might say to myself, "Joshua, I love you. I really do. You have made a lot of mistakes, and I just want to tell you that is okay by me. I want to let you know that you are completely forgiven and I am on your side."

In other words, talk to yourself using the new thought or image that you are attempting to incorporate as a habit in your subconscious mind. This method can be used in a number of ways:

    a.   In your mind;

    b.   Aloud;

    c.   In a letter;

    d.   On a tape; then listen to it as you go to sleep each night.

Visualizations

A visualization or image is really the same thing as a thought. *Every thought has an image that is related to it.* The concept of personal power might be visualized as a sword. The concept of self-love might be visualized as a rose. In the field of psychology there is much talk about positive thinking; positive imaging should be mentioned as well.

The subconscious mind can be programmed effectively by using either affirmations or imagery. If you want to create through imagery, you just imagine yourself the way you want to be. If you want more money, visualize yourself with the money you want. The key is to use all your inner senses: see yourself with the money, feel the money, smell the money, hear the money, taste the money. Make your visualization so real that you are actually in your visualization — not just watching yourself, but actually there. The more realistic you make your visualization, the more effective will be the manifestation by the subconscious mind of what you want.

Visualization Exercises

Following is a series of visualization exercises to practice in your quiet meditative times. A lot of the theory of these exercises will be discussed in later chapters of this book. However, for now I just want you to get an overview of the kinds of visualizations that are available to you.

Begin by finding a spot in your house where you can have some privacy for at least twenty to thirty minutes. Find a comfortable chair to sit in and begin by closing your eyes and taking three deep breaths. After each breath say to yourself inwardly, "Relax now."

Begin imagining that you are in a beautiful place such as the mountains, a meadow, the ocean, or a forest. Imagine that you are actually experiencing this natural setting. Don't just see yourself there; be there! Imagine yourself as being perfectly healthy, vitally alive and strong. Use all five of your inner senses. See the scene, smell it, hear it, touch it, taste it, and feel it. Try to make it so real that you feel you are actually there.

Next, imagine yourself alone in this beautiful place, feeling very powerful and in command of yourself. Imagine how it would feel to be the captain of a ship or the President of the United States; imagine being the chief executive of a major company or the conductor of a major symphony orchestra.

Experience the personal power and the authority you have. Realize that you *are* the captain, queen, executive director, commander, and orchestra leader of your thoughts, feelings, behavior, body, and environment. Imagine being the master of these things instead of letting them be your master.

Recognize that you don't need to be afraid of your power because you are going to use it in a loving, spiritual manner. Notice how good it feels to have personal power and authority over yourself rather than letting everything else in the universe be your master.

Imagine now that whenever you own this power there is an image or symbol that automatically appears in your presence. Choose a symbol that works for you: It might be a sword, a scepter, a crown, a torch, a special ring, special clothing, or a piece of jewelry. Experience your personal power and self-mastery while being aware of the presence of your power symbol.

Now imagine, with the power of your mind, that you are creating a white and golden bubble around you that extends outward about two to three feet. Imagine that it is a protective bubble. Make it thick and strong. Imagine that this bubble is semipermeable in nature. In other words, negative energy is kept out while positive, loving, and spiritual energy is allowed through it.

Next, fill the inside of that bubble with personal power, unconditional self-love, and unconditional self-worth. See yourself filled now with your personal power, emotional invulnerability, and unchanging self-love and self-worth.

Imagine that someone enters the natural setting in your mind's eye and tries to pick a fight with you by making a negative comment. See that negative energy sliding off you like water off a duck's back, and then send love to that person.

Now see yourself at work, and imagine one of your coworkers being irritable and uptight. See that negative energy sliding off you. See your boss coming toward you in a bad mood and hear him or her snap at you. See that negative energy sliding off you.

Imagine yourself now at home with your spouse. See your spouse being in a bad mood and see that energy slide off your bubble. Follow the same procedure with your children, parents, or anyone else with whom it would be appropriate.

When you have finished, go back to your natural setting and imagine that your subconscious mind is bringing up some negative programming. See yourself pushing it out of your mind and denying it entrance. See yourself batting it out as you would a baseball when hitting a home run out of the ballpark.

Experience how good it feels to maintain mental and emotional discipline. Experience how good it feels to have your subconscious mind dancing to your tune and following your every order as a faithful friend and servant would.

Imagine yourself in different situations, taking command over your thoughts, emotions, behavior, and body, instead of letting the content of your subconscious mind run you. Experience how good it feels to be the master of your life, in service to a spiritual purpose.

See yourself powerful, loving, causal, an example and inspiration to others. See yourself being like a light to the world in your strength, self-love, love of others, and emotional invulnerability. Everywhere you go, people are being uplifted by your presence. See yourself fulfilling your spiritual purpose of spreading good energy, happiness, joy, cooperation, forgiveness, harmony, peace, and love. See yourself setting this good example everywhere you go.

Visualize yourself in your natural setting building a gigantic bonfire. See yourself taking all the negative, egoistical thoughts, emotions, behaviors, and physical ailments and throwing them into the bonfire. See them all being burned up. See yourself only as powerful, strong, positive, loving, balanced, and spiritual. Experience it as an unbelievable weight that is being lifted off your back. Experience having finally returned to your true self, freed from faulty thinking and illusion. In your mind's eye, see the fire two hours later having burned everything up. All that is left in the middle of the ashes is a one-pound chunk of gold. Alchemy has taken place.

By gaining all the wisdom from your past mistakes, you have changed base metal (experiences) into gold. Everything that has happened has been positive, since you have learned from it.

Taking an Elevator to Your Subconscious Mind

The Subconscious Mind as a Computer Room

Close your eyes and imagine taking an elevator, a flight of stairs, or an escalator down into the recesses of your subconscious mind. In this first visualization exercise, imagine that your subconscious mind looks like a computer room. Imagine that there is one master computer sitting on a large desk with a chair in front of it. Sit down in the chair and see the keyboard in front of you. The computer screen is also in front of you.

Imagine that there is a particular key you can press to see the existing programs that are already in your computer. Scan the "bad" habits or thinking patterns that are still in your computer (subconscious) and see these faulty patterns being printed out on the screen in front of you.

Choose three thinking habits you want to change. See them clearly on the screen; then see these habits vanish from the screen. Now type in the new thinking habits you want to be stored on the computer disks. See them printed clearly on the screen. Then press another button on your computer keyboard that signifies indefinite storage in your computer bank. When you have finished, take the elevator back up to your conscious mind.

The Subconscious Mind as a Movie Projector

Close your eyes and again take the elevator down into your subconscious mind. This time see it as a movie studio. In the middle of the room there is a projector. In front of the projector is a large screen. Walk up to the movie projector and see yourself switching it on. On the screen in front of you appear three bad habits that have been operating within your videotape machine. See these faulty patterns being projected onto the screen in full Technicolor.

After watching the movie of your bad habits, shut off the projector. Remove the videocassette. As you look at the cassette, you see that it is entitled "Three Past Bad Habits."

See yourself go to a metal wastebasket filled with paper and light a match to the paper. See a small flame engulf the paper. Then throw the videocassette into the wastebasket. See it start to melt. See it burn up.

Then go to a shelf on the wall, get a blank videocassette, and put it into the video machine. Examine the movie camera and press the button that says "record." As you do so, imagine on the screen in front of you, in full Technicolor, the new habits you want in your life.

See in great detail every aspect of these new habits. When you are finished, shut off the movie camera, take the cassette out of the camera, label it, and put it on the shelf with the other videotapes you have in storage. Then take the elevator back to your conscious, reasoning mind.

The Subconscious Mind as a Garden

Close your eyes, take the elevator down into your subconscious mind, and see a beautiful garden in front of you. Examine your garden and see what is growing out of the soil (your subconscious mind). Are there a lot of beautiful flowers, plants, and trees, or is it overrun by "weeds"?

Walk through your garden and begin pulling out the weeds that don't belong there. Each time you pull out a weed that doesn't belong, look at it and see what negative thought or image or habit it represents.

Go through your garden weeding until you are satisfied. Then take the weeds you have collected and burn them. Go to the shed in your garden where you store packages of new seeds (new thoughts and images). While in the shed, decide what new seeds you want to plant in your garden. Then see yourself very carefully planting these new seeds in the soil in an orderly manner.

Imagine time passing by. Every day for twenty-one days, see yourself coming back and watering, talking to, and fertilizing these seeds. Each day you come back, see the seeds sprouting into the positive thoughts, images or habits latent within them.

See your garden now, after twenty-one days. Do whatever you have to do within the garden of your subconscious mind to make it healthy and strong. Make note of which plants, flowers, and trees represent what within your garden. Be clear that the soil of your subconscious mind will nurture any seed-thought you plant, be it positive or negative, so be sure not to let any bad seeds land in the soil of your subconscious mind. If any bad seeds have landed there and are starting to grow, be sure to pull them out daily.

Take the elevator back up to your conscious mind.

The Subconscious Mind as an Audio Tape Recorder

Close your eyes, take the elevator down into your subconscious mind, and see it as an audio recording studio. See the master tape recorder on the table before you. Press the "play" button and listen to the existing cassette of the bad habits or emotional patterns that are existing within your tape recorder.

After listening to three of the bad habits that have been playing, press the "stop/eject" button of the tape recorder. Take that tape out and burn it. Get a brand new audiocassette tape and place it into the tape recorder. Press the "record" button and begin talking into the microphone, either aloud or internally, to make the new audio recording you want to be playing in your subconscious mind.

This is your opportunity to do your affirmations or to just talk to your subconscious and tell it what you would like to manifest within your reality. When you feel complete, stop the machine, put the new cassette back into its container, and file it with your other cassettes. When you are finished, take the elevator back up to your reasoning mind.

While working with these visualization exercises, it is a good idea to do them on a regular basis just as you would with affirmations. It takes twenty-one days to cement a new habit into the subconscious mind. If you spend ten to fifteen minutes, morning and night, for twenty-one days using these exercises in conjunction with the affirmations you are working with in relation to the same specific habit, that will do the trick.

Physical Health Visualization

Close your eyes and see yourself the way you want to look. Let yourself be completely present within the visualization. See yourself exercising. See yourself in the sunshine and fresh air. See yourself eating all the right foods. See your good thoughts and feelings and behavior creating perfect health within the cells of your body. See the good color in your skin tone. See the blood and energy within your body circulating vibrantly.

See and feel the glow of perfect radiant health emanating from the cells of your body. See yourself identifying with your true spiritual nature while your physical body reflects the health and Light within you. See yourself with high energy and vitality. See yourself waking up every morning fully rested and refreshed, filled with physical energy and vitality. See yourself at your perfect weight.

See yourself with the perfect body contours you want. Your physical body is nothing more than a reflection of the thoughts and images you hold about it, in conjunction with the food you eat. See yourself thinking and imaging only healthy, positive thoughts and images and eating only health-ful foods.

Realize that you are the master of your subconscious mind and your body. See yourself telling them what to do. See your subconscious mind and physical body doing those things. Use all your senses in your imagina-tion to experience what perfect health and physical fitness at the highest level feel like. If you can maintain that image within your mind's eye for twenty-one days, you can have it within your physical experience.

Attracting Money Visualization

Close your eyes and imagine how it would feel to have all the money you want or need. See yourself opening your savings account book and see this numerical figure typed clearly in it. See yourself going to the bank on a weekly basis and depositing larger and larger sums of money. Imagine yourself getting a job promotion or a larger paycheck. Imagine winning a sweepstakes or inheriting a large sum of money.

Visualize clearly the material object you want. Make it so real that it is as if you already have it. Use all your inner senses. See it, feel it, taste it, touch it, smell it, and hear it. Use this object on a regular basis as you would if you actually had it physically. See yourself counting your money or checks.

See yourself being grateful to God for the abundance He has bestowed upon you. See yourself giving part of your money to charity or to a worthy cause because the universe has been good to you and you want to give back to the universe.

Physical Health Affirmations

You can program your subconscious mind to create a physical body that manifests perfect health by continuously affirming that perfection. Below are some effective examples; or make up affirmations that are tailored to your specific needs.

1. My physical body is in perfect radiant health.

2. My physical body now manifests the health and perfection of Christ.

3. Every day, in every way, I am getting better and better.

4. I am physically fit and have an abundance of energy.

5. I sleep soundly every night and wake up fully rested and refreshed early every morning.

6. Father, I thank you for my long and healthy life in your service.

7. Father, I thank you for the unlimited increase in the power and energy of my physical battery.

8. God, my personal power, and the power of my subconscious mind are now healing, energizing, and strengthening my physical body.

9. My physical body is now healing with Godspeed.

10. God, my personal power, and the power of my subconscious mind are now returning my body to perfect radiant health.

11. Be still, and know that I am God; my physical body now manifests the health and perfection of Christ.

12. Father, I thank you for the balanced functioning of my glandular system.

13. My glandular system is now operating at its full Christ potential.

14. My thymus gland and immune system are now operating at their full Christ potential.

15. I am a daughter/son of God, so I cannot possibly be sick.

16. God, my personal power, and the power of my subconscious mind are now revitalizing and awakening my physical body.

17. I love physical exercise and am now filled with an abundance of physical energy.

Affirmations of Faith, Trust, and Patience

Faith in God, trust in yourself and the universe, and patience are qualities that will facilitate the manifestation of your goals. Below are some affirmations that will help you to strengthen these qualities.

1. I have perfect faith in my higher self.
2. I have perfect faith that God is now providing for my every need.
3. I trust God.
4. I hereby surrender all problems and challenges into God's hands.
5. Why worry when I can pray?
6. With God helping me, I will certainly succeed.
7. I have perfect faith in my own power as well as perfect faith and trust in God's power.
8. I have invited God's help and I know His invisible hands are now working in my life to answer my prayers.
9. I have invited God's help; I have perfect faith, trust, and patience, and I know that He will provide me with what I want or something better.
10. I have asked and I know I shall receive.
11. I know God will answer my prayer, in His time not mine, and I have perfect faith, trust, and patience until that time comes.
12. If my prayer isn't answered in exactly the way I want it to be, I know that it is a lesson He would have me learn.
13. I have perfect faith, trust, and patience; I know that God will answer my every prayer.
14. Prayer, personal power, affirmations, and visualizations are an unbeatable team.
15. I have perfect faith in my self, my superconscious mind, and the power of my subconscious mind to attract to me everything I need.
16. I have perfect patience.

My Favorite Affirmations

The following affirmations are guaranteed to make you feel better if you say them regularly and with enthusiasm.

1. Mental strength, physical strength, spiritual strength!
2. Personal power, positive anger, mental strength!
3. I am the power, I am the master, I am the cause.
4. I'm mad as hell and I'm not going to take it anymore.
5. Get thee behind me, Satan!
6. I have perfect faith and trust in God!
7. Personal power, positive anger, eye of the tiger, and faith, trust and patience in God!
8. Personal power, causality, steel-like mastery!
9. The power of my three minds makes me an omnipotent force in

this universe!

10. God, my personal power, and the power of my subconscious mind are an unbeatable team!

11. My mind power and spirit power are an unbeatable team!

12. Be still and know that I am God.

13. Father, I thank you for the miraculous healing of my . . .

14. Water off a duck's back, water off a window pane, invulnerability, invincibility, rubber pillow, filter . . .

15. God, God, God, Christ, Christ, Christ, Jesus Christ, Jesus Christ, Jesus Christ.

16. Absolute total supreme mastery over . . .

17. Tough love, tough love, tough love!

18. Mental power, physical power, spiritual power!

19. Faith and trust in God! Patience with God!

20. I will fake it 'til I make it. I will fake it 'til I make it.

21. Every day, in every way, I am getting stronger and healthier!

22. God is my copilot!

23. With my power and God's power and the power of my subconscious, I cannot and will not be stopped!

24. All-out war against Satan, and for God and love and positivity!

25. I will be more powerful from this moment forward than I have ever before been in my entire life!

26. As God is my witness, I will not be stopped!

27. The Force is with me and I am with the Force!

28. The Source is with me and I am with the Source!

29. I am sustained by the Love of God!

30. I can do all things with God, Christ, and my higher self who strengthen me!

31. As God is my witness, I will never give my power to anyone or anything ever again!

32. God, my personal power, and the power of my subconscious mind!

33. Not my will, but Thine; thank you for the lesson.

34. I may lose a few battles, but I am going to win the war!

35. I declare all-out war to get my life together!

36. I am going to be the absolute master of my life from this moment forward!

37. God goes with me wherever I go!

38. I love God with all my heart and soul and mind and might, and I love my neighbor as myself.

Read the affirmations again and this time say them with enthusiasm!
Read each affirmation from three to seven times!

11

Hypnosis and Self-Hypnosis

*Most of my work is not hypnotizing
people but, rather, dehypnotizing them.
A great many people are already walking
around in a kind of hypnotic state.*

Dr. Joshua David Stone

Hypnosis and self-hypnosis are widely misunderstood in this society. To the ordinary person, they are tainted with negativity caused by a misuse of the tool by stage hypnotists and misinformation spread by the media.

Hypnosis is actually a very common phenomenon that happens to all of you throughout your day. Every time you are feeling like a victim or are on automatic pilot, you are in a state of hypnosis. Every time you let your subconscious mind run you, you are hypnotized. Every time another person's thoughts or feelings affect you, you are in a subtle state of hypnosis.

When you go to sleep at night you go through stages of hypnosis. When you read a book, watch television, or drive your car, you go into a state of hypnosis. If you are a person who is a victim instead of a master of your life, you are living most of your life in a state of hypnosis.

Hypnosis can be described in a number of ways. It is a form of relaxation. It is suggestibility. It is allowing yourself to recall being a victim in the controlled, protected setting of a qualified hypnotherapist's office. Hypnosis occurs when the subconscious mind is running the conscious mind — when you are doing things by habit, daydreaming, fantasizing, or on automatic pilot.

Hypnosis is not bad. It is a normal state that you go into and out of every day. It becomes dangerous only when you are not consciously choosing, controlling, or in some way monitoring and directing the process. Hypnosis is usually thought of in terms of a hypnotist hypnotizing another person, but in reality, there is no hypnosis except self-hypnosis. If you were in my office and I were to give you suggestions to relax, the only effect they could have is the effect you, the patient, would let them have. I, as the hypnotherapist, cannot force suggestions into your mind.

Remember, you cause your own reality. I don't cause your reality unless you let me, so you are actually hypnotizing yourself by allowing yourself to accept my suggestions. You cannot be hypnotized against your personal power or will.

Let me give you another example. Let's say that you and I have a chance meeting at the market. Imagine that I am someone you really admire, someone to whom you have given, psychologically, your power. I tell you that you don't look well, that you look as though you might have the flu. If you don't have your power, if your bubble of protection is not up, and if your discriminating mind is not functioning, my suggestions will go right into your subconscious mind. Ten minutes after I leave, you could start feeling sick. I will have unintentionally programmed you to be sick. Maybe what I said was just an inaccurate observation, but if you believe it and let it in, it will become your reality even though it isn't true. This kind of thing happens all the time.

If someone criticizes you and you feel hurt and rejected, you have been negatively hypnotized. You have let another person be the programmer of your emotions. Most of my work as a counselor is not to hypnotize people but to dehypnotize them. Many people are living in a state of hypnosis, and I am trying to get them out of it.

Myths

People would be much more open to using hypnosis if it were called by a different name. If it were called deep relaxation, guided imagery, meditation, or biofeedback, people wouldn't be so wary.

One myth about hypnosis is that we lose total control. The classic fear is that someone will program us to rob a bank, have sex with him, or some other crazy thing. It is important to understand that 95% of the time, if you have been hypnotized, you are aware of what is going on.

Secondly, you would never do anything that goes against your moral or ethical values. A good example of this is a stage show in which a suggestion is given to five people under hypnosis that they are naked. Two of the people go and hide behind the piano, not wanting the audience to see them. The other three strut around, unembarrassed. Why? The same suggestion was given to all five. Each person responds according to his programming. The two behind the piano had been programmed to be shy about their bodies while the other three had not.

If you hypnotize a sane person and tell him to rob a bank, he won't do it. If you hypnotize a psychopathic killer and give him this suggestion, he might do it, but it is not something a sane person would do. It is possible to pull yourself out of hypnosis in an emergency.

People on stage shows like to act crazy and they enjoy the feeling of being under hypnosis. You have to remember that they have volunteered to go on stage, and only extroverts would volunteer in the first place.

Another myth about hypnosis is that you might not come out of it. If the hypnotist left the office, the worst that could happen is that you would fall asleep and then wake up from the experience as if you had just had a nap.

Depths of Hypnosis

There are three basic depths of hypnosis: light, medium, and heavy. These are also called hypnoidal, cataleptic, and somnambulistic states. In biofeedback terminology these states have been called altered states of consciousness: the Beta level is full consciousness; the Alpha level is the state between waking and sleeping, the hypnotic state, or the meditative state; the Theta level is the early stage of sleep, deep hypnosis, or deep meditation; the Delta level is deep sleep.

Occasionally, a person will go into a heavy, or somnambulistic, trance, but most clinical work is done at the light or medium level. The deeper the level of hypnosis, the more suggestible a person becomes. If a suggestion is given to a person in a conscious state, the reasoning or critical faculty immediately rejects or accepts it. In hypnosis it goes immediately into the subconscious mind. This is the reason for giving yourself suggestions while in an altered state of consciousness. An ideal time for programming is during meditation or when you are waking up or falling asleep. Programming with suggestions and affirmations still works when you are in a conscious state, but it requires more repetition.

Some people are convinced that they can't be hypnotized. This is another myth. Everyone who can go to sleep or relax (which, obviously, everyone can do) can be hypnotized. There are those who cannot be hypnotized but it is because they have chosen, either consciously or unconsciously, not to be hypnotized because of some fear of hypnosis or of the hypnotist.

People who are in a hypnotized state often don't think they are. I have seen stage shows in which people were so deeply hypnotized that it was unbelievable, yet when they were awakened and asked if they thought they had been hypnotized, they said no. I think this happens because of increased awareness under hypnosis.

Meditation and hypnosis are very similar. They are both altered states of consciousness. One of the main differences is the goal of the experience:

The intention of hypnosis is to give suggestions to the subconscious mind; the intention of meditation is to quiet the mind and/or approach the spiritual world. But the actual states are not unlike each other.

Types of Hypnosis

There are two ways of hypnotizing people. One is called the maternal approach, and the other is the paternal approach. The maternal approach is the one that is used for most clinical psychotherapeutic work, and it is the one I use. It is the soft, gently guided relaxation method.

It is also possible to hypnotize people with shock methods. I have never used these methods myself, but I have seen lots of demonstrations of them. People can be shocked into a state of hypnosis almost immediately. An example of this is when a hypnotist has someone stand next to him and puts his hand on the subject's neck. He jerks the neck, without hurting the person, and shouts, "Sleep!" I have seen many people go instantly into hypnosis. It is fascinating to watch.

Benefits of Hypnosis versus Self-Hypnosis

It could be of great benefit to you to learn self-hypnosis. There is nothing wrong with hypnosis, but you don't want to have to pay a large sum of money every time you want to do reprogramming.

The methods for self-hypnosis and hypnosis are exactly the same. The only difference is that in self-hypnosis you do it to yourself instead of having the hypnotist give you the suggestions. It is occasionally nice to have someone else do it for you; then you can totally surrender to the experience without keeping a part of yourself awake in order to give directions.

If you record your instructions on tape, then you can surrender to the experience completely. Once self-hypnosis is learned, you can go very deep with no problem.

Children and Hypnosis

Children are excellent subjects for hypnosis. Children have such vivid imaginations that they go right under. Using imagery is one of the quickest ways to put someone into hypnosis.

Physical Signs Indicating Hypnosis

There are a number of signs that indicate when a person is under hypnosis. Usually the heart and breathing slow down and the limbs become heavy. There is a disinclination to move. Sometimes the eyelids will begin to flutter. A hypnotic sigh is a deep breath that indicates a deepening is taking place. Sometimes a person will describe a feeling of lightness as opposed to a feeling of heaviness. There is also usually a reluctance to come out of the experience because it is so pleasant.

Hypnotic Hallucinations

When a person has been hypnotized he can be made to have what are called positive and negative hallucinations. A positive hallucination is the situation in which the subject can see, hear, taste, smell, or touch something that is not really there. A subject can be programmed to see a vision, hear a sound that hasn't occurred, smell or feel something that isn't present. This is because the subtler subconscious senses predominate when the subconscious is in control, as it is under hypnosis. A negative hallucination results from the suggestion that the subject not see, hear, taste, or smell something that is right in front of him. So it is possible to make a person sense something that is not there or not sense something that is there.

In stage shows, a person is given a glass of water and is told that it is a martini. To the person under hypnosis the water tastes, smells, looks, sounds and feels like a martini, even though it isn't. What is really happening here is the projection of thought and imagery onto the material world.

What is the difference between this kind of hallucination and interpreting a given circumstance as a problem rather than a lesson? When you see problems rather than opportunities, you are creating something that is not present, being pessimistic rather than optimistic, thinking egoistically rather than spiritually. You are seeing something that does not really exist; you just think it does. You create hallucinations all the time.

This happens with imagery, also. I am sure you have all had the experience of looking for something and then realizing it was right in front of you. This is because you had programmed yourself to think that it wasn't there, so you didn't see it. You see with your mind, not with your eyes.

Posthypnotic Suggestions

The posthypnotic suggestion is another interesting phenomenon. A person can be given a suggestion to respond to a certain cue after he has been awakened and taken out of hypnosis. An example of this might be the suggestion that two minutes after the subject's head touches the pillow at night he will fall deeply asleep.

Time Distortion

Time can feel distorted while under hypnosis much as it can in a dream. Dreams seem to last a long time when, in actuality, they do not last longer than thirty to sixty seconds. Under hypnosis a person can be programmed to think five minutes is half an hour or that an hour is ten minutes.

The Future of Hypnosis

In the future, hypnosis, self-hypnosis, and the understanding of programming and suggestion will be a basic part of every aspect of society. The understanding of these dynamics affects everything — relationships, health, work, spiritual life, and on and on.

Hypnosis can be used in many areas and for many problems. It can be used for any type of physical, mental, or emotional problem. The possibilities include using it as a replacement for anesthesia, using it to cure insomnia, headaches, and phobias, using it for physical healing, past-life recollection, dentistry, surgery, weight control, smoking, constipation, stage fright, pain alleviation, childbirth, habit removal, emotional healing, sexual dysfunction, crime and law enforcement, sports, the learning of languages, amnesia, and the finding of lost objects, to name a few.

Since the subconscious mind runs the body, any physical problem can be dealt with through hypnosis. A dentist might accomplish the effect of anesthesia by having a patient imagine there is a bucket of ice water next to him. The patient imagines immersing his hand in the bucket of ice water until his hand becomes totally numb. The dentist then makes the suggestion that whatever that hand touches becomes totally numb as well. He has the patient touch his face, and the face becomes totally numb. The dentist does his dental work and then gives suggestions for the numbness to go away. Amazing, isn't it?

All past-life memories are in the deeper layers of the subconscious mind. Through past-life regression a person can be guided back to look at and experience past lives.

There are two kinds of regressions: complete regression and partial regression. In partial regression, the subject just observes what happened in a past life or even in early childhood. In a complete regression, the subject goes back and reexperiences a traumatic event. Either partial or complete regressions can at times be extremely helpful in releasing deep subconscious blocks.

Surgeons and nurses can stop the flow of blood and promote healing by giving suggestions during surgery. It is also important for surgeons and nurses to be careful about what they say when a person is under anesthesia. A study was done in which a person was under heavy anesthesia for six hours; a week later, under hypnosis she could relate every single thing the doctors and nurses had said. An inappropriate comment or a bad joke about the patient's body can serve to program his subconscious.

The criminal justice department uses hypnosis, and there is continual legal debate regarding whether the evidence obtained under hypnosis is admissible in a court of law. While in a waking state witnesses may remember nothing about a bank robbery, whereas under hypnosis they can recall even the license number of the car the robbers were driving.

The subconscious is the seat of memory and it picks up everything that is going on, even though the conscious reasoning mind does not. Einstein said the human uses only something like 8% of his brain. Most people use their subconscious minds and superconscious minds barely at all, and they use only a fraction of their conscious, reasoning minds.

Hypnosis as a Tool; Possible Dangers

It is important to realize that hypnosis is a tool. It is not a therapy, philosophy, or psychological methodology in itself. There are many hypnotists who are not spiritual, are not licensed as counselors, and are not qualified to do some of the things they are doing. Hypnosis can be misused.

It is important to find someone who is qualified and, preferably, who is a licensed counselor. Find someone with whom you have a good rapport and whom you trust. There is a certain surrendering to another person involved, which is fine as long as the person you are seeing is qualified to deal with any other emotional issues that come up.

A lot of hypnotists, I find, are over-identified with the subconscious mind and don't know the first thing about personal power, let alone the spiritual laws I have been discussing in this book. Be aware that most hypnotists do not have a great understanding of spiritual philosophy. In exploring hypnosis, you are entering into the psychic world. You want someone who really knows what he or she is doing, not someone who is treating hypnosis as a hobby.

This section is in no way trying to discourage you from exploring hypnosis and self-hypnosis. It is just as it is with counseling: if you go to a lousy counselor or psychologist you run a risk of becoming emotionally damaged. The same is true for hypnosis. You will be fine as long as the person doing it is trustworthy, qualified, and licensed.

A False Statement

There is one false statement that I find in almost all books on hypnosis. The statement is attributed to Emile Coué, a famous French hypnotist who did fantastic work. It was he who coined the famous affirmation, "Every day, in every way, I am getting better and better." He said, "When the will and the imagination are in conflict, the imagination will win out." This statement is completely false, in my opinion, even though every book on hypnosis quotes the statement. The imagination is the seat of the subconscious mind, so what the statement is saying is that the subconscious mind is more powerful than the conscious mind. Nothing could be more false.

The most powerful force in this universe is human will and personal power. Never forget this. If it were not true, no one could ever achieve self-mastery. The subconscious is definitely more powerful if you are under hypnosis, but it is not if you are not under hypnosis. The example often used is that of walking across a stream on a narrow board. Even if the subconscious is giving you fearful thoughts of falling in, your conscious reasoning mind can override them with will and personal power, thus keeping you centered and steady.

This kind of statement elucidates what I said earlier about hypnotists being overly identified with the subconscious mind and not having a complete understanding of the conscious mind and the superconscious mind.

Demonstrating the Power of the Mind

A study was done at the University of Chicago that demonstrates the power of the mind on performance. The study involved three groups of men shooting basketballs at a hoop. The first group practiced one hour a day for a month. The second group didn't practice at all. The third group practiced an hour a day in their minds only, not physically. At the end of the month the three groups actually shot baskets physically.

The group that didn't practice made something like 29% of their baskets. The group that practiced in their minds made 79%; the group that practiced physically made 80%. Obviously, practicing in the mind helps physical performance. The ideal would be to practice both physically and mentally.

The Process of Induction

In the chapter on making contact with your higher self, I outlined a process for self-hypnosis that you might try. The following is similar but is a little more detailed. It can also be used for hypnotizing someone else, if you would like to try that. At the end is the technique for awakening yourself or someone else from hypnosis.

Begin by having the person focus his eyes on a wall, above eye level. Have him take five deep breaths, and on every exhale, say the words, "Relax now." After the fifth breath have him close his eyes. Do a progressive relaxation, going through each part of the body and telling it to relax.

Have him imagine a golden-white bubble of Light hovering above his head. Have him imagine that this golden-white Light bubble has special properties. Everything it touches is cleared, cleansed, balanced, attuned, healed, and relaxed. Have him imagine this bubble moving down through his body from the top of his head to the tips of his toes. Then have him imagine he is floating in the clouds in this protective bubble. Then have him imagine floating in space in the protective bubble.

Have him imagine, while floating in the bubble, that there are ten distinct levels of depth of relaxation. Count downward from ten to one, and after each count, use "hypnotic patter," helpful phrases you will find listed after the induction techniques.

After reaching level one, have him imagine a beautiful meadow or mountain or an ocean scene, visualizing it as clearly as possible using all five senses. Use imagery such as a stream, a hot tub, a hammock, sunshine, flowers, trees, birds, clouds, wind, a waterfall, a cabin, a waterbed, animals, grass, favorite foods, swimming, and natural sounds.

Then give the actual suggestions to him. Have him visualize actually being that which he wants to be or manifesting what he wants to have in his life. Read a suggestion or ad lib it. When you are finished with the suggestions, have him relax in the natural setting.

To wake the person up, repeat the following:

I am now going to count upward from zero to five. The count of five will always mean that you are feeling physically relaxed, emotionally calm, mentally alert, and refreshed, energized, and revitalized in every way.

"Number one, you are beginning to wake up.

"Number two, you are waking up more and more, becoming refreshed and energized.

"Number three, you are waking up even more now. Your consciousness is becoming grounded back into your physical body in this room.

"Number four, your eyes are becoming crystal clear behind your eyelids. At the next count your eyes will open and you will feel refreshed and energized in every way, with a tremendous feeling of well-being, happiness, and joy.

"Number five, you are wide awake, eyes open, with a tremendous feeling of well-being, happiness, and joy, completely energized and refreshed, physically relaxed, emotionally calm, and mentally alert."

Regression Induction

The following exercise is the process you can use to do a regression for yourself or others to an early childhood memory or even to a past life. It can be used after you have gone through the entire hypnosis induction and the person is in a medium to deep hypnotic state.

There are two kinds of regression: One is a direct experience in which the person actually feels the emotions of the situation. In the other kind, the person observes the experience as though watching television or a movie.

If you feel it would be better for the person to have a partial regression, just say, "You are an observer feeling no pain. You are just an observer." Keep repeating this until the person moves into that more detached space. Once he is witnessing a particular circumstance, have him share out loud what he is seeing.

To induce the regression, say, "Now your body is very heavy and deeply relaxed. Your body is so heavy it feels as though it is sinking very gently into the couch. However, your mind is free and light, floating and alert, yet deeply comfortable and relaxed. I want you to imagine now that you are a pinpoint of consciousness floating up away from your body and hovering near the ceiling of this room.

"You are looking down now from a vantage point near the ceiling of this room. You are floating, insubstantial as smoke, through the roof of this building and out into the clear night sky. The stars are sparkling brightly and the moon is full. Below you the city is glittering with lights [if applicable].

"You are floating higher and higher, up into the velvety blackness of space. You feel marvelously light and free as you soar up and away. You are a point of light soaring up and away as an eagle would float and soar.

"Now we are going to go back into the past. Before you is a tunnel, which is the corridor to the memories of early childhood and past lives. You are now walking through this tunnel. At the end of this tunnel is a gate. I am going to count down from five to zero. At the count of zero I will snap my fingers, and you will walk through the gate. There you will experience or observe the childhood occurrence or past-life event that is the cause of your present-day problem."

Count downward — five, four, three, two, one — snap your fingers, and say, "Back to the cause!" Wait about fifteen to thirty seconds and ask the person to share with you out loud what he is seeing. When that experience is over, count downward from five to zero again and have him go back to another experience that is a cause of the problem or lesson you are exploring.

When you feel the person is ready to come out of the regression, tell him again that you are going to count down from five to zero and snap your fingers. At the count of zero, he will come back through the gate to this side. Have him relax. Give him some positive healing suggestions before bringing him out of hypnosis.

Hypnotic Patter

Following is a list of what I call hypnotic patter. When you are hypnotizing others or yourself or are making a tape, there are gaps between deepening techniques. These are good times to use hypnotic patter, words and imagery that encourage deeper relaxation.

Totally relaxed
Letting go
Releasing
Deeper and deeper

Loose, limp
Heavy veil
Deep hypnotic sleep
Deeply relaxed
You are now feeling the drowsy pulsation of approaching sleep
You feel as if you do not have a bone in your body
Jelly
Melting into the couch, chair, or floor
Drifting downward
Heavier and heavier
Slowing down
Saturated with relaxation
Totally physically relaxed
Drowsy and dreamy
Pleasant, comfortable, safe, protected and supported
Jaw and forehead and muscles relaxing
Eyes relaxing
Blanket of relaxation
Peaceful, comfortable, a very enjoyable feeling
Continue to relax more and more, keep going deeper and deeper
    to sleep
Completely and totally relaxed, every muscle totally relaxed
All the muscles in your body are like loose rubber bands
You have given yourself permission to let your mind just drift and
    wander to pleasant scenes within your imagination
Drowsy slumber
Drowsy relaxation
Pleasant comfortable relaxation
Jaws separate and chin and cheek muscles go loose and rubbery
Restful and tranquil
Rag doll
Feeling of well-being
Confident and sure of yourself
Letting go
Numbness
Peaceful, tranquil, calm
Well-being

In bringing a person back from the hypnotized state, you can use the following patter: "When you open your eyes you will feel . . . "

Refreshed
Energized

Rejuvenated
Well-rested
Full of enthusiasm
Energy
Vitality
Able to deal with the lessons and challenges of the day
Revitalized and invigorated
The wonderful feeling of perfect, radiant physical health.

Deepening Techniques

There are a couple of other deepening techniques. The first is to use anything that occurs as a means of deepening the experience. For example, let's say you hear the noises of cars outside. A suggestion can be given such as, "Any noises you might hear in the outside world will tend to relax you even more and deepen your experience."

Another way to deepen the hypnotic state is to do what is called a hypnotic test or challenge. An example of this is giving a suggestion to the person that his arm is getting very heavy, so heavy that it cannot be lifted. It feels as if it is stuck like glue to the table. It feels as if there are a thousand pounds of lead lying on top of it. When he tries to lift it, he can't. This realization tends to deepen the state even more.

Structuring Suggestions

When structuring suggestions to give to yourself or others, there are a couple of helpful ideas that will make your suggestions more effective.

The first is always to word your suggestions in the positive rather than in the negative. It is better to say, "Your arm is now healed" than to say, "Your broken arm is now healed." Leave out the negative image.

Secondly, if your reasoning mind or subconscious mind has a hard time believing your arm is healed now, it is possible to create an affirmation that induces healing in the immediate future. For example, "Every day, in every way, my arm is getting better and better."

Thirdly, it is helpful, in getting your point across, to use intense, emotional words that have strong imagery. For example, instead of saying that a person's arm is strong, you might say it has steel-like strength and power.

The more motivated you are to achieve your goal, the more effective will be your suggestion. Keep the language simple, but be very specific and use lots of repetition.

Communicating with the Subconscious Mind

There are a number of ways of communicating directly with the subconscious mind in a waking state. A lot of people use applied kinesiology, which is commonly called muscle-testing. Any muscle can be used. It is common to use the fingers; putting your thumb and little finger together to form a circle is one way to do it. Hold these fingers firmly together and try to pull them apart by inserting the thumb and index finger of your other hand inside the circle.

This is done initially to test the strength so you can use the same pressure while testing. The second step is to make a statement such as, "My body has enough vitamin C in it." If this is true and you try to push your fingers apart, you won't be able to do so. If it is false, the fingers can be pulled apart without much pressure. Any question about yourself can be answered using this technique.

Under hypnosis, communication is possible through the asking of questions with yes or no answers. One finger is designated as the "yes" finger; another finger is designated as the "no" finger; a third finger is designated as the "I don't know" finger. Instructions are given to the subconscious under hypnosis to lift the finger that answers the question.

After some initial testing to see if the subconscious has understood the instructions, questions can be asked directly of the subconscious as distinguished from asking the conscious reasoning mind for the answer.

Depth of Hypnosis

It is possible to find how deeply under hypnosis a person is by using the subconscious finger-raising method. While under hypnosis the subconscious is told to image a yardstick numbered from one to thirty-six. Number one means wide awake and thirty-six means somnambulism, or deepest hypnosis. The subconscious is told that you are going to count backwards from thirty-six to one. When the level of depth the person is currently experiencing is reached, he is to raise his finger. You begin very slowly to count from thirty-six to one, and when you reach the level, the subconscious will cause the finger to be raised. This is the best method for finding the depth, if that should be important.

Becoming an Effective Hypnotist

It is important, in becoming an effective hypnotist for others, as well as for yourself, to speak with confidence. If other people sense you are fearful or hesitant, then that is the way they will feel.

The second point to remember is that before hypnotizing someone it is important to develop a good rapport and to clear up any fears or myths about the hypnosis experience he or she has. This will greatly enhance the hypnosis experience.

12

Physical Immortality

Sickness is a defense against the truth
A Course in Miracles

M ost people involved with spiritual pursuits and/or religion believe in the immortality of the soul. In other words, you as a soul extension, or incarnated personality, are an eternal being and although your body dies, you don't. You just keep reincarnating over and over again until you achieve the liberation of ascension.

Many people don't realize, however, that the physical body is immortal, also. It is not immortal for most people because humanity has a collective belief in the reality of death. Death is a belief, just as eternal life is a belief. Collective humanity, for most of its existence, has been materialistically identified; hence, it has listened to the voice of the negative ego on this matter instead of the voice of the soul.

The negative ego tells you that you have to age and die. Spirit tells you that it is eternal and immortal. Spirit says that the physical body is the temple of the soul and that it ages because you program it to do so with your mind. You must remember that the subconscious mind runs the physical body. This can be clearly proven by using hypnosis. The subconscious mind, given suggestions under hypnosis, can cause the physical body to do miraculous feats. However, having no conscious reasoning, it will be just as happy to create perfect health as to create illness and aging, depending on what you program it to do. This programming can come from yourself or from the information with which you allow other people to program you.

What I am suggesting is that it is possible to program your body to youth instead of to age. It is also possible to program your body to remain eternally the same. Many great masters have done this. Babaji has re-mained the same for one thousand eight hundred years. Saint Germain lived for three hundred fifty years. Lord Maitreya resurrected Jesus' body and lived for another thirty-one years. Other masters can materialize or dematerialize their bodies at will.

Thoth (Buddha), in Egypt, was said to have lived for two thousand years. Jesus, in his last lifetime when he ascended, lived for three hundred years. Did not Jesus say, "Everything that I can do, you can do, and more"? *A Course in Miracles,* which Jesus wrote, says, "Sickness is a defense against the truth." The truth is that you are the Christ, or Eternal Self. God doesn't get sick so neither need you, since you are God.

So what causes sickness? It is the negative ego. Sai Baba says that "God equals man minus ego." The ego doesn't exist in God's reality and ideally, it shouldn't exist in yours. When you get rid of the negative ego you recognize that you are perfect because you are made in God's image.

The key to spiritual psychology is to get all levels aligned properly. You know that spirit and soul are eternal. The next lesson is to choose only eternal thoughts, eternal feelings, and an eternal physical body. The Hermetic law states, "As within, so without; as above, so below." If the spirit is eternal then, by definition, you can make the "without," or the body, eternal. Since your true identity is the Christ, by definition you should have only Christed thoughts, Christed emotions, and a Christed body; a Christed physical body is an immortal physical body.

The process begins on the thought level. It is your thoughts that create your reality and that includes your physical body. Any negative thought will manifest in your physical body. The same holds true for positive thoughts. Humanity is under a mass negative hypnosis in believing they have to age and die. Everyone believes it, so everyone does it.

Have you ever noticed that people often die when they have set their mental clocks to do so? They think seventy-five years is old, and they say to themselves, "I want to make it to my granddaughter's sixteenth birthday." They set it up in their minds to die at a certain time and, sure enough, that is exactly what happens.

The key to physical immortality on the mental level is to get rid of this death urge and replace it with a life urge. The fact is, your body is already immortal. You just think it isn't, and it follows the command of that thought. The only thought you should allow in your mind concerning your physical body is that you are in perfect, radiant health, that you are youthing every day, and that you can live eternally, or as long as you choose to.

The soul is eternal, so the physical body should be seen as eternal also, to maintain the proper alignment of the four-body system. This process begins with the acceptance of this philosophy on the level of the conscious mind. Then it must be programmed into the subconscious mind. This last point is important. Some people believe consciously in immortality, but their subconscious minds are not convinced. It will work only if all three minds believe it — and the superconscious, or soul, already believes it.

To achieve physical immortality you must have absolute control over your subconscious mind. You also must maintain vigilance over the thoughts you allow into your conscious mind, both from self and from other people. It is very easy to get negatively hypnotized on this subject because belief in death is so rampant.

It has been proven that there is a death hormone that the pituitary gland produces, as well as a life hormone. The pituitary is producing the death hormone in most people because they are unconsciously programming it to do so through death thoughts and emotions. By getting rid of all these death thoughts and emotions and replacing them with only life thoughts and emotions, you program the pituitary to produce only the life hormone.

The use of positive affirmations in this regard is essential. Constantly tell yourself that you are eternal spirit and that your thoughts, emotions, and physical body reflect this eternal and immortal nature. To achieve physical immortality you must have mastery over your subconscious mind and over your three lower bodies (physical, emotional, and mental), as well as mastery over your negative ego. The negative ego's main belief is that it is separated from God. If you believe you are one with God, that you are literally a son or daughter of God, the next logical step, of course, is to believe that you are immortal on all levels.

You have absolute mastery over all levels of your being, in the service of God, when you believe in physical immortality. Physical immortality is not for weak-minded people and neither is the spiritual path. Physical immortality begins with the purifying of your four bodies of all negative energies.

On the emotional level, you need to get rid of all negative feelings. Again, remember that your thoughts (and that includes your emotions) create your reality. When you think only with your Christ mind, instead of with the negative ego mind, then you live in joy, happiness, unconditional love, even-mindedness, and inner peace at all times. The world is a projection screen and you are seeing your own movie. The movie is made up of your perceptions and interpretations of life.

There is a way of thinking that will bring you this joy, peace, and love all the time: it is the science of attitudinal healing. Negative emotions debilitate the physical body; positive emotions energize the physical body. Living in unconditional love activates the thymus gland which is the seat of the immune system. Physical immortality is another by-product of being on the spiritual path.

Purification on the physical level means eating a healthful diet, cutting down on the amount of meat you consume, eliminating all drugs, alcohol, and artificial stimulants, doing some physical exercise every day, breathing deeply, and getting as much sunshine and fresh air as possible. There are physical toxins, emotional toxins, mental toxins, and energetic toxins in the etheric body. All four bodies must be cleansed of these toxins.

In essence, to achieve physical immortality the goal is to have only God-thoughts, God-emotions, a God-energy body, and a God-physical body. God is perfect and you are perfect. The microcosm is like the macrocosm. When all four etheric bodies become purified and are in alignment with the soul and spirit, perfect, radiant health occurs.

As you move through the seven levels of spiritual initiation, more and more Light and energy are found running through your four-body system. At the third initiation, which is called the soul merge, a great increase in energy and physical health occurs. At the fifth and sixth initiations, which are the ascension process, complete merging with the monad (the spirit, or I Am Presence) occurs, and that guarantees physical immortality.

At ascension, the monad descends and turns all four bodies into Light. The physical body is just densified spirit, and the spirit is just refined matter. You are here on Earth to spiritualize matter; you begin doing that by spiritualizing your physical body and raising it back to Light.

Constantly hold in your mind that you are God. You can't get sick, you can't age, and you can't physically die. Hold the thought and feeling that you are in perfect health, that you are getting younger every day, and you will live eternally. When any negative thought, emotion, or energy tries to tell you anything to the contrary, get rid of it and immediately do a positive affirmation or visualization, seeing yourself as the eternal spiritual being you truly are.

Call to your mighty I Am Presence in order to get rid of that negative egoistical belief and to consume it in the violet flame. Constantly call to your soul, asking it to merge with you on Earth. You are here to create Heaven on Earth. You are here to *be* God on Earth, on all levels. This is within your reach. Jesus said, however, "Be it done to you as you believe."

Your physical, emotional, and mental bodies are your servants, not your masters. Command them in the name of the Christ (which is who you are, in truth), and they will do as you order. Command your pituitary to stop creating the death hormone and to create only the life hormone, and it will do as you command.

The Bible says, "Ye are gods and know it not." The philosophy of physical immortality has now come into its own. It is time now to ground spirituality into the Earth and into the physical body. For too long people have been leaving their bodies in order to touch spirit instead of touching spirit, bringing it back, and grounding it into Earth.

The entire universe responds to your every command because you are God! God doesn't determine when you die; you do. The key to physical immortality is to live as spirit in your every thought, word, and deed. In essence, become God; then sickness, aging, and death will disappear. Since God does not get sick, age, or die, neither will you.

Write down on a piece of paper all your thoughts and feelings about death and about being physically immortal. Rewrite any thoughts that aren't of God in terms of positive affirmations that correct the faulty beliefs you are holding. Then listen for any further faulty beliefs that arise and write them down. Correct them on paper with new positive affirmations until you have cleared out your conscious and subconscious minds.

Also be open to cleansing any past-life beliefs about death that are stored in your subconscious mind. Cleanse all fears of death. In truth, there is nothing to fear because death does not exist except in your own mind.

Forgiving yourself and all others is a prerequisite for physical immortality.

In more advanced stages you will begin to see yourself and everyone else as Light, for, in truth, that is what you really are. What this comes down to is where you put your attention. Do you focus your mind on death, sickness, negativity, and aging or on perfect health, positivity, eternal life, and youthing?

The problem with most people in the world is that they live on automatic pilot and do not control the focus of their attention. Your attention, ideally, should be kept at all times on spirit, on Christ, on God. Each person you meet on the street must be seen as God or you will not achieve God-realization yourself.

One of the by-products of holding the consciousness of physical immortality is that your physical body begins to change from having two strands of DNA to having twelve strands of DNA; having twelve strands of DNA is the state of enlightenment. Affirm to yourself that this transformation is occurring right now and pray that it be so.

Hold the thought and image in your mind that you have been "reborn" in this moment and that you now have twelve strands of DNA. Did not Jesus say, "Except that ye be born again you will not find the kingdom of God." Physical immortality is the consciousness of being born again into your true eternal Christ nature on all levels of your being. Realize in this holy instant the truth of this statement, and from this day forward do not allow any thought or feeling to the contrary to enter your consciousness. If something starts to interfere, say, "Get thee behind me, Satan," and replace the thought with a Christ-like affirmation. This is what Sai Baba calls "self-inquiry." It is the process of discriminating between what is truth and what is illusion, what is permanent and what is impermanent, what is negative ego and what is God.

Sai Baba says that 75% of the spiritual path is nothing more than this practice. This is the key practice in working toward physical immortality and in working toward ascension which, in truth, are one and the same. Once physical immortality has been achieved (which is any moment you choose it to be so), you have a choice: you don't have to stay on Earth for eternity; you can stay here for as long as you choose to do so, instead of letting your physical body decide for you.

Physical immortality, hence, calls for remaining in your personal power and in self-mastery at all times. You could give away your power to your physical body, your desires, emotions, mind, senses, or to other people. To achieve physical immortality you must give your power to no one. You are God. You do not have to be afraid of your power because you are using it only in the service of God and your brothers and sisters, only in the service of love.

Another key to physical immortality is controlling your sexuality. You must learn to become the absolute master of this energy so you choose when to identify with it and when to raise it. Overindulgence in sexuality depletes your physical body and takes years off your life. Sexuality should be used only in the service of love and intimacy and in moderation. The kundalini will never rise if your energy is constantly moving out of your second chakra.

When you raise the kundalini it can then be used to heal the organs and glands and the physical body in general. Fundamental to physical immortality is a deep desire for immortality and for God-realization. If you allow yourself to be run by the desires of the lower self, it weakens you physically, emotionally, mentally, and spiritually.

Understand that physical immortality is a process, as is the spiritual path. It is a process of moving from polarization and identification with the lower self to polarization and identification with the higher self. In the beginning stages it is an all-out spiritual war. In the later stages it becomes much easier as all your habits are reprogrammed.

A further suggestion for the physical level is the use of water, both inwardly and outwardly. Baths and showers can be seen as baptisms and cleansings of the entire four-body system every day. The drinking of large amounts of water purifies the kidneys and liver and the entire system. Disease cannot grow in a purified body.

It can clearly be seen here that physical immortality and ascension require a total commitment. Anything less won't get you to your goal. As Yogananda said, "If you want God [physical immortality] you must want Him as much as a drowning man wants air."

Physical immortality is God-realization. Some people believe it can be achieved just with the power of the mind. I don't, personally, believe that. Holding only positive thoughts without a belief in God will certainly help your health; however, I don't believe that it is sufficient for achieving physical immortality.

Physical immortality is the integration of all levels of your being. You can't skip any levels. Just working on the mental or spiritual while eating a terrible diet and getting no physical exercise is not going to do it unless you came in as a God-realized master. For 99.9% of the rest of the world, all levels must be mastered and purified. Balance and moderation in all things is the ideal.

It is not disease and old age that kill most people; it is the belief in disease and old age that kills most people. Even cancer specialists agree that one of the keys to curing cancer is the will to live. If you don't have that, all other treatment is useless.

Every night as you are falling asleep and as you are waking up in the morning, give yourself autosuggestions affirming your physical immortality. Your subconscious mind is more receptive at these times. Other practices that will help in your achieving of physical immortality are meditating, praying, chanting the name of God, singing devotional songs, fasting, growing your own food, eating organic food, reading uplifting spiritual books, having a clean and orderly environment, not talking about your age, and not going to funerals.

The idea is to keep your consciousness in an elevated spiritual state at all times. If your mind is constantly attuned to God, how can sickness, aging, and death enter? They can't. If you are constantly praying, meditating, and chanting God's name, only perfection can exist. Living this way gets easy after a while; it becomes a habit, a way of living.

The Fountain of Youth

I recently discovered a book called *The Ancient Secret of the Fountain of Youth* by Peter Kelder which tells the amazing story of Colonel Bradford. While stationed in India near the Himalaya Mountains, he heard stories about a group of lamas, or Tibetan priests, who had discovered the fountain of youth. He eventually returned to India in search of these lamas and their fountain of youth, and he found them. In their monastery, he was taught their secret to staying young: keep the chakras revolving at a high rate of speed and at rates that are synchronous with each other. When chakras begin to slow down, aging occurs. The slowing down of the chakras prevents the vital force, or prana, from flowing properly. The key to the fountain of youth was to get the chakras spinning normally again.

Colonel Bradford was taught five exercises by the Himalayan masters. The exercises are easy to do and can all be done in a few minutes, once you learn how to do them. They have the effect of speeding up all the chakras so that they are spinning like the chakras of a twenty-five-year-old and of causing them to revolve in harmony.

When Colonel Bradford returned to America he literally looked thirty years younger, according to Kelder who didn't even recognize him. There is also a special way of breathing while doing the exercises, which remind me a little bit of certain Hatha Yoga postures, but they are very specific in their purpose and effect.

These five exercises must be practiced every day if they are to have their full effect. If you are physically fit, you can do them in ten minutes once you have learned them. I have an incredibly good feeling about them and have no doubt they do exactly what he says they do.

Colonel Bradford was also given a sixth exercises which was to be used only to raise sexual energy for youthing the body.

I cannot recommend highly enough that you get this small book. You can read it in thirty minutes; it will take you a little while to learn how to do the exercises properly. Then all you need is, literally, ten minutes a day, a small investment for such a large return. Djwhal Khul, Kuthumi, and El Morya were all Tibetan lamas — the masters of the Himalayas truly knew what they were talking about.

13

An Esoteric Understanding of Sexuality

Those acts are wrong that are not shared in love.
Those acts are wrong that are selfish.
Those acts are good, however,
that cause a sharing between two souls.

Universal Mind
through Paul Solomon

One of the most confusing subjects for aspirants and disciples on the spiritual path is that of sexuality. In my opinion, there are very few books that really explain this subject in an adequate manner. It is a subject that is complex for a number of reasons.

First of all, the ego and soul have completely different views of how sexuality should be used. Secondly, sexuality is affected by some of the following variables:

1. Your chronological age,
2. Your soul age,
3. Whether you are single or married,
4. Whether you are in a relationship,
5. Your initiation level in this lifetime,
6. Your goals and purposes in this lifetime,
7. Your karma from past lives and your purpose for incarnation in this life,
8. Your degree of physical health or lack thereof,
9. Your commitment to ascend in this lifetime.

To begin this discussion of sexuality, let us first look at the difference between the ego's view of sexuality and the spirit's view.

The ego uses sexuality in service of the lower self; the spirit uses sexuality only in service of the higher self and soul.

The ego is interested only in selfishly pleasuring itself; the spirit is interested in love and in pleasuring the other as well as itself. The ego treats the other as an object, seeking to use that physical body for self-gratification; the spirit sees the other person as the Eternal Self inside the temple of a body.

The ego has only physical vision; the spirit has spiritual vision as well. The ego is controlled by desires, senses, thoughts, emotions, physical sensations, and sexual energy; the spirit is master of these aspects of self and uses them in service of God.

The ego, being focused on lust, directs all sexuality through the second chakra; the spirit recognizes sexual energy as just one octave of energy within the seven-chakra system and seeks to raise this energy up through the chakra system for such uses as creativity, physical health, love, service, deeper meditation, spiritual illumination, and God-realization.

The ego is obsessed with sexuality and looks at every person within this frame of reference; the spirit sees all people first as God incarnate.

The ego uses kundalini energy for sexual pleasuring; the spirit seeks to raise the kundalini energy, of which sexual energy is a part, to the crown chakra.

The ego seeks to have orgasm only at the second chakra level; the spirit, by practicing tantric sexuality, seeks orgasm at all seven levels.

The ego sees sexuality as the most important thing in life and gets moody, angry, upset, and irritable if it does not get what it wants; the spirit, having preferences but no attachments, remains within total joy, peace, and equilibrium no matter what. The ego can't conceive of being happy without sexuality; the spirit's happiness is a state of mind and has nothing to do with sexuality. In fact, spirit seriously considers celibacy as a viable option, whereas the ego constantly gets into relationships that are not right spiritually because of the sexual urge. The spirit, being solidly centered in self-mastery, is perfectly willing to be celibate for a whole lifetime if the right spiritual mate doesn't manifest.

The ego dissipates enormous amounts of sexual energy through masturbation; the spirit, although seeing nothing wrong with masturbation, seeks to raise some of this energy into ojas shakti, or brain illumination.

The ego uses sexuality with the goal of having an orgasm; the spirit uses sexuality for intimacy and the sharing of spiritual love and might even choose not to have an orgasm. The spirit sees foreplay as more important than orgasm.

The ego is interested in pornography and is in the state of consciousness that creates it; the spirit does not use sexuality in this manner but uses it instead for the glory of God.

The ego is making love only to the physical body; the spirit is making love to the spirit living within the physical body.

The ego puts its own pleasuring first; the spirit puts the other person's pleasure first. The ego is interested in having an orgasm as soon as possible; the spirit is interested in sharing love as long as possible.

The ego uses fantasies of others during masturbation or sexual involvement with a mate; the spirit is extremely self-controlled in the use of fantasy, recognizing that all minds are joined and that what one fantasizes affects the other.

The negative ego that controls the incarnated personality leads a person to have affairs because of lack of sexual mastery; the spirit, understanding the law of karma, never does anything that would hurt another person, that is dishonest, or that will build negative karma.

I could go on a lot longer, but I think the basic picture is clear. In summary, those sexual acts are sinful or wrong that are selfish and not shared lovingly. Those acts are good that cause a sharing of love between two souls.

It must be understood that sexual energy is just one of seven octaves of energy within the human body. There is nothing wrong with pleasure from a spiritual perspective. Is pleasure the only way you want to use your energy, however? There is no judgment from spiritual realms if this is your choice at any given moment, but it is important to see the tremendous accomplishments, creativity, and spiritual growth that could be attained if the energy were raised.

Another important point to consider is that, according to the channeling of the Universal Mind through Paul Solomon, for whom I have enormous respect, "the physical act as itself would prevent the higher act of the soul from taking place." In other words, once the lower self or animal nature is given expression, it prevents you from being a channel for the higher self or soul.

In Paul's channelings, the Source also states that the sharing of fluids between two people creates a spiritual bond or cord of energy that cannot be broken for that entire lifetime. The cords can be broken in a psychological sense, once the relationship has ended, but not in a spiritual sense. These cords are like electrical wires, and energy passes back and forth through them. This is why, in many spiritual teachings, the giving of the self sexually is for the completion of the self for that lifetime.

When you understand the karmic bonds you are creating with people every time you have sex, I think you will be a little more discriminating about whom you have sex with. If you are a psychological victim rather than a master of your mind and emotions, you can be victimized by energies flowing through these cords. Your moodiness, depression, and anger might not be your own, but might belong to a person with whom you have slept whose energies continue to flow to you through these cords. Since the energy flows both ways, the lifestyle of the mate or partner continues to flow back to you as well as from you, so it is wise to choose with care.

You all have these cords and the ideal would be to achieve mastery of your energies so you are not victimized by the energies flowing through them. In the highest sense, you want to be such a generator of Light and love that your divine energy flows back through these cords to uplift those people you have been involved with. This is nothing that you have to do consciously; the general lifestyle of being a Light for the world will automatically take care of it.

It is also important to understand that the state of consciousness you are holding when you are having sex is what you are implanting into your partner. In other words, the man is not only implanting his physical seed but is also implanting either the lustful energy of the lower self or the love of the higher self.

This applies to other forms of sexual activity too, not just intercourse. Remember, your partner is God, as you are. The question to ask yourself is whether what you are giving to your partner is what you would be willing to give to God, for in truth, that is exactly what you are doing.

So understand that the physical act is only a physical act. What is judged by self and God is your mental, emotional, and spiritual intentions for entering the sexual involvement.

In situations in which an extramarital affair has taken place, a karmic bond is created among all three people. This is nothing to be taken lightly, for this karmic lesson will have to be resolved, either in this life or throughout eternity, for the ultimate balancing of karma that must be achieved before taking ascension, or the sixth initiation.

Before getting involved in sexual activity you should consider whether the involvement will cause a feeling of regret or guilt in you or your partner. The ego usually wants immediate gratification and doesn't consider the bigger picture. This is why the masters have often said that unless you are willing to give yourself to the person for a lifetime you should not issue forth your seed. That is why it is better, if you are single, to masturbate or to allow the sexual release to come in nature's way, rather than to create an inappropriate karmic bond.

There is another tool that might be considered. When there is sexual arousal in the lower chakras, bring your hands together in prayer. Then let your hands point to each chakra, raising the energy so it can be used for a higher purpose. This can create the experience of having an orgasm on seven different levels of your being. You might feel a convulsing of the muscles at each of the seven chakras and the overall experience will be much greater than an orgasm on just one level.

Sex between single people is not wrong. It is just that all the things mentioned in this chapter need to be considered. Most people in the world have absolutely no understanding of these esoteric laws.

Then there is also the spiritual lesson of how to avoid temptation. The key here is keeping your mind and consciousness attuned to the things of God, the love of God, and the realization of God. As Djwhal Khul has said so often, "Keep your mind steady in the Light." When your mind is on God, temptation does not even arise. It is when your mind leaves God and reverts to body consciousness that temptation occurs. That is why you should have an ongoing routine of spiritual practices that you do every day. It is well stated in the old saying, "An idle mind is the devil's workshop." The mind needs to be constantly preoccupied with praying, meditating, making spiritual affirmations, creating visualizations, repeating the name of God, chanting, singing devotional songs, practicing the presence of God, seeing the Eternal Self in every person as in yourself, reading spiritual materials, getting physical exercise, maintaining a healthful diet, spending time with spiritual people, going to church, temple, spiritual classes and lectures, and so on.

When your life is filled with these activities, temptation will hardly ever even be an issue. This applies to other areas of your life as well. When you are with a person and temptation arises, immediately thank God for that person and see him or her as the Eternal Self, or God. It comes down to an issue of where you put your attention. If you let your subconscious mind, five senses, desire body, and negative ego control your attention, that is a problem. The ideal is for the conscious mind always to focus the attention in the service of soul, spirit, and Christ consciousness.

When your attention begins to slip into body consciousness that is inappropriate, then shift it back to God as though you were changing the channel of your television set. It must be understood that energy follows thought, and all feelings are created by your mind. So the key to achieving sexual mastery is learning to master your mind. This process could also be called attitudinal healing. Sexual temptation always begins with a thought or feeling in your mind. The trick is to nip it in the bud because what you give energy to grows. This takes great vigilance. When it begins to happen, just ask yourself, "Do I want God or my ego in this situation?" When you look at it from this perspective, I am sure you will choose God.

It must be understood that sexual energy is one of the most powerful forces in the universe. The only force more powerful is your conscious will, your personal power in the service of God. You need to ask yourself whether you want animal consciousness or ascended master consciousness.

Do you want to serve your lower self or your higher self?

One of the best methods for overcoming temptation is to immediately begin chanting the name of God, either silently or out loud. As *A Course in Miracles* says, "Deny any thought that is not of God to enter your mind."

When mistakes are made in regard to your sexuality, just forgive yourself and get back on track. Until higher initiations are taken, there is a battle that goes on between the lower self and the higher self. Don't waste time on guilt and regret. When mistakes are made just gain the golden nugget of wisdom from the mistake, learn the lesson, and remember what Jesus said to Mary Magdalene: "You are forgiven. Go and sin no more."

Mahatma Gandhi, in his autobiography, tells of the tremendous battle he had with his own sexuality until he finally gained mastery over it. When temptation begins to occur, stop doing the things that are producing that temptation. It all comes down to what you want in this lifetime. If you truly want God-realization and ascension so you can be of greater service to humankind, then you must choose God in every moment of your life. If you keep choosing God over negative ego, then you will achieve liberation over the course of your lifetime. It must be emphasized that what you see in the world is just a projection of your own thoughts; you are seeing your own movie. See each person as God in all situations, and you will realize God in yourself.

As you are walking down the street, if you are seeing through just your physical eyes, you will be judging physical bodies according to the ego's *Playboy* or *Playgirl* images that have poisoned the collective mind. This sick indoctrination is everywhere — magazines, newspapers, television programs, and movies. The outer world worships the physical body. If you want to realize God, then you must see only God in your daily life, in all people, animals, plants, and rocks and in yourself. If you don't see God in your brother and sister you will never realize Him within yourself. Sexuality is much more than just a physical act. Mental, emotional, and spiritual adultery occur in the mind as you walk down the street or watch a movie.

Vow of the Brahmacharya

The vow of the Brahmacharya, made to self and God, states that you will use sexuality only in the way that God would have you use it. Making a vow is something our Western culture doesn't often partake in as a spiritual practice, and that is unfortunate. The taking of certain spiritual vows provides an enormous freedom.

I took the vow of the Brahmacharya in my own life long before I knew what it really was. It provided me with a liberation and an acceleration of my spiritual growth a thousand times beyond anything I had ever before experienced in my life. The taking of a vow closes and locks a door.

Most people don't lock their psychic doors, so when they get tired or weak or sick or when they lose their personal power, the lower self sneaks back in. The taking of the vow of the Brahmacharya closes the psychic doors and prevents this from happening. The second half of this chapter will be dedicated to understanding what this most profound spiritual practice really means.

Temptation in itself is not sin; temptation is the opportunity to sin. The key is to know when praising God through a loved one stops and when Earthly desires begin. Keep your mind attuned to God and your physical body active through physical exercise. Let any sexual releases occur in nature's way during sleep, as they are needed. No sin or karma is incurred in this manner. Also, this allows the enormous power of sexual energy and the kundalini force to be raised through all seven chakras for the purposes of God-realization, physical health, mental illumination, creativity, healing, and greater service to humankind.

As Paul Solomon said in one of the channelings included in a book called *Excerpts from the Paul Solomon Tapes*, ". . . and thy body and thy mind will remain pure in the Lord. Then you might present before Him that body that is a living sacrifice, holy, acceptable unto God."

The term Brahmacharya literally means "conduct that leads to the realization of Brahman," or of the Eternal Self. It means self-restraint, perfect self-mastery over sexual energy, and freedom from lust in thought, word, and deed.

Brahmacharya also means celibacy, although I am not using it in that strict sense of the term. I first encountered the term when reading Mahatma Gandhi's autobiography. He describes how he took the vow of the Brahmacharya and says that it was one of the keys to the unfolding of his entire spiritual life. He also uses the term in a much larger context than just sexuality. For him, the vow of the Brahmacharya was a commitment to a lifestyle of self-mastery and self-discipline in all areas of his life in order to achieve self-realization.

Reading this section of his autobiography was especially meaningful to me because this vow of the Brahmacharya was something I had taken in the same larger context about four years earlier, although I had never heard of the exact name of such a rite. It was one of the most meaningful things I have ever done, and it has truly brought me "a peace that passeth understanding."

I am no longer in conflict, battling myself at times of weakness. The door to certain types of activities and states of mind belonging to my lower self has been closed and locked and it no longer takes any energy to maintain it. In essence, it has become a habit, and the spiritual depth of the vows I took allows no possibility of my opening that door.

I once heard it stated in a channeling that perfection does not mean never making a mistake; perfection means not ever making a *conscious* mistake. Conscious mistakes are under our control, whereas unconscious mistakes are not. Part of my vow of the Brahmacharya is to direct my consciousness, in thought, word, and deed, back toward God when I become aware of making unconscious mistakes.

Krishnamurti used the term "choiceless awareness." I do not know what context he used it in, but I relate to the term. I need make no choices between my lower and higher selves; that choice was made at the time of my vow of the Brahmacharya. The only choice I have is to be guided by the holy spirit, my monad, the ascended masters, and God. All other doors are consciously locked shut.

The vow of the Brahmacharya applies to married people, people in relationships, and single people. To me, the vow of the Brahmacharya for single people who are seriously on the path of initiation means that you will be celibate until the time when you find your soulmate or twin flame or right spiritual mate. It means you will avoid sexual involvement unless you have found the right person on all levels — physical, emotional, mental, and spiritual.

Many people I know who are single get involved over and over again with people they do not match spiritually. Over and over again the same result occurs. If you put God first, then you have to have a partner who also puts God first, although the form of religion or spiritual path does not matter.

The vow can mean something different if you are chronologically younger and need experience in relationships as part of your spiritual growth. The vow is also different if you are at an earlier stage in your spiritual evolution and are just stepping onto the path. So there are no hard and fast rules.

If you study the teachings of Brahmacharya in the yoga books and Hindu scriptures, you will see they are quite strict about the use of sexuality — believe it or not, a thousand times stricter than are the standards I have expressed in this book. To them I would be an ultraliberal Brahmacharya. My attempt here is to find the right balance of Heaven and Earth, yin and yang, with the proper integration of the Christ consciousness.

What I speak of here is not easy, especially in the beginning stages of your spiritual path. After the third initiation, I believe it gets easier, and after the fourth initiation, much easier. Integral to mastering your sexuality and learning how to sublimate and transmute that energy is learning to have mastery over your thoughts, emotions, ego, subconscious mind, and five senses. In taking the vow of the Brahmacharya you are also committing to mastering these parts of your self. Of all these desires, though, the sex urge is the strongest. To make it even harder, our environment doesn't support us but hinders us in this venture. I believe the AIDS virus and other sexually transmitted diseases are the outer reflections of past misuse of this most precious divine energy.

It is essential to learn how to have mastery and raise this energy if your goal in life is God-realization and ascension. To achieve this you must have iron determination, undying patience, spiritual tenacity, and perseverance. Every day, pray to God and ask Him for help in this venture. Why do it by yourself when you can have God helping you? Over time it will become much easier, as the practices become habit.

You will learn to keep your remembrance on God at all times as you learn to own your personal power and mastery. In Buddhism there is the term "exceptional Bodhicitta" which means generating a state of unbelievable desire for enlightenment and God-realization so you can be of greater service to humankind in this lifetime.

If every morning you cultivate this Bodhicitta, or "mind of enlightenment," temptation will not be able to affect you. I would describe this as an all-consuming spiritual fire. When your yearning for God is not just a matchstick but an all-consuming fire that burns during every moment of your life, then sexual temptation will no longer even be an issue.

In the Edgar Cayce readings it says that one of the forms of karma that is carried over into the next life from overindulgence in sexuality is epilepsy.

Reabsorbing the semen helps to enrich the blood and strengthen the brain. It is almost universally accepted by medical doctors who are experts in this field that the choice elements of the blood go into the composition of the spermatic secretions. Overindulgence in sexuality just drains and weakens the richness of your blood supply.

The vow of the Brahmacharya is one of the key doors to Nirvana. For a liberated sage, the world is full of Brahma (God) only.

The vow of the Brahmacharya involves lustful thinking as well as lustful actions. The concept of mental adultery is more tricky to grasp than that of physical adultery. How do you look at men and women on the street, in movie theaters, on television, in magazines? There is nothing wrong with looking at the physical body of the opposite sex as long as you are looking from your heart and seeing the Eternal Self first.

The ego would have you look with your physical eyes first, with an eye of judgment as to another's sexual attractiveness. See the Christ in all people first and then their physical vehicles and you will be seeing a whole new perception of reality. The ego creates separation through the judgment of appearances; the spirit sees all people as being exactly the same. The self within you and the self within me are the same self. To create differentiation because of physical looks is nothing but illusion.

One method that is helpful is to see each person you meet as your favorite spiritual master; in truth that is who they are. Another technique is to see women as the Great Mother, Kali, Quan Yin, the Virgin Mary, Isis. See men as Jesus Christ, Sai Baba, Djwhal Khul, or the Lord Maitreya. See each person as a brother or sister in your spiritual family.

Mental Brahmacharya is the vow to keep a pure mind. You have succeeded at mental Brahmacharya when not a single lustful or lower-self thought enters your mind, but instead your mind remains focused on God and the Eternal Self.

When you indulge in sexual fantasy or lustful thoughts, even though you don't act physically, you are still having sexual activity on the mental plane and are creating karma. Remember what Edgar Cayce said: "Thoughts are things." You give enough energy to these sexual fantasies and they take on a life of their own.

This is not meant as judgment, for certainly we all have done this. It is just meant to remind you of these subtle but very important spiritual laws you know to be true. The vow of the Brahmacharya leads to purity on all levels.

Another interesting effect of sexuality is that orgasm weakens the legs. All boxers know this. That is why their trainers force them to be celibate for at least six weeks before a fight. This can be tested with a dowsing rod or a pendulum; you will find it to be true.

I once had a client who took a healing class that I happened to attend also. When a healing was done on him his legs were found to be ice cold. I happened to know because of being his counselor that he had been masturbating two or three times a day for almost five straight years. I knew immediately what the coldness was from.

The Vedas declare that "by Brahmacharya and peace the devas have conquered death." It was a key to Gandhi's success. The *Mahabarata*, the book that contains the *Bhagavad-Gita*, which might be the greatest book ever written, says, "Know that in this world there is nothing that cannot be attained by one who remains from birth to death a perfect celibate. . . . In one person, knowledge of the four Vedas [the holiest book of India], and in another, perfect celibacy — of these, the latter is superior to the former who is wanting in celibacy."

Lord Sankara, who was one of the greatest Hindu avatars of all time, has said, "Brahmacharya, or spotless chastity, is the best of all penances. A celibate of such spotless chastity is not a human being, but a God, indeed. . . . To the celibate who conserves the semen with great efforts, what is there unattainable in this world? By the power of the composure of the semen, one will become just like myself."

Lord Krishna, the past life of the Lord Maitreya, has said, "Sensuality destroys life, luster, strength, vitality, memory, wealth, great fame, holiness, and devotion to the supreme."

The Upanishads, which are the wisdom teachings of the Vedas, say, "And those students who find that world of God through chastity, theirs is that heavenly country; theirs, in whatever world they are, is freedom."

Lord Buddha guided people away from marriage because of their lack of control of their lower selves. A person who has not attained mastery over his energies should "avoid married life as if it were a burning pit of live coals. From the contact comes sensation, from sensation thirst, from thirst clinging; by ceasing from that, the soul is delivered from all sinful existence."

I will add to this, however, that the true master who has taken the vow of the Brahmacharya can then be married and live in total purity because his or her sexual energy will be used in an appropriate and moderate manner.

In our society it is so common to hear of a man pouting or being angry at his wife for not giving him sex. A master who has taken the vow of the Brahmacharya would be just as pleased to raise the energy. From a spiritual perspective there is nothing wrong with enjoying sexuality and mutual pleasuring as long as it is loving, is not a selfish act, and is done in moderation and in the recognition of your mate as the Eternal Self incarnate.

The vow of the Brahmacharya, for couples, has to do with staying in the Tao of appropriate sexual involvement, given your mutual sexual ideals and priorities. For couples who are approaching the higher initiations and ascension, I would recommend less sex and more tantric sexuality.

At medium levels of initiation you will just have to use your intuition to guide you about how much is appropriate. There was a time in my life when it was appropriate to live out my sexuality. In my life currently, even though I am married and I deeply love my wife, sex is not as important as it used to be. I could, with no effort at all, be celibate for the rest of my life. This has given me great freedom, for now I am not attached to sexuality.

You might consider not having an orgasm even though you choose to make love sometimes. All the energy that is built up will then be used for other purposes. This may seem strange; however, the question that arises is, what is the most enjoyable part of lovemaking? Is it just the orgasm or is it the whole process?

A person who takes the vow of the Brahmacharya is called a Brahmachari. Hindu scripture states that "by the practice of Brahmacharya, longevity, glory, strength, vigor, knowledge, wealth, undying fame, virtues, and devotion to truth increase." The preservation of the semen is one of the secrets of physical, emotional, mental, and spiritual success.

In the teachings and yoga sutras of Patanjali, the key ideals are non-killing, non-stealing, truthfulness, and celibacy, or Brahmacharya. They are the keys to success in material and spiritual life.

You might think I am being too strict in what I am suggesting. In many of the Eastern and Western spiritual teachings it is recommended that people have sexual intercourse only for the sake of creating progeny. I don't think it is necessary or appropriate for married couples to go to that extreme. I don't believe there is anything wrong with enjoying sex under the proper circumstances and as long as it is done in moderation. I am just giving you the whole picture; you need to find your own middle ground within this understanding. Humanity in this society is fed a lot of misinformation about sexuality by poorly informed, materialistically oriented doctors, psychiatrists, psychologists, and counselors. I am presenting sexuality according to the soul's perception, not according to some materialistic, worldly view.

The practice of Brahmacharya will also allow married couples, when they do want to have a child, to attract a much higher-level soul to incarnate in the physical vehicle they both provide.

In my personal opinion, all adolescents in school should be required to take classes in Brahmacharya, since adolescents, by definition, are completely out of control in terms of their emotional bodies, negative egos, and sexuality. I can't help but think about the news story that spoke of high school boys who were having sex with girls as a game to see who could get the most "points." What was even more disgusting was that the boys were proud of themselves even after they were busted. They didn't think they had done anything wrong.

This is symbolic of a certain segment of our collective consciousness. It is the result of the lack of spiritual training in school. If adolescents were taught the value of Brahmacharya, there would be a drop in the number of abortions and unwanted pregnancies, a slowing in the spread of AIDS and other sexually transmitted diseases, and a halt in the spiritual and moral decline of today's youth. Look at the karma that is being created in these young people's lives that could be avoided though proper spiritual and moral education.

The lack of awareness of Brahmacharya goes along with drinking alcohol, taking drugs, viewing pornography, and, in general, giving free reign to the lower self. I am sure that 98% of all adolescents don't have a clue about what the lower self and higher self even are. This is not their fault; it is the fault of society. Educators are not properly educating the young souls in their care.

The vow of the Brahmacharya also involves your diet, the people you spend time with, the movies you see, the television programs you watch, the magazines and books you read. The vow involves the building of character and virtue. It involves a clear knowledge of sexual health on the physical level, including proper hygiene and birth control.

It is helpful to realize that the Atman, or Eternal Self, is sexless, and that this is your true identity. Many psychologists will tell you that the control of sexuality is repression and that repression is bad. As a psychologist, I say that is ignorance. The control and raising of sexual energy is conservation and conversion of one form of energy to another. In this case it is the conversion of lust into ojas shakti, brain illumination, and supernatural physical health.

Ojas is actually spiritual energy that is stored in the brain. It can be utilized for divine contemplation and spiritual pursuits. If you have a great deal of ojas in your brain, you can turn out enormous amounts of creative, mental, and spiritual work. There is a luster and clearness in your eyes and a magnetic aura in your feet. You can influence people by speaking very few words. Appolonius of Tyanna (Jesus Christ's next incarnation after his life as Jesus, during which he took his fifth initiation) took the vow of Brahmacharya at the age of sixteen and lived to the age of one hundred or more, never breaking his vow.

Sai Baba has recommended that people become celibate after the age of sixty-five, even if they are married. If you have had any serious physical health problems I would highly recommend taking a vow of celibacy or of extreme moderation for a designated period of time. All that energy will then be used to heal your body as well as your mind and spirit.

There is enormous worldly pressure in our society to get married or to find a mate. From the soul's perspective, it is a totally viable option to remain single and celibate and be perfectly happy. You do not need a mate to be happy. Your soul and monad are your true mates, in reality.

So many people who are single are seeking their spiritual mates. This type of relationship is not always easy to find. I would say this is especially true for women, as there are more spiritual women around than there are spiritual men.

If you have not found your spiritual mate, try the celibate path until your mate appears. In my personal experience, being celibate is an incredible high, once you give yourself to it and let go of all the egoistical programming.

If you would like to find your ideal spiritual mate, I am now going to tell you "the secret of the ages": how to find that person. The secret is to give yourself 100% to your spiritual path and to service to humankind. Find complete joy and happiness in your union with God, your union with self, and your union with your brothers and sisters in Christ. Fully own that you are 100% whole and complete within yourself and one with God. Live your life from this state of consciousness and when the time is right, your spiritual mate will turn up right in front of you without your even having to look for him or her. This is because God attracts God.

Again I emphasize the need to avoid allowing your mind to function on automatic pilot, for that is when temptations develop. The problems always begin on the mental plane first. Jesus said that if you have looked at a person lustfully, you have already committed adultery in your heart. See, hear, taste, touch, smell, think, feel, sense, intuit only God. You will not be successful unless your life is one constant sequence of spiritual practices. After a while, this isn't experienced as work but rather as the greatest joy, for there is no better feeling than constantly affirming and experiencing God. When you see a beautiful form in the shape of a physical body, remember who created that form and who is living inside that form.

Ramakrishna, the God-realized avatar, was married and, believe it or not, even consummated his marriage. Sri Anandamayi Ma, the bliss-permeated saint from India, was married and did the same. I bring up these examples to give you the full perspective of choices available on your spiritual path.

One of the keys to developing the siddhas (the higher spiritual gifts) is to raise the sexual energy. In the beginning, try to make a vow of Brahmacharya for a week or a month or three months. This is very much like fasting. We all know how good fasting is for the physical body; fast from sexual activity for a little while to see how you feel.

Every time you do have sex, examine how you feel afterwards to see if you were in the Tao. If not, don't judge yourself harshly, just learn from the experience, make the correction in your mind, and commit to staying in the Tao in the future.

The vow of the Brahmacharya is a great spiritual experiment and an ongoing, evolving process. At different times in your life, the nature of your vow may be different. The main point is to be the master of your sexuality and not let it master you.

I would like to end this chapter with a story about Socrates and his disciple from a book called *The Practice of Brahmacharya* by Swami Sivananda.

> One of the disciples of Socrates asked his teacher, "My Venerable Master, kindly instruct me how many times a householder can visit his legal wife."
>
> Socrates replied, "Only once in his lifetime."
>
> The disciple said, "Oh, my lord! This is absolutely impossible for worldly men. Passion is dreadful and troublesome. This world is full of temptations and distractions. Householders have not a strong will to resist temptations. Their indriyas are very revolting and powerful.

The mind is filled with passion. Thou art a philosopher and yogi. You can control. Pray, kindly prescribe an easy path for the men of the world."

Then Socrates said, "A householder can have copulation once in a year."

The disciple replied, "Oh venerable sir, this is also a hard job for them. You must prescribe an easier course."

Socrates then replied, "Well, my dear disciple, once in a month. This is suitable. This is quite easy. I think you are satisfied now."

The disciple said, "This also is impossible, my revered Master. Householders are very fickle-minded. Their minds are full of sexual samskaras (programming) and vasanas. They cannot remain even for a single day without sexual intercourse. You have no idea of their mentality."

Then Socrates said, "Well said, my dear child, do one thing now. Go directly to the burial ground now. Dig a grave and purchase a coffin and winding sheet for the corpse beforehand. Now you can spill yourself any number of times you like. This is my final advice to you."

This last advice pierced the heart of the disciple. He felt it keenly. He thought over the matter seriously and understood the importance and glory of Brahmacharya. He took to spiritual sadhana (practice in right awareness). He took a vow of strict unbroken celibacy for life, became a yogi, and achieved self-realization. He became one of the favorite disciples of Socrates.

14

Psychic Self-Defense

*The commonest form of psychic attack
is that which proceeds from the ignorant or
malignant mind of our fellow human beings*

Dion Fortune, Mystic

This chapter might be one of the most important in this entire book. Instead of calling it "Psychic Self-Defense," I could also have entitled it "How to Build a Strong Physical, Emotional, Mental, and Spiritual Immune System."

You might think of the immune system as being a part of the physical body only. This is not the case, however. It is just as important, if not more so, to develop a psychological and spiritual immune system. The effectiveness of your physical immune system will, in actuality, depend to a great extent on the strength of your psychological and spiritual immunity.

Whether spiritual people like to admit it or not, life is a battle. Even the great Paramahansa Yogananda said, "Life is a battlefield." In the *Bhagavad-Gita*, Krishna implored Arjuna to "give up his unmanliness and get up and fight." You have to learn to be a spiritual warrior in life. *A Course in Miracles* emphasizes the importance of being "vigilant for God and His kingdom." The fight exists on a number of levels. First, you are fighting to remain conscious and alert and not fall into what I call automatic pilot. Second, you are fighting to keep your mind clear of negative thoughts. You are fighting to keep glamour, illusion, maya, and negative ego from taking over your consciousness. You are fighting to stay centered and balanced. You are fighting to maintain unconditional love, joy, even-mindedness, and inner peace.

Sometimes you are battling to heal yourself of physical disease or of dis-ease on emotional, mental, and/or spiritual levels. Sometimes you are battling fatigue. You are battling to control your subconscious mind and to master your three lower vehicles, or bodies. You are battling to remain in the consciousness that you are God.

One of the biggest things you must fight, along with the energies within yourself that do not come from soul, are the negative energies from other people and the environment.

The spiritual path is like climbing a mountain — climb up three steps, fall back two. This is how everyone grows. You have learned, in this planetary mystery school called Earth life, that you must remain strong. This battle does get easier the higher you go in the initiation process. In the early stages there is a great battle going on with "the dweller on the threshold" (negative ego, glamour, illusion, and maya). As you gain mastery, these energies are subjugated and new, positive spiritual habits are formed. In essence, over a long period of battling and suffering, you finally reach a point of learning how to stay strong physically, mentally, emotionally, and spiritually, and how to avoid being knocked off center by an onslaught of negative energies from the inner or the material world.

In this chapter I am going to give you the understanding and the tools to win this battle easily and gain self-mastery, so that life becomes much easier and more enjoyable. I am going to teach you how to protect yourself just as a martial arts instructor would, except on subtler, spiritual and psychic levels.

Before I can do this, however, I must give you a wakeup call. Many of you are living your lives on automatic pilot, like automatons, totally unaware of all the negative forces that are at work: negative ego, glamour, illusion, and maya, and onslaughts of negative physical, environmental, psychological, and spiritual energies that confront the average person on a daily basis.

This chapter will help you to develop an arsenal of psychological and spiritual tools to win the war against these negative energies. It will also point out the enormous barrage of negative energy that is coming from the environment, other people, the astral plane, the mental plane, and the etheric plane. You cannot win the battle until you understand what it is you are fighting.

In beginning the practice of psychic self-defense I ask you to read this material with detachment so as not to become overwhelmed. After listing what you are battling, then I will teach you how to become invulnerable to their effects. For never forget that, in truth, you are God, and as you realize this potential you are no longer a victim of anything; you are then a total master and the cause of your reality.

Let us begin with the physical body and the physical immune system and what it has to contend with. Some of the things I am about to mention you might already be aware of, but some of them you might tend to forget about in terms of protecting yourself.

Assaults on the Physical Immune System

The first thing the physical body has to deal with is pollution, especially if you live in a big city, although in truth there is pollution almost everywhere on this planet now. In a city such as Los Angeles, there is air pollution, and the drinking water is toxic. There is an enormous amount of sound pollution, with car alarms constantly going off along with all the sounds of a big city. These noises affect you much more than you realize.

The oceans are polluted. The fish are filled with mercury. There are fast food restaurants and ice cream parlors on every corner. Needless to say, the food is dead and not good for your body.

The government fluoridates the water supply; drinking fluoridated water shuts down the immune system. Toothpastes are also filled with fluoride. Dentists fill cavities with mercury, one of the most toxic substances to the human body, with only plutonium or nuclear radiation being worse. After ten or fifteen years the mercury fillings crack and leak into your system, creating havoc. I would highly recommend having them replaced with gold or composite fillings.

The government performs nuclear tests which leave their traces in the atmosphere for forty years. Then there is nuclear waste which no one has any idea what to do with. The latest brainstorm is to use some of it to irradiate our fruits and vegetables, a practice that has already been approved by a "protective agency," the FDA, which is the biggest joke in the universe.

When food goes through the checkout counter in the supermarket, it is zapped again with some kind of radiation so the price is recorded automatically. Please realize this energetically poisons the food.

Then, of course, the farmers use massive amounts of pesticides on all the fruits and vegetables you consume on a daily basis. The soil and water are filled with nitrates. Medical doctors have no training in diet or nutrition or holistic practices so instead they pass out drugs and antibiotics like candy. The antibiotics wipe out all the friendly bacteria and poison the liver, throwing the entire physical body and immune system out of balance as the yeast grows like crazy. Then the average person goes back to the doctor who runs medical tests with all kinds of high tech machinery, dyes, and radiation that poison the patient even more.

The dentist takes x-rays which provide a little more radiation. The government sprays the city from helicopters with Malathion, a pesticide, to kill the Mediterranean fruit fly. The FDA, our great protective agency, says that it does no harm to the human body. But they do tell you to cover your car when the spraying occurs because Malathion will take the paint off a car. And yet it won't affect the human body adversely?!

It is finally coming out that people are getting cancer from being too close to electric power lines. You are constantly being bombarded with radiation from television sets, computers, toasters, microwave ovens, electric blankets, and on and on. There are many ways to protect yourself from low-grade electromagnetic frequencies.

I saw on the news last week that cellular phones in cars are now known to cause cancer on the side of the head the phone is held to. I also saw another special on television that talked about how police officers are getting cancer of the groin from holding radar guns in their laps while tracking cars.

The immune system must battle aluminum poisoning from using aluminum pots and pans and aluminum foil. A homeopathic doctor pointed out that I was getting aluminum poisoning from cooking my fish in foil. They are finding a correlation between Alzheimer's disease and aluminum poisoning, metal poisoning in general, and chemical poisoning, as well.

Children are getting sick from the lead in the paint in many houses and other buildings. The gasoline fumes from all the cars also cause lead poisoning. If you live in a city, God knows what toxic chemicals and metals you have in your system. People who drink the local water can get too much copper in their systems from the copper pipes.

Because of the way we have polluted the planet, we have caused a massive hole in the ozone layer which allows too many ultraviolet rays from the sun to get through. They are causing skin cancer and they have other toxic effects, too.

The destroying of the rain forests has caused the oxygen level of the entire planet to be in danger of being thrown off balance. The massive amounts of cement that cover the earth don't allow the Earth Mother to breathe properly, which obviously has adverse effects. The ground water is being polluted by toxic landfills.

Fast-food restaurant hamburgers are killing people because of the amount of bacteria in the meat. *Sixty Minutes* did a special on the chicken industry, and even the FDA found 50 to 60% of all chicken is tainted with salmonella bacteria. In addition, cancer in chickens tends to be hereditary.

The food that most people eat is filled with preservatives, chemicals, and additives, which are totally toxic to the liver. Besides this, 95% of the food in a supermarket is "dead food." There is no longer any life force in it. Humanity's apparent inability to work with the nature kingdom and with nature spirits in a loving, cooperative manner has caused these wonderful beings to leave the farms where produce is grown; hence, the food is filled with only one-tenth the life force it could have.

Some people live on coffee and sugar and artificial stimulants like chocolate and soda pop, which give you a brief rush and then totally deplete your energies. The medical profession gives children vaccines and insists on vaccinations for adults who want to travel out of the country. Vaccines are absolutely poisonous to the immune system and are one of the biggest frauds that has ever been perpetrated on the public.

To make it even worse, the military-industrial complex, which looks at people as nothing more than objects, performs chemical warfare experiments using these vaccines to test out their experiments. One of these is, of course, AIDS, which was created by the military-industrial complex. Don't be so naive as to think that this is the only disease they have purposely released on the unaware American public.

Average people don't eat well or exercise enough and do not have strong mental or emotional or spiritual immune systems, so they get sick a lot. They have to battle to keep their resistance up against all the viruses and bacterial infections floating around, not even taking into consideration the sexually transmitted diseases.

The burning of fossil fuels is actually causing, for the first time in history, acid rain. No plant life can grow in acid rain. Another thing immune systems must battle on the physical level is the lighting in most buildings and offices. Fluorescent light bulbs are toxic to the human body.

Another factor that people have to deal with, which most are not aware of, has to do with the field of psychotronics and radionics. These are machines that send out energy waves that are supposed to be used for healing purposes. Of course, the military-industrial complex has gotten hold of them and is using them for warfare at times. This is also being experimented with in other countries. Segments of the population are being bombarded by these unseen electromagnetic energy waves, and sometimes even certain individuals are targeted.

In a similar vein, but less sinister, is the effect of all the radio, television, phone, and satellite waves that we are constantly bombarded with. Some of these may be subtle, but they all have their effect. Then there is the low level of negative ions in the stale air of city buildings. The greenhouse effect is causing temperatures to rise and is also causing extreme weather conditions which can be hard on the physical body, especially in some areas of the country.

These are just some of the factors your physical immune system is battling on a daily basis, the factors that are in the front of my mind. I am sure there are millions of other factors that I have not listed. It is amazing that immune systems do as well as they do, considering the assault they are under in modern society.

Assaults on the Psychological and Spiritual Immune Systems

On psychological and spiritual levels, you first have to deal with the negative thoughts, feelings, emotions, and energies of other people. They can act very much like hypnosis if you are not in a vigilant state of consciousness. Then there is the onslaught of violence and other negative energies that come from society in general in the form of advertising, magazines, television, newspapers, and the media as a whole. The world has basically institutionalized negative-ego, lower-self consciousness. It is everywhere and it permeates every aspect of society.

You have to deal with all the bad news that is constantly reported and glamorized in the media. The lyrics of pop music are filled with the consciousness of addictive love. You have to deal with the bad moods, irritability, anger, depression, worry, insecurity, fear, and criticism of your co-workers and family members. If you do not have strong psychological and spiritual immune systems, all this stuff gets into your subconscious mind and depletes your energy, making you feel bad.

Then you have to deal with what the Eastern religions refer to as the monkey mind: when the mind is out of control, then emotions will be out of control, and the physical body will be adversely affected. You have to deal with your own negative ego, glamour, illusion, and maya. You also have to deal with biorhythms and negative astrological configurations.

When you become weakened physically, psychologically or spiritually, you become open to psychic attack from the lower astral plane. In cases of severe weakness this can result in a type of possession which must then be cleared. Some people are battling obsessive thought, anxiety, and/or personality disorders. All these things become cleared as self-mastery is gained and the four bodies and three minds become aligned.

Other types of things you are battling on psychological and spiritual levels are alien abduction and alien implants. Most of these abductions are performed by the negative extraterrestrial group called the Grays from Zeta Reticulum and the Orion sector. I will teach you how to protect yourself from these invasions.

Lightworkers are often under attack from the Dark Brotherhood, also known as the Black Lodge. They are not to be feared as long as you have the tools to remain in self-mastery.

Some people have to deal with poltergeists, or Earth-bound spirits who have gained a small amount of vital force and like to play tricks on unaware humans. Then too, you have to deal with people I like to call psychic vampires, for they drain your psychic life force.

You have to learn how to deal with what are called the negative elementals that are created by your thought forms. They latch on to your aura and drain you. You have to learn how to deal with psychological and spiritual illness. Just as physical disease is not contagious (for you can't get sick if you have a high resistance) the same is true on a psychological or spiritual level. There is no such thing as a contagious psychological or spiritual disease; there are only people who have low resistance within their psychological and spiritual immune systems.

This chapter will provide you with the understanding and tools to avoid catching the physical, psychological and spiritual diseases of other people. The object is to stay healthy and bring sick people up to your level, not to fall down to their level. You must see them as God sees them, which is perfect and whole. As *A Course in Miracles* says, "Sickness is a defense against the truth."

You must learn to protect yourself from psychiatrists, psychologists, ministers, and traditional medical doctors because so much of their training is filled with negative-ego concepts that overemphasize material reality and cut them off from the true realities of spirit.

You must even protect yourself from the New Age movement and use great discernment, for there are many false prophets and cult movements in operation. You must protect yourself and be particularly discerning in the field of politics where negative ego is rampant.

You must protect yourself from the media, for the newspapers and TV stations are run by the Trilateral Commission and Council on Foreign Relations (the secret government). Nine-tenths of what the government tells the public is just deception and lies. The Warren Commission says that Oswald killed Kennedy and that it wasn't a conspiracy. They insist UFOs don't exist when there are actual extraterrestrials of many species living as guests of the government. They deceive you with a phony space program. They tell you what you want to hear and then things like Vietnam, Watergate, Contragate, a phony drug war, and the loss of civil liberties are going on behind your back.

Other energies you need to protect yourself from are the energies that are actually embedded in the walls. The great spiritual master Ronald Beesley used to say that hospitals should be burned down every five years. So much negative energy has been embedded in the walls that it is amazing anyone ever recovers at all. This is true also of a new home or office building.

Another way to be poisoned is to fall asleep at night watching TV. Whatever you are watching or listening to gets programmed right into your subconscious mind as you sleep. While you are sleeping you are in a state of hypnosis and you are hypersuggestible. The same thing happens under anesthesia during surgery. Everything the doctors and nurses say is programmed right in. In the future, this understanding will be used for a positive purpose to accelerate healing.

Another way you are influenced if you are not vigilant is through subliminal advertising. It is supposed to be illegal, but it happens all the time. Subliminal messages in either visual or auditory form are placed within commercials, television, movies, music, radio and the like to program people unconsciously.

The military-industrial complex is involved in all kinds of experiments in mind control and psychic warfare. If people really knew what was going on behind the scenes in this world they would never, ever let themselves go on automatic pilot even for an instant. Not only is the government using psychic warfare, radionics, and brain-washing techniques, but so are the negative extraterrestrials. We are basically in an all-out war right now with negative alien civilizations that are trying to take over this planet, and people are not even aware of it. This war is not like the movie *War of the Worlds* with its physical bombs; it is a war of mind control.

There are probably only a handful of people on Earth who are not filled with alien implants. Why do people have a hard time remembering they have been abducted? It is mind control again, and the negative extraterrestrials are masters of it. I will provide tools for getting rid of all your alien implants and preventing the mind control and abduction from taking place.

Then there is the whole field of black magic — the using of God's universal laws for evil and selfish purposes. You must not be so naive as to think that this can't happen, for it can and frequently does. It is nothing to worry about as long as you keep your immune systems on all four levels working effectively.

Another thing you have to protect yourself from is what I call disinformation. The secret government, with the help of agencies such as the CIA, has infiltrated all aspects of society that are opposed to their selfish purposes. Then they have CIA-type agents disseminate disinformation to confuse the public. An example of this is the lectures presented at the conventions about extraterrestrial contact. I'll bet a quarter of the people lecturing are hired to present material that will confuse and fragment the movement that is trying to educate the populace.

In addition, it is good to avoid letting people touch your jewelry. Very innocently, people come up and touch a ring or bracelet and an energy transfer takes place. Now if it is someone you love, it might be okay; however, to let strangers do this is to carry their energy with you from that moment on. Another lesson of a similar nature is the practice of hugging people. I certainly believe in hugging, but as you become more sensitive and as your energy fields become more refined, it is better to have less physical contact with certain people.

Any one of these things alone is not that important. However, when you put them all together, the effect is quite significant.

I will share with you an interesting story I remember reading in one of the Edgar Cayce books. There was a machine the Universal Mind recommended for the running of electric energy through a body to accelerate healing in the case of a broken leg, for example. It was a fantastic machine and many people had great success with it. One man who bought one was getting terrible results, and it was causing all kinds of other problems when he used it. He finally asked for another channeling from Edgar Cayce to find out what was going wrong. The Universal Mind told him the problem was that the man who made the machine had been extremely angry the day he had made that particular machine. The anger was stored in the machine, and every time it was used, the maker's negative anger surged through the man's body. This makes you think a bit, doesn't it?

The same principle applies to the food you eat. You say you like fresh vegetables and you think they're good for you. Have you considered the process they go through before they reach you? First, if they are not grown organically, they are planted in depleted soil. Pesticides and chemicals are used. The pesticides and chemicals keep away all nature spirits, so the life force in the vegetables is at a bare minimum. They are picked before they are ripe so as to make more money for the grower. What was the mood of the person who picked them? Was he angry or depressed? If so, that energy was transferred into the vegetables.

How about the person who carries them to the truck and unloads them? How about the produce person who puts them on display in the market? How about the grocery clerk who picks them up to weigh them and register the price or put them through the little radiation machine? Many vegetables are being irradiated, and no written statement to notify the general public has to be displayed. All that is required is some logo that only one person in a million would even recognize.

In the same category is cooking food in a microwave oven. Hanna Kroeger, whom I consider to be one of the finest herbalists and healers on the Earth today, has said that microwaving food is an absolute blasphemy. It is certainly not a New Age form of cooking. It radiates the food in a most unhealthful manner. You can test this yourself with the use of a pendulum.

Now begins the fun part. In the next section I will begin the intensive training in psychic self-defense.

Psychic Self-Defense on the Physical Plane

It is always good to burn high-quality incense or, even better, sage when you want to clear the psychic atmosphere of a room. This is a quick and easy method. However, if you want to clear the energy completely, the best method of all is to put three or four tablespoons of Epsom salts into a small frying pan or cooking pot that you no longer need for regular cooking. Then pour in enough rubbing alcohol to just cover the Epsom salts. Place the pot in the middle of the room you want to clear and light a match to it. My wife and I like to sit and watch it burn as though it were a campfire. The results you can get are absolutely miraculous. The entire atmosphere is cleansed of all negativity.

To amplify your energy field, you can wear certain amulets or gemstones that are designed for protection and strengthening. One of the best of all is a simple crystal pendant. Crystals amplify energy, and wearing a crystal or carrying one with you will serve this purpose in a most effective manner.

To protect yourself from low-grade electromagnetic frequencies, I recommend getting a Tesla watch. It is a special kind of watch invented by Nikola Tesla that actually creates an electrical field around you that protects you from the energy leakage from TV sets, computers, power lines, and so on.

If you go to your neighborhood homeopathic pharmacy or metaphysical bookstore you can buy different kinds of copper coils that are much cheaper and that also work. You can just carry them in your pocket or wear them as a necklace. Your homeopathic pharmacist will know what I am talking about. You can also find them at the Whole Life Expos that come to most cities in the United States.

Don't keep your television set right at the foot of your bed. When you shut it off at night it is still emanating radiation and the chakras in your feet will just soak up the energy.

Homeopathic pharmacies also have certain kinds of remedies for the specific purpose of strengthening your energy field and offering protection. There are also Bach flower remedies for this purpose.

An item every person should have is a soma board. It costs only ten dollars and was created by Hanna Kroeger, the master herbalist and healer. A soma board is filled with herbs and crystals, and it lasts forever. The idea is to put your food on the soma board before eating it. It completely clears and neutralizes all the negative vibrations that have been put into the food along the processing route I spoke of earlier. Hanna Kroeger's address is:

> 7075 Valmont Drive
> Boulder, Colorado 80301
> (303) 442-2490 or (303) 443-0755

Hanna Kroeger is one of the most amazing people I have ever met and the finest herbalist. She is totally of the Christ consciousness and must be close to eighty years old. I strongly recommend that you get her books. She has a cure for AIDS, believe it or not, that costs $25 and works. She has cures for cancer and just about every other disease known to man. She is a master of pendulum use; my wife and I have checked out her claims with our own pendulums and she is totally right.

She has an apprentice teacher in the Los Angeles area by the name of Sherry Cash, who works out of the Balanced Life Centre ((818) 348-8818). Sherry has all her books and products. She is a healer and can test you for all Hanna's products with her pendulum.

One aspect of strengthening your energy field is to get rid of all the residual toxins, viruses, and bacterial infections that have been stuck in your body since childhood. Seeing someone like Sherry Cash as well as a good homeopathic doctor who does some kind of vega machine testing is essential.

A vega machine is just one of many similar machines that holistic, homeopathic, and naturopathic doctors are using to test a person for things like pesticide poisoning, mercury poisoning, metal poisoning, chemical poisoning, parasites, viruses, bacterial infections, and, in fact, any physical problem or weakness you might have.

In my opinion, these are the doctors of the future. With the help of these machines and homeopathic medicine you can be checked out in one hour for just about every disease known to man without having to take blood tests or the invasive tests of traditional medicine. I am not saying you shouldn't have a traditional medical doctor; I am just suggesting you do both.

Pesticides, chemicals, metals, mercury, and an infinite number of other possible toxins can be cleaned out of your system in a month or two using homeopathics and/or herbs. Since we are on the subject of food, I also recommend buying organic vegetables and asking the person in charge of the produce at your regular market if the produce has been irradiated. If it has, don't buy it. As much as possible, buy beef and poultry that has been raised naturally. That way you will never have to worry about bacteria poisoning or meat that is filled with antibiotics, stilbestrol, and other chemicals.

Hanna Kroeger has another invention called an iron ring, which you can read about in her books. You stand in it for ninety seconds and it clears from your aura all the environmental pollution you have accumulated. You can make one yourself for less than five bucks with some strong wire.

I am taking it for granted here that everybody knows the importance of a good diet, rest, and exercise in building strong immune systems and keeping the dark forces at bay.

I recommend drinking six to eight glasses of pure water each day. This clears a lot of toxicity out of the body. It is important not to eat right before bed. Edgar Cayce said that was the cause of nightmares for many people. It is also of the greatest importance to avoid coffee, sugar, and artificial stimulants, as they have a very great weakening effect on the body over time. They are all right on rare occasions or in emergencies, but not on a regular basis. The question of whether to eat meat is an individual choice. Some types of physical bodies need it more than others. If you do eat it, don't eat too much of it, and try to let it be as fresh and natural as possible.

The idea of the spiritual path is to achieve even-mindedness and evenness in physical energy so as not to be on a roller coaster. It must be understood that food does affect your emotional state. This is working with what is called the law of similars.

There are a number of other physical techniques you can use. All these tools and understandings are subtle, but together they have a very pro-found effect.

Never cross your legs when sitting or standing. It immediately cuts off the flow of energy through your chakra system, and as long as your aura is strong you cannot be affected by negative entities.

If you work with a computer it is essential to get some kind of protective computer screen. Hanna Kroeger also sells an inexpensive computer pillow which will protect you from radiation.

Whenever you eat it is a good idea to bless your food. I learned a prayer for this purpose from Paul Solomon's channeling of the Universal Mind. Hold your hands over the food while you address it: "As you are created by God, adore thy Creator in what you shall do within my body and temple as I build it to His glory. Amen."

A simple technique to open and energize your chakras is to cup your hand in front of you just below the first chakra. Slide your hand upward through all your chakras and then over the top of your head, feeling the subtle magnetism move with your hand. Do this from three to seven times and it will energize you if you are feeling sluggish.

If you ever feel yourself under a psychic attack of some kind or if there is a negative energy in your home, there are a number of physical things to do. One is to shower and set the intent as you shower that you are also cleansing all seven bodies. A dark entity can get in only if you are weakened or vibrating at a similar level of consciousness. Showering cleanses the aura and the body. Put on clean clothes and wash your old clothes. You can put spiritual books around your bed in a "ring pass not."

In a case of severe psychic attack it is a good idea to eat frequently, as often as every two hours. Food makes you less sensitive, and at a time like that you want to be as grounded as possible. It is also a good idea to be around positive people.

My wife and I were guided to hang a mirror as a protection, given all the meetings we have. When people come into the room they see them-selves in the mirror, which prevents evil spirits from entering.

In the Chinese art of Feng Shui, the art of environmental design, there are many suggestions, such as the importance of closing closet doors and of putting up screens in certain areas of the house. Terri and I were guided to put a small rug in front of where we sit when we do workshops. We were also guided to put a fountain in our living room.

Another idea was to put a pie tin on the outside of our home to collect and reflect the noise and to attract prosperity. In Feng Shui, every room in the house has a specific function. For example, my office turned out to be the room of knowledge and wisdom, which is perfect. Our bedroom turned out to be the room of marriage, and Terri's room turned out to be the room of prosperity.

You might invest in an air-freshening machine or a negative ion generator. A Native American technique is that of smudging a house when you move in and at certain other times. You can buy smudge sticks at a metaphysical bookstore.

An excellent technique for strengthening your energy field and killing bacteria and viruses is to sunbathe. This vitalizes the etheric body. Something as simple as getting enough sleep instead of burning the candle at both ends is also important; moderation in all things.

Playing spiritual music, devotional songs, or mantras can be very uplifting and protective if you feel negative energy around you. Sometimes just going into another room will help.

It is also a good idea to arrange your bed so that it faces east, for that is the direction of the strongest spiritual current. It is also recommended for meditating. It might be important for some people to study a martial art like aikido, tai chi, or any of the others you might be guided to. They all have physical, psychological, and spiritual effects.

The less alcohol and the fewer drugs, the better. Read labels. Eat to live, don't live to eat. It is also a good idea to supplement your diet with a natural food source vitamin and mineral which will have a strengthening effect on your auric field, along with other appropriate supplements. Considering this modern society and the depleted food, additional vitamins are necessary in order to get all the nutrients you need.

Maintaining the proper chemical balance in your body is essential. Imbalance can cause severe mood swings and other problems.

When you move into a home, it is wise to scrub the walls with a strong cleaning agent throughout the house and, if possible, paint the walls. This will eliminate most of the negative energy that has become imbedded in the walls from past tenants. Search for and clear any negative energy vortexes. This can be done with a pendulum. Go through the house with your pendulum, and when you find a spot that makes the pendulum reverse its swing, you can breathe into it to make it spin in the proper direction again. If you sleep in a negative vortex, it can cause restlessness. This should also be done when you are traveling and staying in a hotel.

An Epsom salts and baking soda bath has an absolutely fantastic effect, clearing out radiation and low-grade electromagnetic frequencies from your field as well as any lingering hypnotic connections with other people.

Psychic Self-Defense on the Mental, Emotional, and Spiritual Planes

The first technique I would like to recommend is what Christian Science has called putting on your mental armor. This is something that should be done every morning when you get up and any other time you feel the need for it. Just as you put on physical clothes every morning, it is also important to put on your psychological and spiritual clothes. This means putting on your personal power, self-mastery, invulnerability, unconditional love, attunement to God, self-love, and centeredness. In other words, you psychically clothe yourself in the psychological attributes you want to wear that day.

This must be done consciously and with intent each morning. Most people just bumble into life on automatic pilot, wearing the qualities of energy they happen to wake up with. This is not self-mastery. Putting on your mental armor could also be called putting on visual armor. Visualize any — or all — of the following:

> A bubble of protection around yourself;
> A protective tube of Light surrounding you;
> A grounding cord;
> Your chakras being lighted up in their appropriate colors;
> A robe of Light and vitality;
> A sword as a symbol of your personal power;
> A symbol such as a rose in your heart as a symbol of self-love and love for others.

This prepares you and aligns your mind with the way you want to create your day. In essence, this is a type of meditation that will also greatly strengthen your auric field.

One of the most powerful prayers of protection is the Lord's Prayer:

> Our Father which art in heaven, hallowed be Thy name.
> Thy kingdom come, Thy will be done on Earth, as it is in heaven.
> Give us this day, our daily bread, and forgive us our debts, as we forgive our debtors.
> And lead us not into temptation, but deliver us from evil,
> For Thine is the kingdom, and the power, and the glory forever.
> Amen.

Another one of my favorite prayers of protection is one by Isabelle Hickey:

> I ask and pray to be clothed with a robe of Light composed of the love, wisdom, and power of God, not only for my protection, but so that all who see it or come in contact with it will be drawn to God and healed.

Another prayer of protection is from the Fellowship of Universal Guidance, founded by Bella Karish:

> Father-Mother God, I ask that I be cleared and cleansed within the universal white Christ Light, the green healing Light, and the purple transmuting flame. Within God's will, and for my highest good, I ask that any and all negativity be completely sealed in its own Light, encapsulated within the ultraviolet Light, cut off and removed from me, impersonally, with neither love nor hate.
>
> I return all negativity to its source of emanation, decreeing that it never again be allowed to reestablish itself within me or anyone else in any form. I now ask that I be placed within a triple capsule of the universal white Christ Light of protection, and for this blessing, I give thanks. Amen.

Whenever you desire protection it is very appropriate to call on Archangel Michael and his legions of Angels of Protection. Archangel Michael's specific purpose is to provide this protection for Lightworkers when asked. This can also be visualized using a blue ray of protective Light.

Djwhal Khul has recommended visualizing a golden egg and then painting the outside of the egg black, if you really want super protection. Leave a little hole at the very top of the egg for the tube of Light and your antakarana that connects you with your soul, monad, the ascended masters, and God.

If you feel you are under psychic attack or if you feel negative energy around you, one of the most powerful tools of protection is to hold a crystal or a piece of jewelry that has a lot of your energy in it and chant the name Elohim or Jesus Christ for fifteen minutes. This can be done silently or out loud. Repeating the name of God and visualizing God's form while you do it is a sure-fire method of removing all negative energy from your field. I recommend doing this as a daily practice even if you don't need protection.

When you are around people who are negative, visualize a glass window in front of you. In serious cases put up a brick wall. The Berkeley Psychic Institute uses the protective device of imagining a red rose in front of you, protecting you. When negative energy comes toward you, the flower will absorb it and start to wilt. When it does, put up a new rose. If you want, you can put a ring of roses all around yourself. Check the roses two or three times a day when you are dealing with a lot of negative energy.

One of the most powerful mantras you can use is the soul mantra made known by Djwhal Khul.

> I am the Soul,
> I am the Light Divine,
> I am Love.
> I am Will.
> I am Fixed Design.

This immediately connects you with your soul, and I would recommend using this mantra before using any other methods listed in this chapter. Other mantras I would recommend in emergencies are Aum or Om Mani Padme Hum, So Ham, I Am God, or I Am that I Am. It is fun to switch around.

You can chant just the name of the spiritual master or saint you have the most affinity for and visualize his or her form while doing it. You can also visualize his or her form descending and superimposing itself on your body; or you can miniaturize the form and place it within your heart.

When feeling negative energy around you before bed, call forth and visualize the ascended masters around your bed in a protective circle, and ask them to serve as guards and sentinels. You can also place a grid of crystals, either in your imagination or in physical form, around your bed, and program them for your purpose.

When you feel negative energy in your aura, do your soul mantra and then call forth from your soul, monad, God, and the ascended masters a shower of Light to pour down your antakarana, or rainbow bridge. In essence you are taking a Light shower. When you ask for this Light shower, you can also ask that the Light fill your room, your entire house, and the homes of people you love. There is no limit to the Light. It is an inexhaustible supply. It is there for the asking.

If you really want to clear your aura, do the soul mantra and then say, "In the name of the Christ I call forth the spiritual vortex." Visualize a vortex coming down from your monad and moving through your entire auric field, clearing away all auric debris. This is not just imagination; it will actually be there. The power of the mind is incredible, and it is even more powerful when you invoke the soul or mighty I Am Presence to help.

Phyllis Crystal, a psychologist and devotee of Sai Baba, tells a story of a young man whose car had been broken into frequently. She told him to visualize a beach ball around his car to protect it. To his amazement he had no more break-ins. She then told him to put a beach ball around himself for protection. He did this. Two or three weeks later he was visiting a clairvoyant friend who suddenly stopped their conversation and said to him that she kept seeing a beach ball around him and wondered what it was for.

Edgar Cayce, in his channelings of the Universal Mind, kept saying over and over again that "thoughts are things." God created the universe with the power of His mind. You are creating your universe with the power of your mind. As you develop spiritually you learn to take the things you think and imagine and actually lower their vibrations so they become physical. This is one of the things you will be able to do when you become an ascended master, and maybe even before that.

Other effective tools are to make the sign of the cross, the sign of the pentagram, or the sign of the Kabbalistic cross. These may seem kind of superstitious and not that effective, but there is enormous power in these psychic and spiritual techniques.

Another extraordinarily powerful prayer is the rosary of the Virgin Mary. This is not just a Catholic prayer, and she has said this herself through channelings of Earlyne Chaney. She told Chaney that saying the rosary was so powerful that it could even protect a person from a nuclear bomb. Earlyne Chaney didn't believe her. Three months later she was told a story of seven priests who lived in Hiroshima during World War II. Their church was something like eight blocks from ground zero of the atomic bomb that was dropped. After the explosion everything was destroyed for an entire mile in all directions — except this church. Sociologists were baffled. The only thing they could come up with was that these seven priests had said the rosary three times a day.

I have enclosed a copy of the rosary. I love this prayer, and I am not Catholic. I think it is one of the most powerful prayers in existence. Some of the words in the Catholic interpretation bother some people; if that is the case, just change a word or two to make it comfortable for yourself. It is not necessary to use an actual rosary, but if you want to, you can.

There is something else I would like to recommend: you can order a New Age version of the rosary that was channeled from the Virgin Mary through Sylvia Clarice. This particular rosary is called the Ascension Rosary, and it is fantastic. Djwhal Khul has confirmed its efficacy. The Ascension Rosary comes in booklet form and costs ten or fifteen dollars. You cannot get it in bookstores, so if you are interested write to

The Mother Matrix
P.O. Box 473
Mt. Shasta, CA 96067.

Prayers of the Rosary

The Sign of the Cross

In the name of the Father, and of the Son, and of the Holy Spirit. Amen.

The Apostles' Creed

I believe in God, the Father Almighty, Creator of Heaven and Earth; and in Jesus Christ, His only Son, our Lord; who was conceived by the Holy Spirit, born of the Virgin Mary, suffered under Pontius Pilate, was crucified, died, and was buried. He descended into hell; the third day He arose again from the dead. He ascended into Heaven, sitteth at the right hand of God the Father Almighty; from thence He shall come to judge the living and the dead. I believe in the Holy Spirit, the Holy Catholic Church, the communion of Saints, the forgiveness of sins, the resurrection of the body, and life everlasting. Amen.

The Our Father

Our Father, who art in Heaven, hallowed be Thy name. Thy kingdom come, Thy will be done on Earth as it is in Heaven. Give us this day our daily bread, and forgive us our trespasses as we forgive those who trespass against us. And lead us not into temptation, but deliver us from evil. Amen.

The Hail Mary

Hail Mary, full of grace; the Lord is with thee: blessed art thou among women, and blessed is the fruit of thy womb, Jesus. Holy Mary, Mother of God, pray for us sinners, now and at the hour of our death. Amen.

Glory Be to the Father

Glory be to the Father, and to the Son, and to the Holy Spirit; as it was in the beginning, is now, and ever shall be, world without end. Amen.

The Hail, Holy Queen

Hail, Holy Queen, Mother of Mercy, our life, our sweetness, and our hope! To thee do we cry, poor banished children of Eve; to thee do we send up our sighs, mourning, and weeping in this valley of tears. Turn, then, most gracious Advocate, thine eyes of mercy toward us; and after this our exile show unto us the blessed fruit of thy womb, Jesus; O clement, O loving, O sweet Virgin Mary.

V. Pray for us, O Holy Mother of God.

R. That we may be made worthy of the promises of Christ.

Let Us Pray

O God, whose only begotten Son, by his life, death, and resurrection has purchased for us the rewards of eternal life, grant, we beseech Thee, that meditating upon these mysteries in the most Holy Rosary of the Blessed Virgin Mary, we may imitate what they contain, and obtain what they promise: through the same Christ our Lord. Amen

Another good protective tool is to image your golden bubble or golden egg and then breathe love and peace into it. Send any negative energy down your grounding cord into the Earth for transmutation.

Probably the most important protective mechanism of all is a psychological understanding of denial and affirmation. *A Course in Miracles* says, "Deny any thought that is not of God to enter your mind." If you do this one thing, you will automatically be protected. The thoughts can be coming from your subconscious, a possessing entity, or from other people in the world. If you push these thoughts out of your mind and replace them with positive affirmations, your subconscious mind will be reprogrammed within twenty-one days.

Another variation on the same theme is a technique I learned from the great mystic Dion Fortune. She suggested visualizing the negative thought or image as a mirror which you shatter; then immediately visualize a positive spiritual image like a temple or spiritual master.

There is another very effective tool I learned from Phyllis Krystal's book, *Cutting the Ties that Bind.* When you are dealing with someone with whom you need to maintain a boundary, imagine yourself in a circle. Then imagine, around the person you need the boundary with, another circle that is touching but not entering your circle. Do this with golden Light and make it a thick line. The two circles end up looking like a figure eight. If you like, you can draw the circles in a figure eight motion. (The figure eight is the sign of infinity.) Then draw a line of blue Light within the golden Light. I would enlarge upon this by suggesting that the two circles could be made into two golden spheres of Light with blue inside of them for even more protection.

Another important tool for cutting the inappropriate ties that bind you to other people is to image the codependent ties as cords of energy that radiate from your chakras. Imagine a gigantic scissors or the flaming sword of Lord Michael or the light saber of a Jedi knight. Use this instrument in your visualization, and also use your physical arm to slice through these codependent cords. When they have all been cut, pull them out of your chakras and burn them. Then say the soul mantra and call forth a golden sun to come down and fill any emptiness with the love and wholeness of God. You can call down as many suns as you need until your aura is healed, whole, and full.

If you ever sense dark spirits around you, just say, "In the name and power of Jesus Christ, I command you to leave." It is very important when dealing with dark spirits in this world or from the other side that you have no anger or fear. Remember what Master Yoda said in the *Star Wars* movies: "Don't give in to your anger or fear, or you will be seduced by the dark side of the Force." Maintain a state of even-mindedness, divine

indifference, detachment, and neutrality. That way you are giving the
confused spirits no energy. They feed off anger and fear. See them as God
even though they don't see themselves that way. With your full power and
full love, command them to leave. As the commercials say, "Just say no."

If a person you know is possessed, say the following prayer:

> Oh beloved God, Christ, Holy Spirit, mighty I Am Presence, my
> monad, my soul, Sathya Sai Baba, Babaji, Jesus Christ, Master
> Djwhal Khul, Vywamus, ascended masters, and any other saint or
> spiritual master on the spiritual plane!
> You are healed and forgiven.
> You are one with your soul and higher self.
> You are filled with the love of God.
> You are filled and surrounded with the Light of God.
> You are free from fear and suffering and free from the vibration of
> the Earth plane.
> I ask the above-mentioned spiritual masters and God Himself to
> take you to your rightful place.
> Go in peace.

Say this prayer three times with full power after doing your soul
mantra first. In very serious cases you can call an organization called the
Teaching of the Inner Christ in San Diego; someone there will guide you
to a minister who will perform the needed exorcism. The phone number is
(619) 233-7745.

With all the tools in this book you should have no problem doing it
yourself. Possessing spirits are usually just confused souls who don't know
how to let go of their material focus and move back through the tunnel to
the other side.

It is important to remember that negative energy or entities can enter
your field only when you have allowed your own negative ego and lower
self to predominate. If you keep them small and quiet, then all the other
negative energies and entities will stay away also.

Another good visualization for protection is to see yourself in a
pyramid of Light or to see a wall of Light. Sai Baba has referred to this as
a divine buffer. It is also important, when dealing with the Dark Brotherhood or dark spirits, that you not try to send them love to win them over.
They will use your love as a power source and send their energy back to
you. Be loving in a neutral way.

Another simple tool is to detach yourself as though you were watching
a movie. Pretend you are seeing any negative people through a pair of
binoculars turned backwards.

A very powerful exercise you can do every morning when putting on your mental armor is to visualize an army of ascended masters and saints behind you, supporting you as you start your day.

Some of my favorite affirmations for strengthening myself are:

> If God be for me, who or what can be against me!
> I can do all things with Christ, who strengthens me!
> God, my personal power, and the power of my subconscious mind are an unbeatable team!

One of the best ways to keep away dark forces is to avoid thinking about them. The more you think about them, the more you attract them. If you keep your physical, mental, emotional, and spiritual vibration at a high level they never enter your existence.

Never allow yourself to be put under anesthesia without doing many prayers of protection first. If someone touches your jewelry, use the Light invocation of Deal Walker, the crystal man:

> I invoke the Light of the Christ.
> I am a clear and perfect channel.
> Light is my guide.

Hold your jewelry, say this mantra three times out loud, and channel the Christ Light vibration back into the jewelry to cleanse and spiritualize it. The soul mantra is good for this also. The most common protective tool is to just call forth the white Light. All you have to do is make the request to your soul and it will immediately come pouring in.

The law of the mind is this: where you put your attention is where you live. The idea is to keep your attention steady in the Light. Most people do not exercise enough control over where they allow their attention to focus.

The other psychological quality that is needed for protection is that of spiritual discernment. When you start falling back into automatic pilot, you become very impressionable and hypersuggestible. On a psychological and spiritual level it is very important not to give away your power so easily. For example, don't give your power to your physical body when it gets tired. Don't give your power to astrological forecasts. Don't give your power to your dreams; I know people who have let a bad dream wreck their whole day.

In essence, I am saying don't give your power to anyone or anything, and that includes God. This is not blasphemy; God does not want your power. God wants you to own your power while simultaneously surrendering to Him and His will, rather than the ego's will. God helps those who help themselves. Don't give your power to your thoughts, feelings, physical body, negative ego, subconscious mind, other people, weather, astrology, biorhythms, past lives, inner child, subpersonalities, outside energy, ascended masters, spirit guides, or a guru. Any spiritual teacher worth his or her weight will be encouraging you to own your power and to recognize your equality.

If you learn to stay in your power, all these other tools are unnecessary, for you won't need them. You become victimized only when you lose your power. Abductions and implants occur because there is an opening in your aura that allows them to happen. Close it. Get back your personal power and what Edgar Cayce calls your positive anger, and they will cease to become a possibility.

One of the confusions of many spiritual people is thinking they should be open all the time. Nothing could be further from the truth. Everything in life is to be balanced. There is the yin and the yang, the feminine and the masculine; there is a time to be open and a time to be closed. You must learn to open and close your energy field at will.

When there is negative energy around, you must be able to close down and protect your psychological and spiritual space. You can still be loving, even when you are closed to negative energy. To be open all the time is a prescription for victimization by the energies of others.

The chakras are like camera lenses that can be opened and closed at will. If you make up your mind that there is no way in God's universe that negative extraterrestrials are going to abduct you, they won't. Be still and know you are God. Can God, the Father, be victimized? Well, you are made in His image and likeness, so you can't either — unless you allow yourself to be by not claiming your full power.

With respect to getting sick physically and emotionally, if you think you are vulnerable, you are probably right. If you use your powers of creation to program your physical and emotional bodies that they will not get sick, they won't. If you think you are the Christ and one with God, then that is who you are.

It gets back to that lesson of where you put your attention. You must learn to keep it where God would have you put it. You often allow yourself to be far too weak in this respect. That is why Djwhal Khul states over and over again the importance of keeping the mind "steady in the Light." When you are in a state of anything other than perfection, then the lesson is to immediately say an affirmation or prayer to bring yourself back into that perfected state that God sees you in.

If you are dealing with a negative feeling, visualize yourself vomiting it up and killing it with a spear or sword. Then place a beautiful angel or your spiritual teacher inside of you to replace what was there before.

A good prayer for exorcising a possessing entity is found in Isabelle Hickey's book, *It's All Right*: "In the name and through the power of Jesus Christ, leave my magnetic field and go back to the Source and be lifted up into the Light." A prayer she recommended for protection is, "In the center of all Light I stand. Nothing can touch me there."

Max Freedom Long, who gave the long-lost Huna teachings of Hawaii to the Western world, created a mantra for the Huna researchers who had a fear of negative forces: "I refuse to accept any suggestion from any negative source; I merit only good and only good will come to me. I have the protection of my high self about me at all times and it surrounds me with a robe of Light. I fear no evil. Nothing but good can touch my life in any way. I remain serene, safe, and calm in the full knowledge that I am protected every moment, night and day."

Another protection mantra, one Edgar Cayce recommended before meditation, is, "I put around myself the protection found in the thought of the Christ."

A very powerful prayer of protection is found in Dion Fortune's book, *Psychic Self-Defense:* "Visualize yourself holding the flaming sword of Lord Michael in your right hand and say, 'In the name of God, I take in hand the sword of power for defense against evil and aggression.' Imagine yourself growing in height to double or triple your present size. Now draw a magic circle upon the ground all around you with the point of the sword. See a line of flame following the point of the sword.

"Upon completion, clasp your hands in prayer and raise them above the head while facing east and pray, saying, 'May the mighty Archangel Raphael protect me from all evil approaching from the east.' Turning to the south, say the same thing but invoke Archangel Michael. Turning to the west, invoke Archangel Gabriel. Then to the north, invoke Archangel Uriel. Then back to the east."

This formula is especially effective for protecting your sleeping space. The idea is to draw the circle around your bed. The circle will last from sunset to sunrise. To begin and end this prayer it is necessary to make the Kabbalistic sign of the cross. This is an extremely powerful tool, much like making the sign of the cross in Catholicism.

Touching your forehead, say, "To Thee, O God (touching your solar plexus) be the kingdom (touching your right shoulder) and the power (touching your left shoulder) and the glory (clasping your hands) unto the ages of the ages. Amen."

To seal your aura using the sign of the cross, Dion Fortune, in the same book, says to "stand upright and cross yourself by touching forehead, breast, right shoulder and left shoulder, saying, 'By the power of the Christ of God within me, whom I serve with all my heart and soul and mind and might, I encompass myself about with the divine circle of His protection, across which no mortal error dares to set its foot.' "

If you like, you can also use just the sign of the cross. If you would like triple protection you can then use the sign of the pentacle, or five-pointed star. It is very effective in protecting a house from intruding spirits. It can be created in the air in front of you; then immediately visualize it in all the windows and doorways of the house. It can be created in the following manner:

If you want to seal your aura because you are with someone who is trying to drain your vitality, interlace your fingers and place them over your solar plexus. While doing this, press your elbows against your sides and be sure your feet are touching each other. You have made your physical body a closed circuit and thus you cannot be drained.

Dark forces cannot enter your field if your overall frequency is raised to a high enough vibration. To quickly raise your vibration, say the following prayer I have formulated for this purpose:

> Beloved God, Christ, Holy Spirit, mighty I Am Presence, Mahatma, my monad, Vywamus, Sai Baba, Djwhal Khul, Master Jesus, Virgin Mary, and the Great White Brotherhood:
>
> I hereby call forth a pillar of Light. I call forth my glorified Lightbody. I call forth a complete infusion of the Mahatma energy. I call forth the golden twelfth ray. I call forth an ascension column of Light. I call forth the violet flame of Saint Germain. I call forth the Light of one thousand suns to descend now into my four-body system. I call forth my fifth-dimensional ascended self to merge its aura with mine.
>
> I call forth the ascension flame. I call forth my living Light vehicle, my merkabah, and ask to be placed inside of it. I call forth an axiatonal alignment. I call forth the complete anchoring of my twelfth chakra into my crown chakra. I call for the complete descending of my soul and monad into my four-body system. I call forth a raising of my vibrational frequencies to that of the Christ. I call forth the Aum vibration!

The I Am Discourses of Saint Germain recommend the following tube of Light protection prayer:

> Beloved mighty victorious presence of God I Am in me! Blaze Thou around me now, Thy invincible Cosmic Christ protection of the tube of pure electronic Light essence. See to it, for me, that this protection is all-powerfully active and eternally sustained.
>
> Let no human discordant creation ever reach me through it. Let this tube of Light essence make and keep me invisible and invulnerable to every human shadow, constantly raising and holding my attention upon Thy omnipresence in everyone, everything, everywhere. I consciously accept this done right now with full power!

I will end this chapter with what I believe to be the most powerful prayer on the Earth today. This prayer is guaranteed to provide protection. It is the Great Invocation of the Lord Maitreya, the Planetary Christ.

> From the point of Light within the Mind of God
> Let Light stream forth into the minds of men.
> Let Light descend on Earth.
>
> From the point of Love within the heart of God
> Let Love stream forth into the hearts of men.
> May Christ return to Earth.
>
> From the center where the Will of God is known
> Let purpose guide the little wills of men —
> The purpose which the masters know and serve.
>
> From the center which we call the race of men
> Let the Plan of Love and Light work out
> And may it seal the door where evil dwells.
>
> Let Light and Love and Power restore the Plan on Earth.

15

The Human Aura and the Seven Bodies

*Our life course, our habits,
our health and mental appreciation, in fact
our life history, is written in color, forms, and
lines comprising the energy fields of our
several levels of being or conscious states.*

Ronald Beesley

Just as there are seven dimensions of reality, there are seven bodies around every physical form, each one corresponding to a dimension of reality. You have a physical body, etheric body, astral body, mental body, soul or causal body, Buddhic body, and atmic body. There are other bodies beyond these levels which I call the celestial bodies, but they are beyond our comprehension at this level of evolution.

Each body has a characteristic or quality of energy associated with it. The physical body has to do with instinct; the etheric body with the vital force and vital energy; the astral body with desires, feelings, and emotions; the mental body with the concrete mind; the soul or causal body with the abstract mind; the Buddhic body with intuition; the atmic body with spiritual will.

The Physical Body

Explanation of the physical body is not necessary, for you are all very familiar with it. The physical body is the temple for the incarnating soul extension. It is an instrument, a vehicle for exploring the physical world. Just as the physical body is the vehicle for the manifestation of soul on this plane of existence, so the soul is the vehicle on a higher plane for the manifestation of spirit, or the monad.

A great many of you don't realize the importance of helping the physical body to evolve along with the other bodies, for it is impossible for coarse, dense physical bodies to contact high vibrations. The refinement of the physical body is essential. Many spiritual aspirants work on evolving the other bodies but not the physical body and end up getting sick because of the discrepancy in vibrational frequency.

It is not the purpose of this book to be a manual on how to care for the physical vehicle. However, following the simple suggestions below would be extremely helpful:

1. Adhere to a daily physical fitness program;
2. Eat pure food;
3. Develop good sleep habits;
4. Get at least ten to twenty minutes of sunshine a day if possible. The sun kills all germs and frees you from disease, as well as vitalizing the etheric body;
5. Maintain cleanliness. Use a lot of water, both inwardly and outwardly;
6. Avoid sugar, artificial stimulants (coffee and tea), and drugs as much as possible;
7. Be sure to create play time.

The Etheric Body

The etheric body, or the etheric double, is an exact replica of the physical body. It is the archetype upon which the physical form is built. There is nothing in the manifest universe — solar, planetary, or in the various kingdoms of nature — that does not possess an etheric body.

This etheric body governs and conditions the physical body. The function of the etheric body is to store up the rays of radiant light and heat from the sun and to transmit them via the spleen chakra to all parts of the physical body. The etheric body is a web of fine, interlacing nerve channels called nadis. During incarnation, the network of nadis forms a barrier between the physical and astral planes. If you have taken large amounts of drugs, you can break this etheric webbing which can cause you to be unprotected from lower astral energies.

The etheric body can also be called the energy battery of the physical body. Congestion in part of the etheric body can lead to many forms of disease and to lack of mental clarity. The etheric body is vitalized and controlled by thought and can be brought into full activity by right thinking. Most diseases the physical body suffers from have their roots in the etheric and astral bodies. The principal factors in establishing a healthy etheric body are sunshine, a careful diet emphasizing the proper proteins and vitamins, and the avoidance of fatigue and worry.

The Astral Body

The astral body connects you to the astral plane and to your desires and emotions. If you are run by your astral body — by your feelings and desires — your astral body ends up running your conscious mind instead of your conscious mind having mastery of your emotions.

You travel in this body when you practice astral projection or when it occurs naturally during sleep. You might have dreams of flying in your astral body. Perhaps you have developed the ability to travel consciously in your astral body. The limitation of this is that you are limited to traveling only on the astral plane. If you travel in your soul body or your Lightbody, you have a greater range of dimensions in which to travel.

The great teachings of Hinduism and Buddhism emphasize the need to eliminate desire. This means to make your only desire liberation and God-realization instead of all the material desires of the negative ego. The astral body receives the impression of every passing desire it contacts in the environment. Every sound causes it to vibrate. Your great need as a spiritual aspirant is to train your astral body to receive and register only those impressions which come from the higher self. Your aim is to train the emotional body so that it will become still and clear as a mirror, so that it reflects perfectly. The words that describe the emotional body in its ideal state are still, serene, unruffled, quiet, at rest, clear.

Djwhal Khul, in the Alice Bailey books, has elucidated how to still the emotional body:

1. By the constant watching of all desires, motives and wishes that cross the horizon daily and by the subsequent emphasizing of all those that are of a high order and by inhibition of the lower.

2. By a constant daily attempt to contact the higher self, and to reflect its wishes in the life.

3. By definite periods of meditation daily, directed to the stilling of the emotional body. Each aspirant must discover for himself when he yields most easily to violent vibrations such as fear, worry, personality desire of any kind, personality love of anything or anyone, discouragement, oversensitiveness to public opinion. Then he or she must overcome that vibration by imposing on it a new rhythm, definitely eliminating and reconstructing it.

4. By work done on the emotional body at night under the direction of more advanced souls working under the guidance of a master.

When illusion and glamour have been overcome, the astral body fades out in the human consciousness. There is no desire left for the separated self. Ego disappears, and you are then regarded as consisting essentially of soul, mind, and brain within the physical body.

The Mental Body

The mental body is associated with the mental plane and the concrete mind. The refinement and development of this body are the result of hard work and discrimination. There is a great need for clear thinking, not only on subjects in which interest is aroused, but on all matters affecting your life and humanity. Mental clarity means the ability to make thought forms out of thought matter and utilize these thought forms to help humanity.

It is important to learn how to still the mental body so that thoughts from abstract levels and from the intuitional planes can find a receptive mind whereon they may inscribe themselves.

Two qualities should be developed above all else: first, unshakable perseverance and fortitude; the capacity of perseverance explains why the non-spectacular man or woman often attains initiation before the genius. Second, progress that is made without undue self-analysis. Pull not your selves up by the roots to see if there is growth.

The mental body remains clear when you maintain a good mental diet. Every thought that comes from your subconscious mind or from other people should be examined to determine if it is of God or not of God and if it is truth or illusion. If it is positive and of God, let it into your mind as you would good food into your stomach. If it is negative and not of God, deny its entrance into your mind. It is the ongoing process of remaining conscious and vigilant and not functioning on automatic pilot that will keep your mental body clear.

Keeping your mental body clear will help to keep your emotional body, etheric body, and physical body clear, for it is your thoughts that create your reality. This last point cannot be emphasized strongly enough!

The Soul, or Causal Body

The soul, or causal body, exists on the higher mental plane and its characteristic is the abstract mind. The causal body is the temple of the soul. It is the storage house of all good karma and virtue from all past lives and the present life. The causal body is a collection of three permanent atoms enclosed in an envelope of mental essence. The three permanent atoms are recording devices for the physical, astral, and mental bodies. These atoms also record karma.

In your very first incarnations on Earth your causal body was a colorless ovoid holding the soul like a yolk within an eggshell. As you incarnated over and over again you began to build good karma and virtue into your causal body and it began to become a thing of rare beauty, containing within itself all the colors of the rainbow. Djwhal Khul has called this a form of "divine vampirism" in which the soul sucks the good out of the personal life and stores it in the body of the soul. This building proceeds slowly at first, but toward the end of incarnation when you step more firmly on the path of probation and initiation, the work proceeds rapidly. It is at the fourth initiation, when you have achieved liberation from the wheel of rebirth, that the causal body is burned up and merges back into the monad; the evolving soul extension then receives guidance from the monad rather than from the soul. This is an important point in the initiation of a soul on the spiritual path.

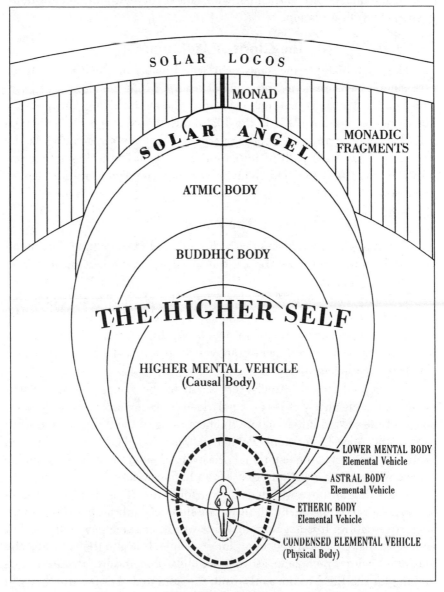

The Seven Bodies

The Buddhic Body

The Buddhic body is associated with the Buddhic plane and the characteristic quality of it is intuition. After passing the fourth initiation you live in the Buddhic body.

The Atmic Body

The atmic body is associated with the atmic plane and the characteristic and quality of it is spiritual will. This is the body you inhabit upon passing the fifth initiation.

The Glorified Lightbody

The Lightbody is the body you will inhabit at the time of your ascension, ascension being the complete merger with the monad, or I Am Presence, on Earth. At that time your entire being, including your physical body, merges into Light. It is the Lightbody that you will officially step into. It is, in a sense, the "wedding garment" that you are creating day by day as you travel the path of initiation. It is made of the Light that you create in your daily life. This body is not fully complete until just before ascension.

The Aura

Everything that has been created has an aura of some kind. In human beings the aura surrounds the central nucleus, or the extension, of the overshadowing soul.

The aura is composed of four fields: the physical health aura, the astral, or emotional, aura, the mental aura, and the etheric body aura. The astral aura is usually dominant in people on this planet, although that is beginning to change as humanity moves deeper into the Aryan root race which is a mental attunement.

The mental aura is usually very small in the average person, but it develops rapidly once you become polarized in the mental body at the later stages of the second initiation and the beginning of the third. Djwhal Khul says in the Alice Bailey book *Ponder on This* that the "mental aura will eventually obliterate the emotional or astral aura and then the soul quality of love will create a substitute that is of a higher nature."

You live and move within your fourfold aura. This living, vital aura serves as a recording agent of all impressions of both an objective and a subjective nature. It is not so much your words, as some people think, but your aura that creates effects upon other people. It is also the aura that the master of your inner-plane ashram watches. Specifically, the master is looking for the Light of the soul within the aura to determine whether you are nearing the path of discipleship. As the emotional reactions lessen and the mental apparatus clears, the progress of the aspirant is noted.

The aura is radiant in nature and extends from all the bodies in every direction. The seven chakras have a great effect on the nature of your aura. A highly emotional person working through an overdeveloped and uncontrolled solar plexus chakra can wreak havoc in a home or office. On the other side of the coin, a disciple consciously using the heart or throat center can carry inspiration to hundreds.

The aura is brought into a radiant condition by right living, high thinking, and loving activity. This leads the initiate to become a center of living Light in which all seven of the chakras are merged into one Light.

You look out onto the world through your aura. The four words that best describe the human aura are color, light, quality, and sphere of influence. Most psychics see only the astral range of the aura. In reality, there are seven layers of the aura to be seen.

Christ's aura was so powerful that all people had to do was touch him or be near his aura and the virtue would pour out of him and heal them. Every person's aura either attracts or repels, depending on the programming and patterning within the individual. Every group has an aura, every country has an aura, and the Earth as a whole has an aura. I once bought a very beautiful statue of the Buddha, and a clairvoyant friend of mine, without my asking, told me that the statue's heart chakra was spinning and open. A master only has to look at the Light reflected in a person's aura to determine his or her level of evolution.

Each color visible in the human aura indicates specific characteristics.

Red . . . . . The color red reflects physical aspects of the mind such as passion, anger, physical desires, emotion, vigor, and vitality. It is related to the first-ray quality of will.

Blue . . . . . The color blue reflects the religious or spiritual aspects of the mind, including contemplation, prayer, heaven, spirituality, altruism, and selflessness and emotions such as love, devotion, and reverence. Blue is a soothing and calming color.

Yellow. . . . The color yellow reflects intellectual pursuits such as logic, induction, active intelligence, analysis, and judgment.

White . . . . The color white represents pure spirit.

Black . . . . Black is the absence of color. It is the opposite pole of pure spirit, hence the term "black magic." It indicates hatred, anger, avarice, revenge, and malice.

Gray . . . . . The color gray reflects negative thoughts and emotions.

Violet . . . . The color violet is a very spiritual color. It usually indicates evenness of mind and indicates a searching for a cause or religious experience. Violet has been associated with transmutation because of its connection with the seventh ray.

Orange . . . A good and vital shade of orange usually indicates thoughtfulness and consideration of others. Orange is connected with fifth-ray energy of concrete science.

Green . . . . The color green usually deals with healing and is helpful, strong, and friendly. It is a color that doctors and nurses often have. It is connected with the fourth ray energy of harmony through conflict.

The following is a color chart of the human aura from a book by Edgar Cayce called *Auras*. What is interesting in this chart is that it also shows the afflictions, or negative aspects, of each color as well as the positive qualities. The planets and musical notes connected with each color are listed too.

The Human Aura				
Color	**Musical Note**	**Planet**	**Interpretation**	**Affliction**
Red	Do	Mars	Force, Vigor, Energy	Nervousness, Egotism
Orange	Re	Sun	Thoughtfulness, Consideration	Laziness, Repression
Yellow	Mi	Mercury	Health, Well-being, Friendliness	Weakness of Will
Green	Fa	Saturn	Healing, Helpfulness	Mixed with Yellow: Deceit
Blue	Sol	Jupiter	Spirituality, Artistry, Selflessness	Struggle, Melancholy
Indigo	La	Venus	A Seeking Nature, Religion	Heart and Stomach Trouble
Violet	Ti	Moon	A Seeking Nature, Religion	Heart and Stomach Trouble

16

The Twenty-Two Chakras

*The chakras are in the nature of distributing
agencies and electric batteries, providing
dynamic force and qualitative energy to man*

Djwhal Khul
through Alice A. Bailey

In the most common understanding of the human chakra system, there are seven chakras. This is a valid understanding if you are considering only third-dimensional reality. The fact is that there are also eight fourth-dimensional chakras and seven fifth-dimensional chakras. There might possibly be chakras beyond these in the sixth and seventh dimensions of reality, but that information is far beyond my ability to explain or access.

This information concerning the twenty-two chakras was sent by Vywamus through Dorothy Bodenburg of The Tibetan Foundation. The diagram on the next page delineates these twenty-two essential aspects of the human being.

The seven main chakras are the ones that connect the etheric body, or energy body, to the physical body; they are within the etheric body, not within the dense physical body. Each chakra has a specific pattern of energy for a specific purpose. Since the Harmonic Convergence, in August of 1987, an energy structure has been developed that will allow the fourth dimension to come into physical existence.

The Third-Dimensional Chakras
The Root Chakra
The first chakra is the seat of the physical body. It focuses your Earthly life, connecting you very specifically to the Earth. It deals with issues such

as grounding and survival. In the early Lemurian period it was the base chakra that was most open. The first chakra deals with considerations about being here on Earth. Its color is red; it is connected with the gonads.

The Chakras					
Third Dimension		**Fourth Dimension**		**Fifth Dimension**	
0	Earth	8	Seat of the Soul	16	Ascension; Universal Being
1	Base	9	Body of Light	17	Universal Light
2	Polarity	10	Integration of Polarities	18	6th Dimensional Divine Intent
3	Solar Plexus	11	New Age Energies		No Correspondence
4	Heart	12	Christ Consciousness	19	Universal Energy
5	Throat	13	Manifesting Vibratory Communication	20	Beingness
6	Third Eye	14	Divine Plan	21	Divine Structure
7	Crown	15	Monadic Connection	22	Source Connection

The Second Chakra

The second chakra is the polarity chakra. It has to do with creativity, masculine and feminine balance, and sexual energies. The back of the second chakra relates to the seat of the subconscious mind. The gland it is connected to is the ludig, or lyden gland, which relates to the lymphatic system. Its color is usually designated as orange. This chakra was focused on in later Lemurian development.

The Solar Plexus Chakra

The third chakra is the seat of the emotional body. The adrenal glands relate to this chakra, and the color usually associated with it is yellow. The Atlantean period of Earth's history focused on the development of this chakra.

The Heart Chakra

The fourth chakra deals with unconditional love. The gland that is associated with it is the thymus gland; its color is usually considered to be green. This chakra has been the focus in the Christian era.

The Throat Chakra

The throat chakra deals with communication, expression, and the use of will. The thyroid gland is associated with this chakra and the color most

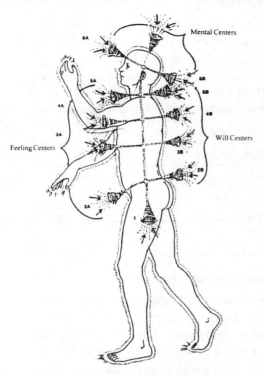

often connected with it is blue. This chakra is the one that is to be developed in the Aquarian Age.

The Third Eye Chakra

The third eye chakra has to do with inner seeingness or spiritual sight and vision. The gland associated with this chakra is the pituitary gland. The color most often associated with this chakra is violet. The third eye chakra also relates to the conscious mind.

The Crown Chakra

The crown chakra has to do with the superconscious mind, the higher self, and/or God. It is truly our gate to bring through the higher energies. The color most often associated with this chakra is white Light, or a rainbow-speckled white Light. The gland associated with this chakra is the pineal.

The Seven Major Chakras, Front and Back Views

This chart is from Barbara Brennan's book, *Hands of Light*, which I highly recommend.

Chakra Colors

The colors that most schools of thought have used for the visualizing of the chakras are listed below. I have also included the updated colors that Djwhal Khul has recently channeled to my wife and me.

Chakra	Standard Color	Colors from Djwhal Khul
Root	Red	Violet
Second	Orange	Indigo
Solar plexus	Yellow	Yellow
Heart	Green	Pink (with a hint of violet)
Throat	Blue	Blue (with orange triangle in center of it)
Third eye	Indigo	Gold
Crown	Violet	Rainbow white

Chakra Toning

Besides using Light and color to work with your chakras and open them, it is also possible to use sound. Djwhal Khul has channeled the sounds that correspond to the seven third-dimensional chakras.

Chakra	Tones from Djwhal Khul		Hindu Tones
Root chakra	O	(oh)	Lam
Second chakra	SHU	(shuck)	Yam
Solar Plexus chakra	YA	(yawn)	Ram
Heart chakra	WA	(way)	Yam
Throat chakra	HE	(he)	Ham
Third eye chakra	HU	(hue)	Om
Crown chakra	I	(eye)	Aum

The Fourth-Dimensional Chakras

I became aware that there are more than seven chakras a couple of years ago when Djwhal Khul told me there are twelve. He said that as a person evolves, the higher chakras begin to move downward, descending into the former third-dimensional chakras. I asked if my higher chakras had descended. He told me that my tenth chakra was in my crown, my ninth chakra was in my third eye chakra, my eighth chakra was in my throat chakra, and so on all the way down my chakra system. I found this piece of information fascinating. Since that time I have been calling my twelfth chakra down into my crown. I have also been focusing the quality of the twelfth chakra, the Christ consciousness, more clearly in my life. In a later conversation with Djwhal, he said I had stabilized the twelfth chakra in the crown chakra, the eleventh in the third eye, and so on all the way down.

It was only recent information from Vywamus that made me aware that there are, in actuality, twenty-two chakras. My current focus in my spiritual path is to anchor my fifteenth chakra into my crown, the fifteenth chakra having to do with the monadic connection.

The sixteenth chakra is the chakra that is anchored in the crown when an initiate ascends. Djwhal Khul has recommended that prior to ascension people not call down any chakra higher than the fifteenth, for there is a danger of burning out the physical body with too high a frequency of energy. It is permissible, however, to call forth the colors of the energies that are associated with the fifth dimensional chakras.

The Eighth Chakra

The eighth chakra is the first chakra of the fourth dimension; it is the seat of the soul. Just as in the third dimension the Earth, designated

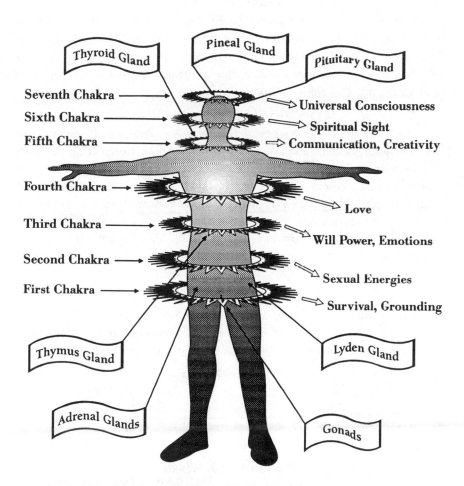

The Seven Chakras and Glands

number zero, represents physical existence, so in the fourth dimension, the seat of the soul becomes the seat of existence.

The colors of chakras eight through twelve are exactly the same as the colors of the higher fourth-dimensional rays. (These rays will be explained in a later chapter.) The color of the eighth chakra is emerald green and purple.

The Ninth Chakra

The ninth chakra corresponds to the base chakra in the third dimension. It is related to the body of Light; it has to do with joy. When this chakra is activated it ignites the body of Light which is now in your cellular and sub-cellular structure. The color of this chakra is blue-green.

The Tenth Chakra

The tenth chakra is associated with the polarity chakra of the third dimension. It has to do with the integration of male and female within self. This chakra starts functioning when the male and female energies are in total balance. It is experienced as a state of effortlessness and an alignment with your soul. The color of this chakra is a pearlescence.

The Eleventh Chakra

The eleventh is the chakra of the New Age energies. It corresponds with the solar plexus chakra of the third dimension. Connecting the third chakra to the eleventh chakra allows you to diminish the present- and past-life trauma stored in the third chakra. The feeling of the eleventh chakra energy is that of a wave, and it will move through your body and out again without staying and without attaching itself to an area of misperception. (Before the fourth dimension was available, an emotional response would attach itself to some misperception already in the body.) The color of this chakra is pink-orange.

The Twelfth Chakra

The twelfth chakra is the Christ consciousness, which is a transformational energy that connects all energy forms. It is associated with the heart chakra of the third dimension, and its color is a shimmering gold.

The Thirteenth Chakra

The thirteenth chakra has to do with the manifesting of vibratory communication. This is the chakra that is used in materializing and dematerializing things and in teleportation. This chakra is also used for healing. It is pale violet-pink in color.

The Fourteenth Chakra

The fourteenth chakra has to do with the Divine Plan. It allows the mind to surrender. The fourteenth chakra is saying that you are allowing the Divine Plan to show you the way without review or evaluation by your mental processes.

This chakra corresponds to the third eye of the third dimension. It brings clairvoyance into the fourth dimension and begins to activate your unlimitedness. The color of this chakra is deep blue-violet.

The Fifteenth Chakra

The fifteenth chakra is concerned with your monadic connection. It corresponds to the crown chakra of the third dimension, your spiritual connection. Opening the fifteenth chakra allows your new spiritual connection which is to your monad. That occurs when you pass the fourth initiation. At the fifth initiation you become merged with the monad, which brings you to the doorway of ascension. When this chakra is operating it is saying that the structure of your soul is stable enough to handle the energy and the scope of the information coming from the monadic level. It is a light golden-white.

The Fifth-Dimensional Chakras

The Sixteenth Chakra

The sixteenth chakra has to do with ascension and becoming a universal being. It is the sixteenth chakra that descends into the crown chakra at the time of ascension. When this chakra has been activated, the master needs to decide whether or not he or she is going to stay in physical existence. The universal being moves among all time frames and dimensions and can adapt to whatever energy form or body is needed.

As the first chakra of the fifth-dimensional chakra system, this chakra of ascension into the monad and becoming a universal being is the new base line, just as the eighth chakra, the seat of the soul, was the base line of the fourth-dimensional chakras. The color of this chakra is light violet-white.

The Seventeenth Chakra

The seventeenth chakra has to do with universal Light, and it corresponds to the ninth chakra, or the body of Light of the fourth dimension. The progression is from the third dimension which is solid to the fourth dimension which is solid and Light to the fifth dimension which is total Light. It is multi-white in color.

The Eighteenth Chakra

The eighteenth chakra is concerned with sixth-dimensional divine intent. This chakra, when activated, creates the ability to bring in the sixth dimension of reality. In looking at the chart of the chakras you will see that there is a gap between the eighteenth and nineteenth chakras that says "no correspondence." The reason for this is that at the fifth-dimensional level there is no correspondence to the solar plexus because it has united with the heart chakra. It is pink-gold in color.

The Nineteenth Chakra

The nineteenth chakra relates to universal energy. The heart energy is the focus in the third dimension; the Christ consciousness is the expanded energy of the fourth dimension; in the fifth dimension, the correspondence is the universal energy. This universal energy is felt by those who are allowing it to come through this chakra, through the monadic level, and through the soul level to the physical body. It is magenta in color.

The Twentieth Chakra

The twentieth chakra focuses on beingness. In the third dimension you need to communicate; in the fourth dimension you are able to communicate in a more expanded way by means of vibration through Light; in the fifth dimension there is no need for an exchange. There is pure beingness in which exchange is not necessary for communication. It is violet-gold in color.

The Twenty-First Chakra

The twenty-first chakra has to do with divine structure. It is creating from a point of evolution, which is really a point of resolution. There is the third eye which allows clairvoyance in the third dimension; in the fourth dimension, there is the Divine Plan. You are now beyond the structure of the fifth dimension and into the learning that took place during the divine structure. Vywamus said in respect to this chakra, "Now I must tell you that none of you has to worry about this in the next two or three years." It is blue-gold in color.

The Twenty-Second Chakra

The twenty-second chakra is the connection with the Godhead. It is platinum in color.

A Final Note

I would like to acknowledge The Tibetan Foundation and Dorothy Bodenburg for a transcript of the material she channeled from Vywamus, which I used as the basis for the information in this chapter. Some of the best channeled material I have ever seen has come out of The Tibetan Foundation which was founded by Djwhal Khul through Janet McClure.

17

The Raising of the Kundalini

*It is easy to awaken kundalini but it is very
difficult to take it to the crown chakra
through the different chakras. It demands a
great deal of patience, perseverance, purity,
and steady practice.*

Swami Sivananda

Along with the twenty-two chakras and the seven bodies, the human spiritual constitution contains etheric nerve channels called nadis.

The Nadis in the Etheric Body

The etheric body, or etheric double, is the energetic blueprint of the physical body. It is the body that distributes the vital force throughout the physical form. It is like the battery of the physical body. The etheric body contains an etheric nerve system consisting of thousands of channels which interpenetrate both the physical and the etheric forms.

Indian literature suggests that we have seventy-two thousand meridians, or nerve channels, that pervade the etheric body. Three of these nerve channels are of particular importance in understanding the kundalini: the sushumna, the ida, and the pingala.

The Sushumna and the Sutratma, or Silver Cord

The sushumna is the central nerve channel within the spinal cord. It flows from the base of the spine all the way up to the third eye area and then merges into an even more powerful Light ray called the sutratma, or silver cord. The sutratma extends through the crown, up through the soul and all the way to the monad. The chakras also reside in the etheric body, so the sushumna runs through and connects the seven third-dimensional chakras.

The Ida

The ida is the feminine channel. It extends from the base of the spine and ends in the left nasal passage. It flows principally along the left side of the spinal column. It travels in a curving, crisscross pathway through the seven chakras.

The Pingala

The pingala is the masculine nerve channel. It extends upward from the base of the spine and ends in the right nasal passage. It flows principally on the right side of the spinal column. It travels in a similar curving, crisscross pathway along the spine and through the chakras. The ida and pingala represent two opposite poles of the same energy.

While the pingala controls the right half of the body, and the ida controls the left half of the body, the sushumna is more neutral. The ideal is to balance the energy in the ida and pingala. The sushumna is most active at sunrise and sunset and between four a.m. and sunrise. This is why Eastern cultures suggest meditating at dawn.

I speak a great deal of the need to become balanced within the four bodies, three minds, seven chakras, and in terms of the yin and yang aspects of self. It is fascinating to see how the ida and pingala represent these facets within the spiritual constitution. If you are too feminine or too masculine, it will show up in the flow of energy through the ida and pingala.

The Kundalini

The word kundalini means "coiled"; it refers to the dormant energy or power that lies, like a coiled serpent, at the base of the spine in the etheric body of every human being. This spiral force, while still asleep, serves to vitalize the physical body and organs.

When this kundalini force is aroused, it will steadily increase the vibratory action of the chakras and of the physical, astral, and mental bodies. The rising of the kundalini has two basic effects. First, it begins to eliminate all that is coarse and unsuitable from the physical, emotional, and mental vehicles. Second, it causes the consciousness to absorb into its sphere of influence the lofty qualities that will raise the energy content of the etheric body.

One of the main objects of activating the kundalini to move up the sushumna is to awaken the pituitary and pineal glands, which results in the opening of the third eye. This results in a revelation of the subtler planes of spiritual life. When dormant, it can be stimulating to the reproductive organs and sexual impulses. Many young souls dissipate this energy by overindulging in sexual activity, hence missing the opportunity to raise a portion of this energy up the sushumna to the third eye and crown.

Many people in the New Age are beginning to practice tantric sexuality, learning to raise this energy up the sushumna and through the chakras to have orgasms, in a sense, on all seven levels of their being. Learning to merge with your partner on the levels of all chakras is a lovemaking meditation. There are many good books on the market today that explore how to do this.

In the Taoist religion men are taught to divert the flow of semen inward and upward rather than to dissipate it outside the body. The Taoists teach that too many orgasms can dissipate your life force. I adhere to a philosophy of moderation in these matters; however, I do know that there is some truth to what the Taoists say.

When the kundalini rises, your personal radiance intensifies and you light up. Swami Vivekananda, one of India's great saints, wrote the following in his book, *Raja Yoga:*

> When, by the power of long internal meditation, the vast mass of energy stored up travels along the sushumna and strikes the head centers, the reaction is tremendous — immensely superior to the reaction of sense perception.

> Wherever there is any manifestation of what is ordinarily called supernatural power or wisdom, there is a little current of kundalini which must have found its way into the sushumna. In the vast majority of such cases, people have ignorantly stumbled on some practice which set free a minute portion of the coiled-up kundalini.

Another one of India's great spiritual masters is Swami Sivananda. In his book, *Kundalini Yoga,* he says,

> It is easy to awaken kundalini but it is very difficult to take it to the crown chakra through the different chakras. It demands a great deal of patience, perseverance, purity, and steady practice. The yogi who has taken it to the crown chakra is the real master of all forces.

> Generally, yogic students stop their spiritual practices half way, on account of false satisfaction. They imagine they have reached the goal when they get some mystic experiences and psychic powers. They desire to demonstrate such powers to the public to get reputation and fame and to earn money. This is a sad mistake. Full realization alone can give the final liberation, perfect peace and highest bliss.

Earlyne Chaney, in her book *Kundalini and the Third Eye*, eloquently states:

> When the union of the ida and pingala occurs through meditation and breath control, and the balanced positive/negative forces rise through the sushumna meridian, the all-powerful force of aroused

kundalini, being drawn upward along with the balanced pranic force, strikes the masculine pineal gland. This stimulates the usually passive pineal into action.

Thus aroused and erected, he projects his energies across the third ventricle to simulate the feminine pituitary gland. Responding to the essence of pineal, the pituitary unites with pineal in their mystical marriage in the chamber of the third ventricle – and the ineffable third eye momentarily opens, bringing transcendental illumination to the devotee. The experience is what Westerners call Christ or cosmic consciousness.

Liberation and Awakening

The awakening of the kundalini does not mean that the disciple has achieved liberation; there are many requirements beyond having kundalini experiences. Even when the kundalini is awakened, it usually doesn't remain that way until the higher initiations are achieved through years of steady spiritual practice, purification, and service to humankind.

There are several indications that the kundalini energy is beginning to awaken:

1. Consciousness of a small area of physical warmth at the base of the spine;

2. Light physical pressure along the spinal column;

3. Moments of dizziness or a sudden increase of vitality or seeing a blinding flash of light;

4. A sense, during meditation, of contact with the higher planes and dimensions;

5. A sense of ascending or rising into the spiritual spheres during meditation.

Dangers of the Kundalini

Djwhal Khul, in his teachings, says that artificial means and exercises for the specific purpose of raising the kundalini should be used with extreme caution. The kundalini is an enormously powerful force, and if raised prematurely or in a forced manner when a disciple is not ready, can cause extreme damage to that individual.

There are basically three schools of thought on this matter. There are Kundalini Yoga masters who freely teach students, whether ready or not, exercises to raise the kundalini. Then there is the school of thought that says to let the kundalini rise on its own in the course of normal, unforced spiritual evolution. The third school of thought is the one that Djwhal Khul and the teachings of Earlyne Chaney have recommended: to be exceedingly careful, and to practice these exercises only under expert guidance after you have purified and balanced yourself and have attained sufficient self-mastery so that you are able to handle this powerful energy.

Djwhal Khul told me the premature raising of the kundalini in a disciple who is not ready can create an imbalance in the four-body system which can take as long as two years to rebalance. The raising of this force, if brought about ignorantly and prematurely, can lead to serious nervous trouble, inflammation of the tissues, spinal disease, and brain trouble. When the kundalini is allowed to progress naturally, through disciplined living, the expert guidance of a qualified spiritual teacher will serve to open the gates to the higher realms.

It is also very important that your emotions be pure and under control when dealing with kundalini energy. Fear and anger or improper motives can cause the kundalini to descend rather than ascend, causing the energy to be used by the negative ego-self.

Summary

For those of you who are interested in learning more about the kundalini and who feel you are ready to begin the gradual process of activating this energy in a safe way, I would recommend reading Earlyne Chaney's book, *The Kundalini and the Opening of the Third Eye*. It is a fantastic book which gives a lot of the basic knowledge, postures, meditations, mantras, and exercises for beginning this process.

Earlyne is a channel for Kuthumi, the Virgin Mary, and the ascended masters, and her information correlates very well with the teachings of Djwhal Khul, who is one of my main teachers. After reading this book, if you are interested in going deeper, I would recommend sending for her lessons. The lessons of Astara, Earlyne's mystery school, present more in-depth practices that are not given to the general public. These lessons are received twice monthly, and over a period of time you can practice Lama Yoga exercises that have been taught to her by Kuthumi. This is a very safe, gradual training for those of you who feel guided to focus on the kundalini activation. It is not necessary to focus on raising the kundalini if you do not truly feel guided to do so. As you evolve spiritually and go through the basic initiation process, the kundalini will eventually rise on its own, as long as you are performing some form of consistent spiritual practice. The form of religion, the spiritual path, or the mystery school you are involved with does not matter as long as the teachings are pure, for all paths lead to the same place.

18

Channeling

Learning to channel
is the single most important spiritual
practice a person can achieve in order to
accelerate spiritual growth

Vywamus

Many people look at channeling as some strange metaphysical and esoteric phenomenon when, in actuality, there is not a person in this world who does not channel all the time. Everyone is a channel; the key point is who or what is being channeled.

You channel all kinds of things, including your physical body, subconscious mind, ego, impulses, instincts, intuition, vital force, monad, soul, spirit guides, and ascended masters; you channel insights, inspiration, imagery, dreams, art, music, creative writing, healing energies, and so on. What I am suggesting here is that most of you are unconscious channels. You are channeling, do not realize it, and are not always in control of what you are channeling.

As you gain mastery over your energies you develop total control over what you channel. The ideal is to become a channel for those energies that serve the soul and God.

Each of you has specific strengths in terms of what you channel. Your greatest strength might lie in channeling thoughts and intuitions. You might be very good at channeling imagery and visualizations. You might be a great channel for music, as the music just comes to you inside your head. Others of you are channels for great art. If you are a healer, you are a channel of energy and vital force. It is important to become attuned to your specific gift in this lifetime and to use it for service to humankind.

Right Brain/Left Brain

You have a right brain and a left brain. The problem is that you are taught in school to deny your right brain, for the most part, and to use primarily your left brain. You are taught to be totally logical, scientific, and deductive in your reasoning. The imaginative, psychic, intuitive part of yourself lies neglected as you are taught to disown it. As a child, this side of yourself was very open. You were clairvoyant (inner sight), clairaudient (inner hearing), and clairsentient (inner feeling and touch). By the time you had gone through traditional schooling, these natural faculties had shut down because they had been programmed to do so.

Albert Einstein used to sit in his rocking chair and gaze at the clouds. That would make him dizzy and put him into a hypnotic state in which he would ask questions about his inventions and answers would come to him.

Thomas Edison would sit in a chair, hold ball bearings in his hand, and squeeze them as hard as he could for as long as he could. After five minutes or so the ball bearings would drop from his hand because the muscles would be exhausted. He would then ask questions about his inventions, and answers would come to him.

Nikola Tesla received images of inventions in his mind. These blueprints were so minutely detailed that often he didn't even need to create physical blueprints for his inventions.

All knowledge already exists in the universe. You just need to learn to quiet your mind, ask questions and listen. All the answers, guidance, and direction you need are available for the asking. If you are busy allowing your mind to chatter away, you prevent this information from flowing through. Each of you has within you the ability to access all knowledge. It is available to everyone. It is just a matter of learning how to tune into it as you would tune a radio receiver.

Edgar Cayce called prayer talking to God; he called meditation listening to God. Maybe you have the idea that you have done your duty if you have said your prayers, even though afterwards you just jump up and go about your business. But what if God were listening patiently and just waiting to give you answers, illumination, or insight right then and there? You have left the attentive state without waiting to receive those answers.

Most of us do not listen as well as we pray. Channeling is the ability to listen, to be receptive, and to allow information to come to you without using your left brain to figure it out first. Part of the ability of channeling is learning to quiet the left brain.

I want to emphasize that if you are reading this book, you know how to channel and have always been doing it.

Voice Channeling

When you think of channeling you might think first of voice channeling in which you attune to the spiritual world and allow a spirit guide, your higher self, or an ascended master to speak through you, using your vocal cords. This is one type of channeling, but it is certainly not the only way it can be done. You can channel by doing automatic writing using a pen, typewriter, or computer and allowing guidance to bring forth information through your hands. You can tune in to spirit and channel images. You can channel telepathically, in thoughts rather than vocally. You can receive poetry or sounds, or spirit can paint or write music through you. All of these forms and many more can be learned and developed with practice.

I recommend that you find a psychic development or channeling class in which you can practice with other people. Then on your own you can begin to try out various forms of channeling and practice, practice, practice. These are skills that do take practice. You will get better and better over time. You might find an unexpected form of channeling to be especially satisfying; thus, trying a variety of them is recommended.

Try to recognize what your strong and weak points might be in terms of the kind of channeling you are most suited for. No one form is better than another; no one person has all abilities. The most important thing is to avoid comparing yourself with other people and to find, instead, the essence of your function, the specific information God would have you express. For example, my wife and I channel in completely different ways; I can't do what she does and she can't do what I do. Together we make a greater whole. Find the way that is best for you.

Psychological Channeling

There are two levels of channeling: you can channel on a psychological level or on a spiritual level. When you are channeling psychologically, you are channeling subconscious parts of yourself. For example, you can channel specific subpersonalities in your subconscious mind. You can channel your emotional body, your mental body, or even your physical body. You can channel your inner child or inner parent. This list is endless. You might try doing it in your journal writing. It is a form of role-playing: Just pretend you are leaving the conscious mind state and becoming a particular part of yourself. Let that part write in your journal. Then go back to the conscious mind state and respond to it. This kind of dialogue is a form of channeling.

Spiritual Channeling

The second level of channeling is spiritual channeling in which you attempt to channel a higher source of information. You can channel spirit guides, your soul, your monad, ascended masters, angels, nature spirits, extraterrestrials. The one warning I would give you is that, as Jesus said, "In my Father's house there are many mansions." What he meant is that there are many dimensions of reality. When you are channeling spiritual guidance, I would recommend channeling only your own soul or monad and beings who are ascended spiritual masters.

People who fool around with ouija boards and the lower psychic arts often begin contacting lower astral entities. I would recommend channeling only beings who are on the monadic, logoic, or higher planes of consciousness in terms of their evolution. Astral-plane entities are not likely to have much more knowledge than you have. Just because a spiritual entity is on the other side does not mean it has evolved. You might be talking to Aunt Betty who just died. She didn't believe in spiritual things when she was living and still doesn't even though she has died.

I am suggesting that you skip the physical, astral, mental, Buddhic, and atmic planes, and attune to the sixth and seventh dimensions of reality which are the monadic and logoic planes of the ascended masters. When you are about to begin channeling, all you have to do is make this request. You just say something like, "I now attune myself to the spiritual dimensions of reality in which the ascended masters dwell and I ask to speak to (Jesus, for example). I do not accept any guidance except from the planes of the ascended masters." It doesn't really matter how you say it. The formation of the request in your mind will protect you. If you set your intent and attunement as I have specified, then that is all that can come in.

If you ever hear a voice or receive guidance that in any way feels unloving or authoritarian, you can ask with whom you are speaking and the entity will have to tell the truth. If you feel that your radio receiver (your mind) has attuned to a lower vibration, just dismiss the connection, say some prayers, and be firmer and more focused in your attunement.

Sometimes praying, spiritual reading, or chanting God's name before you start can help you to attune until it becomes a natural habit. In fact, it is always good to clear and attune yourself to the highest before beginning any endeavor of this sort — or before beginning your day, for that matter.

In summary, don't waste your time channeling astral-plane or mental-plane spirits; go for the spiritual level and higher. Why channel low-vibration entities when you can just as easily channel your soul, your monad, or ascended masters who are longing to speak to you and help you in any way they can? It is their greatest pleasure to do so, and they are there for the asking; however, they never interfere with free choice. The same goes for your soul and monad. They are happy to speak to you and give you guidance and direction, but they must be asked for help. That is divine law.

Prayer of Protection

The following is a good prayer of protection you can use before channeling (or before bed or any other time you need it):

> Beloved Presence of God, my monad, my soul, and beloved ascended masters, I ask to be clothed in a robe of Light composed of the love, wisdom, and power of God, not only for my protection, but so that all who see it or come into contact with it will be drawn to God and healed.

How to Channel

The actual process of channeling is quite easy.

Step 1: Begin by saying the soul mantra of Djwhal Khul:

I am the Soul,
I am the Light Divine,
I am Love,
I am Will,
I am Fixed Design.

Next imagine a tube of Light extending from the top of your head all the way up to the highest spiritual dimensions of reality. Even though you might be imaging this tube for the first time as you read this, the tube has been there all along.

Step 2: Imagine a clockwise spiral coming down the tube from the spiritual plane and moving through the tube, down through all your chakras and right into the Earth. Do this two or three times, moving it with your breath. The purpose of this is to clear your tube and chakra column of any psychic debris before you begin.

Step 3: Invoke an ascended master or your soul or monad. You have already made contact with your soul and invoked its help by doing the soul mantra, so just say something like, "I now call forth _____ !" As you call forth the ascended master you wish to speak to, feel that energy coming down the tube into the top of your head. Feel the contact and ground it into your physical body.

Step 4: You are now ready to channel. To begin you must "kick-start" the process by either saying something out loud if you are doing voice channeling, or beginning to write or type if you are doing channeled writing. The ascended master will glide in on top of your initial words; then just let it flow. Get the left brain's critical mind out of the way and don't worry about what comes out.

You might want to record the message if you are doing voice channeling, so you don't have to think about what you are saying. If it doesn't come through in a clairaudient voice (so that you actually "hear" words), then just say the first thing that comes to your mind.

In the beginning it might also be important to pretend, if your critical mind is doubting the process. Just pretend, let's say, that Djwhal Khul is speaking. By pretending, you are allowing him to glide in on your role-playing. As you let go more and more, it will no longer feel like pretending; it will be the real thing. If you are doing other forms of channeling such as dancing, then you have to take the first step. If you are channeling music, then you have to play the first chords. If you are painting, then you need to start the process by making the first couple of brush strokes, and so on.

Step 5: Finally, you must close and clear the process. Sometimes the teacher will leave first. If not, kindly dismiss the connection and thank the master or your soul for the guidance. It is very important to dismiss the connection, for you do not want to stay in the channeled state all the time; it is not healthy for the physical body. You would become dissociated and perhaps confused. The ideal is to channel and receive your guidance and energy and then ground yourself and live your life demonstrating that which you have learned. To channel all the time would be like meditating all the time and not living.

When you dismiss the channeling connection you are getting back your sense of self and your own personal power and self-mastery. So, in essence, you have the best of both worlds.

19

A Spiritual Perspective on Dreams and Sleep

It is only when we wake from dreams that we know we have been dreaming. Similarly, this life may be realized as a dream only when we awake in cosmic consciousness.

Paramahansa Yogananda

Dreams are a feedback mechanism of the subconscious mind and higher self. Frequently, you don't have the ability to talk to your soul or higher self directly, so the soul uses dreams as one of the ways it seeks to communicate with you. Most dreams, however, are created by the subconscious mind until the incarnated personality begins to awaken spiritually.

Dreams are like a computer printout of your previous day's thoughts, feelings, and actions, but instead of being in words, this printout is in symbols. The key to interpreting dreams is the understanding that every part of the dream is a part of yourself. By examining the organization of the symbols in the dream you can become conscious of what you are creating and causing to happen in your life.

It is very important to understand that the conscious mind is not always conscious. For example, maybe you are being rude to people and are not aware of it. Your dreams can give you an experience of a very rude individual taking his irritability out on people. The subconscious or superconscious mind is giving you feedback; you cannot master a problem unless you know about it.

Perhaps you don't pay attention to dreams because you don't understand what they mean. Dreams are like a foreign language: When you are first exposed to a foreign language it is meaningless, but once you study that language, it is easy to understand. Dreams are the universal language of symbols.

Sometimes you might have prophetic dreams or dreams of past lives, which are categories unto themselves. It is common to have recurring dreams. These dreams are especially important, for they mean that your subconscious mind or soul is trying to make you aware of a certain pattern in which you are stuck.

Most dreams speak to the inner organization of thought and emotional patterns. However, sometimes dreams can also be conveying a clear statement about outer reality. For example, if you dream about a particular person being in a car crash, the dream might be using that person as a symbol for a part of your own personality that is about to crash. Or the dream might be making a statement about the actual person. Maybe your higher self is giving that other person guidance through you. That is why I am a firm believer in sharing with my friends and loved ones any dreams I have about them.

In interpreting dreams, there are personal symbols and universal symbols. It is always safer to assume the symbols in your dreams are personal. For example, the standard meaning of a cat in most dream books is independence. You, however, might have had certain experiences in childhood that gave cats a special and specific meaning for you beyond that.

It is also very important when dealing with your dreams not to give your power to them. I bring this up because I know people who have let bad dreams depress them for a good part of a day. You must find a balance between honoring and acknowledging your dreams and also understanding that you need to own your personal power.

It can be a very helpful practice to reenact your dreams in the morning. Perhaps a dream had a disturbing outcome. For example, maybe someone was breaking into your house and stealing things. You can reprogram this negative pattern by revisualizing the dream in the morning: have the police come and arrest the burglar, and then see all your things in their proper places. This procedure corrects the faulty pattern the dream was indicating to you.

Another common experience in dreams is flying. It can be a symbol of flying in your life in a psychological sense, but it can also be a real experience. At night you very often astral-project; flying dreams are frequently lucid dreams of astral travels.

It is also a normal phenomenon for the masters to contact you in your dreams. When you are dreaming you are experiencing yourself in a spiritual state without your physical body, so it is easy for the masters to communicate with you. Sai Baba, the great master from India, has said that no one ever dreams about him without his willing it.

Carl Jung, the great Swiss psychologist and contemporary of Freud, called some dreams "big" dreams and other ones normal dreams. Big dreams are the ones that are most important to remember because they are often created by the soul or the masters.

Sometimes you feel frightened when you die in a dream because you think it means you are going to die in physical reality. This is usually not the case. When you have a dream of yourself dying, it can be a very positive dream. It can symbolically mean that you are dying to a certain phase of your life or to a part of yourself that is negative. You are being given a message of death and rebirth.

Another confusing symbol is the act of making love in a dream to someone other than your spouse. It does not mean that you should do this in real life, nor is it a dream you should be embarrassed about. When you make love to someone you are symbolically connecting with that part of yourself. Focus on the meaning and symbolism of the person you were making love with.

The Senoi Indians' entire culture is based on dreams. They look at dreams as being almost more important than real life. Every morning upon arising they share their dreams with each other as a sacred ritual. Many wonderful books have been written about this amazing group of people.

It is common to be given direct messages in dreams. You might not need to interpret your dream if the meaning is given in a clear, straightforward message by your soul, a master, or a symbolic person.

Words in dreams often have double meanings or are puns. For example, if you had a dream about bugs flying around, it might have to do with someone who is bugging you.

An important thing to look at in your dreams is where your conscious mind is or where you are in the dream. In other words, are you just watching the dream or are you actively participating? An example of this might be dreaming of yourself as being two hundred pounds overweight, standing in the kitchen eating too much food, as compared to watching someone else who is overweight and eating too much food. There is a significant difference. The dream image in which you are watching evidences disidentification from the process. The pattern of overeating is in play, but you are aware of it. In the first dream you are identifying with the activity.

This example shows the importance of watching the sequence of the dreams you are having. You can watch the development of your consciousness from total identification with a negative pattern, to disidentification, to self-mastery.

How to Remember Your Dreams

Remembering dreams is not difficult. All you need to do is give your subconscious mind suggestions right before going to sleep. This can be done aloud or in writing. Writing is better because the physical aspect of doing it strengthens the message to the subconscious mind. Just say or write, "I am remembering my dreams tonight" ten times. This will program your subconscious mind to wake you up after a dream.

It is a good idea to have a small lamp or flashlight and pen and paper near your bed. If you don't write the dream down or at least make notes, it is likely you will forget it by morning. The interesting thing about dreams is that you often remember them from the back forward. They are like fishing lines you reel in. If you don't catch that initial line it drifts away.

It is of the greatest importance that you write your dreams down in the morning at the latest. Just the act of writing them down is healing and integrating. Often the meaning will come to you later in the day, or days or even weeks later. Your records are also helpful to refer back to when watching your dream sequences.

If you get stuck in interpreting your dreams, pray to your higher self for help. You will be given immediate insights then or later in the day at a quieter and more receptive moment. It is also important to notice how your inner life correlates with your outer life. Remember the Hermetic law: "As within, so without; as above, so below."

Sleepwalking

An interesting phenomenon of the sleep state is sleepwalking. What is happening here is that the person has identified with his or her astral body, but the physical body is moving along with the process.

I once had a client who was a young adolescent. About two hours before bed he was planning to steal his parents' car and go visit his girlfriend. After planning the whole affair, he changed his mind just before bed and decided it wasn't worth the risk of getting caught and being punished. His conscious mind decided not to do it; however, the plan was still in his subconscious mind. He started to sleepwalk and proceeded to get the keys and push the car out of the driveway and down the street. When the car was a block and a half down the street, he got into the car to start it. At that point, he woke up.

There is a good lesson here about the importance of gaining mastery over your subconscious mind in service of the superconscious mind, or soul. This is an example of what can happen when the three minds are doing separate things and aren't in alignment.

Attending Classes at Night

Every night while you sleep you travel in your various bodies. Every night on the inner planes classes are taught by the archangels, the masters, and their initiates. You might not realize that while your physical body is sleeping and obtaining its needed rest, you can be going to spiritual workshops and seminars of the highest order. You can request to be taught on the inner planes while you sleep. You would do well to take advantage of the tremendous opportunity for spiritual growth that is available to you.

When you sleep, one-third of yourself is shut down, and the other two-thirds (the subconscious and superconscious) are left to be active. It is likely that you function on the astral plane while you sleep; however, it is highly recommended that you go to higher dimensions, if possible. Before sleeping, you can ask to go to the spiritual planes.

You can affect where you go during sleep by what you are thinking about before bed. In the *Bhagavad-Gita* it says that where you go when you die is determined by the last thought on your mind before death. The same is true of sleeping; where you go depends upon the last thought on your mind. That is why it is a terrible idea to watch the news right before bed. The ideal is to do spiritual work, reading, studying, journal writing, meditation, or prayer during the last thirty minutes or hour before sleeping. This will assure you of traveling to a higher level — at least to the higher astral plane.

The quality of your physical sleep and the level of your physical rejuvenation will be greatly affected by your thoughts before bed. The physical body is not a machine; it is a synergistic, holistic organism whose quality of sleep is determined by the thoughts you are thinking and the feelings you are experiencing.

Another thing to be careful of is going to sleep angry and filled with negative emotions. These thoughts and emotions can pull you like a magnet into the lower astral planes, which are the hell regions to which traditional religions refer.

Your monad and your soul have a direct connection into your subconscious mind while you sleep. They have this connection when you are awake, too, but the conscious mind, with its critical thinking and unceasing chatter, tends to get in the way. While sleeping you are in a state much like hypnosis, in which you are hypersuggestible and totally open.

Almost everybody goes to school during the sleep state, even if you are not consciously aware of wanting to go to school. It is your soul that is in charge of your course of study. Your prayers affect the nature of that schooling, so do take responsibility for your cocreative part in the process.

Some incarnated personalities do service work during dreamtime. They help souls that have died by letting them know they are no longer in the physical and leading them into the Light and toward the next step in their evolution.

Sometimes when you are tired in the morning it is because you have worked long and hard on the inner planes. Sometimes this work has to do with going over blueprints to build something on the astral plane. Often, things are built on the astral plane before they are brought into existence on the physical plane.

Some people enjoy the activities of the sleep realm more than those of the waking state. The ideal, however, is to bring the spiritual state to your Earthly life.

Entering the Temples of Wisdom

At a specific and special point in your spiritual evolution the sleep state becomes even more important: it occurs when you step upon the paths of probation and initiation. It is at this time that you enter the Hall of Wisdom. You move to a new set of classes and to higher learning. It is like graduating from high school and going on to college. The classes become much smaller, sometimes having only two or three students.

In these classes you might sometimes hear the same lesson for a month straight so it gets completely reinforced in your subconscious mind. It is a way of learning in a more intense manner.

How Much Sleep Do You Need?

Most people average around seven or eight hours of sleep a night. You might sleep even more as a means of escape if your conscious life is traumatic. There is an illness called narcolepsy in which a sufferer falls asleep constantly. This is an extreme case of the subconscious mind not wanting to be present. People in mental hospitals usually sleep either too much or not at all. However, you can accomplish all you need to get done in the sleep state in four hours.

Breakthroughs in the Middle of the Night

Very often, great inventions and other breakthroughs occur in the middle of the night because that is when you are most receptive to the information in the spiritual world. All knowledge already exists; it only has to be attuned to. At specific times the Spiritual Hierarchy puts into the Earth's universal mind certain concepts. Those people with the proper attunement and receptivity will pick these ideas up.

This also occurs on a personal level. All you need to do is state the question you are seeking the answer to. It can be about your personal life or about an invention you are working on or ideas for a script. Your subconscious mind, your soul, or higher teachers will give you the answers you are seeking. Many people think they are creating great paintings, music, theater, inventions, and so on, themselves. They are, more often than not, channeling them from the universal mind or from spirit guides.

Astral-Plane Service

Many people who are currently incarnated on the Earthly plane volunteer to serve on the astral plane while sleeping. They work out of their bodies at night, aiding people who are in transition, teaching, and helping to expand awareness.

Lucid Dreaming

Lucid dreaming is the state of being conscious and aware even though your physical body is sleeping. There are three basic levels. The first level might be called witnessing. Witnessing occurs when you are aware you are sleeping and also very much aware of what is going on in the room. At the second level, you are sleeping and are aware you are dreaming and of the choices that you are making in your dreams. At the third level, you are sleeping and are aware of your dreams and choices, and you also have the ability to use your will within the dream to change it. This is the highest level of lucid dreaming and definitely one to be achieved, if possible. It is the same process used in reenacting your dreams in the morning, except that you are not doing it in the morning, but while the dream is actually occurring.

Soul Extensions

An important process that takes place within your dreams is communication with your eleven other soul extensions. Your monad, or mighty I Am Presence, created twelve souls, and each of your twelve souls created twelve soul extensions, or personalities, who incarnated into the material world. It is primarily during sleep that you have the opportunity to contact the eleven other members of your soul group.

I was told by Djwhal Khul that I was an oversoul or teacher to my eleven soulmates and that I had been instrumental in their collective transformation. This all occurred even though on a conscious level I had been completely unaware of it.

Djwhal Khul also told me that I had a codependent relationship with my other eleven soul extensions. That didn't make sense to me, because I believe myself to be one of the least codependent people on Planet Earth. If anything, I tend to be too independent at times. Djwhal Khul explained that that was true in my Earthly relationships, but that I had been running the karma of my eleven other soul extensions through my physical body and that was weakening me. He explained to me that the Spiritual Hierarchy wanted me to use this body for service, and that I should let my other soul extensions deal with their own karma.

This immediately made total intuitive sense to me and I told my soulmates in meditation that I was cutting the codependent cords and that they were on their own in terms of dealing with their karma; from then on I was responsible for my karma alone. They immediately listened and I have not had a problem since.

Dreams Involving the Emotional Body

Your soul and the ascended masters can teach through symbols, through direct verbal communication, and through emotion. When the emotional body is involved in the dream experience, the communication is far more rich and meaningful. These types of experiences can be very profound because of their emotional intensity. A personal example of such emotional intensity is a dream I had in which I had traveled to India to be with Sai Baba. At one point in the dream I told Sai Baba how much I loved him. I burst out crying with tears of love and devotion. Sai Baba came over to me with a box of tissues and I saw a tear in his eye, too. This dream was extraordinarily meaningful to me.

How to Interpret Dreams

The interpretation of dreams begins with writing the dream down. Then isolate each symbol in the dream and find the experiential meaning it has for you. In Gestalt psychology it is done by physically experiencing, or role-playing, the symbol. No interpretation is made until this is done for all the symbols in the dream.

Carl Jung and Sigmund Freud used a process of free association for each symbol in the dream. This method is the most practical. For example, you might take a particular person who shows up in your dream and free-associate as to the qualities and characteristics of that person. It is important to write down these associations. Once you have completed this process you are ready for the actual interpretation.

It is important to realize that dreams are not telling you what to do; they are just describing in symbols what is actually happening within the patterns of your thoughts, emotions, and behavior.

One of the challenges of dream interpretation is to avoid letting your belief structure and outlook on life govern your analysis of your dreams. It is easy to fall into this trap, thereby exposing yourself to the danger of self-deception. This can be overcome to a certain extent by using your inner guidance and intuition and asking for the help of your soul and monad in the interpreting procedure.

Once the psychodynamics that are occurring in the dream are recognized, it is the job of your conscious mind to decide whether you want to continue the pattern that is in operation. If you don't, then you need to exercise your personal power and will to change the pattern, and do visualizations and affirmations to reprogram all three minds, not just one or two.

Possible Interpretations

If you have a dream that some else is driving your car, then you want to examine who it is and what meaning that person has for you. If the person driving your car is your crazy, erratic grandmother, then the dream means that the crazy, erratic grandmother part of *you* is driving your life.

Being nude in a classroom means that you are not mentally prepared or protected. Finding yourself in a basement or upstairs would have to do with being in the subconscious realm or the realm of the higher self.

I have listed the likely meanings of some other common symbols.

Ocean: the unconscious

Water: feelings

Water leaking all over the place: your emotions are leaking all over the place

You are speeding in your car and the police are chasing you: you are speeding in your life and the law-and-order part of you is after you, but you are not listening

Someone is breaking into the house: a negative thought or feeling in your subconscious mind is breaking into the sanctity of your mind

The color white: the spiritual aspect

Babies: an aspect of self that is just being born; birth of a new state of consciousness, idea, or principles

Fly: irritation

Birds: transcendence

Hair: thoughts

Lamps or lights: spiritual or mental illumination

Wedding or engagement ring: spiritual integration

Feet: understanding

Homes and buildings: the various psychic locations of thought and action

House with rotting floors: poor spiritual foundation

Cellar: buried dimensions of consciousness

Prison: some way you have imprisoned yourself with your mind

Airport: high ideals or religious beliefs because planes take you heavenward

Soap dish: a good, clean life

House on fire: anger

Telephone ringing: message or communication is coming

Missing teeth: possibly a breakdown in your ability to discriminate properly

Bathroom clogged: not getting rid of your psychological "shit"

Dreams are an invaluable source of feedback, guidance, and direction. Take the time to write them down and work with them and they will become an invaluable aid to knowing yourself and accelerating your spiritual growth.

Djwhal Khul's Ten Sources of Dreams

Djwhal Khul, in his book through Alice Bailey, *Esoteric Psychology,* has enumerated ten sources of dreams.

1. *Dreams based upon brain activity.* Dreams having this source are caused by sleeping too lightly. You haven't left your body, so the thread of consciousness (from the soul to the pineal gland) has not been completely withdrawn as it would be if you were in a deep sleep. Hence, you remain closely identified with your physical body. This particular state of consciousness can last the entire night, although usually it is present only during the first two hours of sleep or the last hour before waking up. Djwhal says that these dreams are manifested by a type of physical nervousness and don't have a lot of significant spiritual meaning.

2. *Dreams of remembrance.* These dreams are the remembering of experiences on the astral plane during sleep. It is on the astral plane that you are usually found when the thread of consciousness is removed from the body.

3. *Dreams that are recollections of true activity.* These dreams are exactly the same as waking life: you are lucid and active, yet your physical body is sleeping.

4. *Dreams that are of a mental nature.* This type of dream is a record in the waking consciousness of your experiences on the mental plane as opposed to the astral plane. If you tend to be polarized in the mental body, you are likely to have this type of dream.

There are three kinds of dreams that are of a mental origin:

A. Dreams of an ancient, modern, or recently emerging nature, based on contact with the world of thought forms.

B. Dreams of archetypal geometric figures. Djwhal mentions some of the geometric shapes: point, line, triangle, square, cross, pentagon, and circle. There are seven such symbols for every root race. Given that humankind has moved through the Lemurian, Atlantean, and now Aryan root races, that means there are twenty-one of these geometric forms that you can dream about.

C. Dreams of a symbolic nature. These are presented from the Hall of Learning and from the Hall of Wisdom on the mental plane.

5. *Dreams that are records of work done.* This type of dream records service work done in borderland (between the astral and physical planes), in summerland (where the entire wish life and racial desire exist), and in the world of glamour which is part of the astral plane.

6. *Telepathic dreams.* These dreams are records in the physical brain of real events that are communicated from one person to another. Usually a friend or relative goes through an experience and shares the experience during sleep; it is picked up by the recipient in dream form.

7. *Dreams that are dramatizations by the soul.* These dreams are symbolic presentations by the soul for the purpose of giving spiritual instruction to the incarnated personality. They are very common for aspirants and disciples. These types of experiences can also occur during meditation.

8. *Dreams concerned with group work.* In this type of dream the soul is training the incarnated personality for group service and activity. The group work is carried on in the world of soul life, not on the physical plane. Your experiences in the master's group, or ashram, might be an example of this kind of training.

9. *Dreams that are records of instruction.* This type of dream embodies the teaching given by a master to his disciple. The job of the disciple is to learn to interpret these instructions properly upon waking. Usually the master gives the guidance to the soul and the soul then passes the instruction on to the mind of the disciple, frequently in a dream.

10. *Dreams connected with the world plan.* These dreams are communicated to the world disciples. They deal with the world plan, the solar plan, and the cosmic plan. Such a dream indicates a high stage of evolution on the part of the disciple or initiate.

20

The Laws of Manifestation

*Manifestation is not magic. It is a process of
working with natural principles and laws in
order to translate energy from one level of
reality to another.*

David Spangler

Mastering the laws and methods of manifestation is one of the most
important goals of a disciple on the path. In this chapter I have put
together one of the most comprehensive, yet easy to understand articles on
the subject you will ever find. I have organized the information into a
series of laws, or principles, necessary to achieve mastery of this subject.
The careful study of and meditation upon these principles will be of
incalculable value to you.

1.   The first law of manifestation is that you must learn to manifest
with all three of your minds — your conscious mind, your subconscious
mind, and your superconscious, or soul, mind.

A.   Manifestation on a conscious level is done through the use of
will, or personal power. Most people manifest the things in their lives
this way. They work eighteen-hour days and just power it out. The
conscious level of manifestation is also connected with physical action.
This means making phone calls, physically organizing, seeing clients,
running errands, administrating, and so on. This is a very valid and
important method of manifestation.

"There is no force more powerful in the universe than your will."
This is a famous statement by the Universal Mind through Edgar
Cayce. To manifest efficiently you must own your full personal power
and will and use them in conjunction with unconditional love and the

knowledge that you are God in action.

B.   The second method of manifestation is through the power of your subconscious mind. In reality, you are using this level of manifestation whether you realize it or not. The problem is that in many cases, you are not using it consciously. The other problem is that you often use this level to block manifestation rather than to facilitate it.

The law of the subconscious mind is based on that famous Hermetic law of correspondence: "As within, so without; as above, so below." That which you think and imagine in your conscious and subconscious minds will manifest its mirror likeness in your external circumstances. Your outer world is a mirror of your inner world. This is the law, and it manifests for better or for worse because the subconscious mind does whatever it is programmed to do. It is constantly attracting and repelling according to that which you allow to be put into it.

The major work of the spiritual path is to clean out all of the lower-self, negative-ego, and imbalanced programming that is not of the soul and higher self. When this has been done, you have "the Midas touch" — everything you touch turns to gold. This occurs because your subconscious mind is subservient to your conscious mind, which is subservient to your superconscious mind, which is subservient to your soul mind, which is subservient to your monadic mind, which is subservient to God.

Your subconscious mind runs your physical body completely and will create health or disease, depending upon how you program it. The subconscious will attract to you everything you need, for all minds are joined, in truth. That is why the use of affirmations, visualizations, and autosuggestions is such an important science. (In chapter 10 I have provided twenty-four methods for implanting suggestions into your subconscious mind.)

To manifest effectively, you must be in control of your subconscious mind. Many times, you let yourself be run by your computer (your subconscious mind) instead of letting your computer programmer (your conscious mind) run your computer. Ideally, it's your servant. It has been called the basic self or the servomechanism in other teachings. It is your faithful servant and it will supply you with whatever you need, as long as you program it directly.

C.   The third way to manifest is through the power of the superconscious mind, the higher self, the spirit, God. This is, of course, manifesting not by affirmation or visualization but rather, by prayer. Prayer is the spiritual practice of asking God for what you want and accepting that it has been done once you have made your request.

God, through your higher self and monad, hears and answers all prayers. How, when, and in what form He answers them will be dependent on how you adhere to the universal laws of manifestation.

Why manifest just with will power and physical work when you can pray every day and acquire God's help? Not only do you have God's help through prayer, but you also have the help of the ascended masters, the angels, the elohim, the nature spirits, God working through other people, your higher self, and your monad.

Perhaps you do not pray enough. The ideal is to use all three levels of your mind. Maybe you use only your conscious mind. Maybe you pray but don't get off your duff, expecting God to do everything for you. This will not work, for God helps those who help themselves. Maybe you are constantly doing affirmations and visualizations but don't have the will power to do the physical action and work that are needed.

This law deals with the importance of using all three levels of mind in perfect harmony, balance, and integration.

The kahunas of Hawaii have a method of prayer in which all three minds are utilized. Build up your vital force and energy before you begin the prayer, and perform the process with enthusiasm. Write the prayer on a piece of paper very specifically and with lots of colorful imagery. When you have the prayer worded and imaged in a way that feels right, then say it three times out loud, addressing the prayer to God, your higher self, and whomever else you feel guided to address. After saying the prayer three times, in a powerful but loving way, command your subconscious mind to take the prayer to your higher self. Visualize this happening like the Old Faithful geyser, shooting up into the air through your crown chakra. Then forget about the prayer and do whatever you need to do on a conscious and subconscious level to manifest the prayer. In other words, all three minds are working together in perfect harmony, synchrony and balance.

I have used this method countless times in my life and it never fails to work. (Another method of prayer is to just write a letter to God and your higher self. Your higher self will respond to your letters in your daily life.)

All forms of prayer work; however, I would recommend using this method for important events.

2. The second key law of manifestation is to work from the awareness that you are the soul and not the personality. If you manifest from the consciousness of personality, you see yourself as separated from your brothers and sisters and from creation itself. That is an illusion.

Your manifestation will be one thousand times more powerful if you recognize yourself as the Christ, the Buddha, the Atma, the Eternal Self, for that, in truth, is who you are. You are one with God and all of creation — so what you are trying to manifest is nothing more than a part of yourself! This cannot be too strongly emphasized.

The New Age laws of manifestation deal with this shift in the focus of your identity. Failing to use prayer and failing to identify yourself as soul rather than as personality cuts you off, to a very great degree, from the source of energy for the manifestation of your desires. Ask the ascended masters, angels, your monad, the elohim, the nature spirits, and/or the Ashtar Command if you would like extra help.

3.   Do not be attached to what you are trying to manifest, or you will repel it from yourself. Make your choice for manifesting a preference, not an attachment. With this attitude you will be happy until it arrives.

4.   Surrender your prayer request to God and leave it in God's hands. God is happy to help, but you *must* surrender it. You can visualize your prayer request going up in a bubble of pink or golden Light and melding with God's Light. Then it is your job to go about your business and do what you can on the conscious, personal power level, on the physical action level.

5.   All that exists is perfection, in truth. God created you and you are perfect. Any time anything but perfection manifests, immediately pray and/or visualize and affirm the truth instead of the illusion of the negative ego. Cancel and deny any thoughts that try to enter your mind other than this truth. If you are sick, affirm and visualize only perfect health. If your bank account is low, imagine that it is full.

6.   The thoughts and images that you hold in your mind create your reality. God's universe is abundant and limitless. However, you attract either poverty or abundance, depending on the attitude you hold. This brings us back to the Hermetic law: "As within, so without; as above, so below." Your outer world and physical body are mirrors of the inner world of your conscious and subconscious thinking and imaging.

7.   Have faith. You know God exists and you know that God's laws are perfect and work every time. So after you pray, know that your prayer has been heard and that God's law has been invoked. Nothing but perfect fulfillment of the prayer and law can happen as long as you have faith in God's laws. If you give into doubt and worry, you are blocking the energy you just set in motion.

8.   Be aligned and consistent. All four bodies must be in alignment for a quick manifestation of your prayer request. The mind must be attuned to spirit so that its energy can flow through you.

The feeling body must be attuned to the mind and then to the soul. The physical body must be attuned to the emotional body, which is attuned to the mind, which is attuned to the soul, which is attuned to the monad, which is attuned to God. Another way this could be said is that the subconscious mind serves the conscious mind, which serves the superconscious mind or soul, which serves the monad or spirit, which serves God. Each level is subservient to the one above.

After you pray, you don't want the subconscious mind going renegade and saying, "I don't believe this is going to work." If this starts to happen, push the thought out of your mind and say, "Get thee behind me, Satan." Then reaffirm God's perfection.

9.   Everything in God's universe is just energy, and all energy is God. Even physical matter is nothing but energy vibrating at a slow rate. So all you are really doing in working with the laws of manifestation is changing energy from one form to another.

This law deals with the fact that energy follows thought. What you ask for already exists on a higher level once the prayer, affirmation, and visualization have been done. At that point, you are just waiting for it to manifest into physical reality. The attitude should be one of expectancy, as though it were going to happen any second. You are just waiting for it to move down through the dimensions and ground itself into physical reality. As long as you keep your four bodies and three minds in alignment, there is no reason for that not to happen.

10.   These laws are operating whether you are consciously aware of them or not. In addition, they are perfectly happy to work with the negative as well as the positive; they are not selective or discriminatory. Whatever you give the subconscious, it will use. If you hold a negative thought and image for too long, it will manifest into your physical reality eventually. So if you are not working with these laws of manifestation for the positive, then they are going to work to your detriment.

Edgar Cayce said, "Why worry when you can pray?" Own your own power and affirm and visualize anything you want at any time. If you are starting to worry, it is time to get back to your spiritual practices of proper manifestation. If you continue to worry you might just manifest what you are worrying about.

11.   Every moment of your life you are working with the laws of manifestation, even when you are not praying, willing, visualizing, or affirming. Every thought you think as you go through your daily life and as you sleep is part of the process.

If you never did any specific manifestation work but were vigilant about every thought that you let into your mind, allowing in only thoughts of perfection, prosperity, God, love, balance, and perfect health, then you would have, in truth, everything you need. In this state the three minds are functioning as one mind. Your soul and your higher self are doing your thinking for you, rather than your negative ego or your personality.

12.   Be sure that the desire for what you are praying for is coming from your soul and not from your negative ego. Your soul won't help if what you are asking for is not for the highest good of all concerned. If a prayer doesn't manifest, there is a possibility it is not meant to be and is not truly a part of the Divine Plan for you.

13.   Perseverance is necessary. On this Earthly plane of reality, time is slowed down so you can practice these laws. In the higher dimensions of reality, things manifest instantly. You are on this plane of existence to prove your mastery of these laws so you won't create havoc on the higher planes.

The higher your initiation, the quicker the manifestation. Sai Baba can manifest whatever he wants instantly, while still in a physical body. You will be able to do this too, in the future, but for now you need to demonstrate perseverance and endurance.

14.   Do not put limits on how the manifestation will occur. If you are trying to manifest money, for example, don't imagine it as coming only from work. Maybe it will come from the lottery, or an inheritance, or you will find it, or someone will give you money. God works in mysterious ways, so don't try to out-think God. If you think your prayer can manifest in only one way, then you have limited God and you have limited your subconscious mind's ability to manifest for you.

15.   You need the ability to receive as well as to give in life. I know a lot of spiritual people who are great givers but do not know how to receive. They are offered a gift and they say, "No, I can't accept this." If you act this way, you are blocking your abundance. This is an essential part of having prosperity consciousness.

16.   It is extremely important to be humbly thankful for the abundance God has bestowed upon you. Thank God, your soul, the ascended masters, your subconscious mind, the angels, the nature spirits, for all the wonderful work they do for you. Make every day a thanksgiving holiday.

17.   You cannot fail. How can you fail with God, your soul, the ascended masters, the angels, the elohim, your personal power, the power of your subconscious mind, your physical body, the nature spirits, other people, and your monad all helping you? Add to that the fact that, in truth, you are the Christ, the Buddha, the Atma, the Eternal Self. You are God. Can God lose against the forces of glamour, illusion, and maya? Actually, they don't even exist; you just think they do.

The only thing that can stop your manifestation work is the glamour, illusion, and maya of your own negative ego and lower self. The only thing that can stop you from manifesting anything you want is you. God has given you everything. It waits only for you to claim it. That is the one thing that God can't do for you. You must claim God's abundance; then it is instantly yours.

If you master your thinking and imaging and, hence, your feeling body, then nothing can stop the manifestation from occurring.

18. To have all, give all to all. This is a law of manifestation made known in *A Course in Miracles*. You must learn to receive, but you must also learn to give in order to manifest effectively. You must keep your abundance in circulation. If you become selfish and stingy and stop giving, then the universe becomes selfish and stingy and stops giving to you. When you stop giving to the all, which is God, your pipes get clogged and you are not able to receive as much. Keep giving, keep receiving; that keeps the abundance factor flowing.

19. Every word you speak is a decree and a fiat of manifestation. It is important to be vigilant over your speech. The power of your spoken word is even greater than that of the thoughts you allow to run through your mind. Just because you are not focusing on your manifestation work doesn't mean that you are not doing manifestation work.

20. Affirmations and prayers must be worded in positive language rather than in language that includes negative words and imagery. For example, if you want to heal a broken leg it would be good to avoid saying, "I am now healing my broken leg." It would be better to say, "My leg is now powerful, healed, and whole." The reference to the negative image can have a negative effect on the subconscious mind which will manifest anything that is put into it. The first statement holds the danger of giving it a double message.

21. Build up your vital force and energy before doing your manifestation work. Spirit sometimes uses your energy as well as the thoughts and imagery you send in your prayer request. Vital force can be built up by breathing deeply or doing some physical exercise for a few minutes before you begin.

22. Be enthusiastic when you do manifestation work. Your enthusiasm is part of the above law of building vital force, and it also incorporates your emotional body in the work which will make the manifestation occur much more quickly. The emotional body is connected to the subconscious mind, and nothing will manifest unless the subconscious mind is involved in the process.

23. There is just one universal subconscious mind. Each of you focuses one aspect of that mind, while being simultaneously connected to the whole mind or, as Jung called it, the collective unconscious. This understanding and awareness in your manifestation work eliminates the belief in separation that can slow down manifestation.

24. Be sure you have forgiven all people, situations, and yourself

before beginning your manifestation work. If there is lack of forgiveness it builds guilt and other psychic blocks that make the subconscious mind unable to cooperate fully in the prayer and affirmation process.

25.   Self-love is of major importance. If you are lacking in self-love, it usually means that you feel undeserving. This faulty belief sends a double message to your subconscious mind. If this is a lesson you need to work on, study chapter 4, "Christ Consciousness and How to Achieve It."

26.   Some people pray too much, which is a sign of lack of faith. In reality, once is enough. If, however, worry and doubt are beginning to set in, there is nothing wrong with repeating your prayer to solidify your faith. There is a balance to achieve in this regard that is unique and specific to each individual.

27.   Write down your prayers and affirmations on paper. The physical act of writing sends a stronger message to your subconscious mind than does just thinking your prayers or saying them out loud. The subconscious mind is more strongly influenced when some kind of physical action is taking place.

28.   Do your manifesting work in a state of meditation, an altered state of consciousness. At such a time you are under hypnosis, which allows suggestions to get into the subconscious mind more easily. A good time to do manifestation work is just as you are falling asleep at night (the hypnagogic state) or when you are waking up in the morning (the hyp-nopompic state), those twilight states between sleep and waking.

Avoid talking about your manifestation work. Often, talking with friends about what you are working to manifest can dissipate the energy. In addition, there could be a negative reaction from people that you would have to fight off in order to prevent it from getting into your subconscious mind. (See the chapter on psychic self-defense.)

29.   Remain in a positive environment and with positive people. Until you achieve self-mastery this is the single most important influence on your spiritual path. In manifestation work you are trying to hold a certain thought form, energy, and vibration. You want to be around people who support that process. Being around negative people and in negative envi-ronments tends to deplete your physical, emotional, mental, and spiritual energies, making it more difficult to hold the vibration.

30.   You already have everything. You already are everything. Since you are God, Christ, the Buddha, the Atma, the Eternal Self, the monad, the soul, in truth, everything is yours just as everything is God's. This has always been the case; however, it is difficult to own this because you are so used to believing the ego's interpretation of yourself that tells you that you are just a physical body, a personality, and are separate from creation. If you truly hold the truth that you are the Eternal Self, then all your

thoughts will stem from that basic understanding, and everything you need will manifest whenever you need it.

31. Ask only for what you truly need. If your ego becomes involved and starts asking for things you don't really need, then the prayer request is coming from glamour. This will sabotage your manifestation.

32. Learn to rely solely on God and God's laws for your abundance and prosperity. God, your personal power, and the power of your subconscious mind are an unbeatable team. When they are aligned your security is inside of yourself instead of outside of yourself. No matter what happens outside in terms of disasters of one sort or another, you always know that you can manifest whatever you need with God's help, your own will, and the power of your subconscious mind.

33. It is important to use all five of your senses when visualizing what you want to manifest. See it, hear it, taste it, touch it, and smell it. Make your visualization so real that the meditative reality is just as real as or more real than your physical reality. When the visualization is done in this way you are assured of success.

34. You must ask for help in order to receive it. If you don't ask, your higher self and the ascended masters and angels are not allowed to help. Ask and you shall receive; knock and the door shall be opened. Unless you request help, God doesn't provide it. This is law.

35. The law of the subconscious mind is just the opposite of the previous law. You must tell your subconscious mind what to do. If you don't give it suggestions, affirmations, visualizations, and computer programs, then it will manifest whatever happens to be in its computer banks already along with whatever you allow other people to put into them.

36. Be of service. Just because you are working with prayer, affirmation, and visualization doesn't mean that you don't have to do physical work for a living. The soul's perspective is that work is service to God and that true pleasure is serving God. Once you achieve some level of self-realization, there is no other reason to be here except to be of service to humanity, which is God.

37. Manifestation on the mental level has to do with concentration, staying focused, and keeping your mind steady in the Light. It has to do with not losing the idealized potential that you are in the process of manifesting. As you evolve you will not even have to be patient and wait, for what you choose to manifest will happen instantly as it does for Sai Baba.

38. Manifestation on the emotional level deals with childlike faith and devotion to God. Does not the Bible say that if you have the faith of a mustard seed you can literally move mountains? This childlike faith of many noneducated people is a wonder to see. Who is more prosperous, the

multimillionaire banker who worries about money all the time or the woman with six children who manifests everything she needs through her simple faith in God?

39.   Manifestation on the soul level is concerned with identifying yourself as soul rather than as personality and with staying attuned to the soul consciousness. This allows the energies of the soul to be involved in the manifestation of whatever you need. To work only on mental, emotional, and physical levels and not utilize the soul level would be to cut yourself off from the source of all life.

Without the soul you live in the illusion of separation, immersed in negative ego with all its attributes. When the soul is included, what you want to manifest is already a part of you. Manifestation then, in a sense, is uncovering that which is already yours but has been hidden by the delusion of the personality. The soul is not separate from the object that it is trying to manifest, as the personality would have you believe. What you are trying to manifest is part of the soul, for soul pervades all things. This is why you already have and are everything.

A person such as Sai Baba, who is one with spirit, images a thing and it instantly manifests. The same is true for you, except that the process is slowed down a bit. When you image from a soul consciousness it instantly manifests also, even though you cannot yet see it with your physical eyes. Time and space do not really exist, so once you claim your manifestation it is already yours; you are just waiting for it to come into manifestation on the Earth plane. If you have already developed your clairvoyant ability, you can see it.

It is often easy to lose your concentration before your manifestation has the opportunity to move from the etheric into the physical. The laws are slowed down on the physical plane so manifestation doesn't appear to happen instantly but takes a little time to ground itself into the physical. Hold your focus and manifest through your soul consciousness.

40.   *Miracles are natural.* Miracles are the normal by-product of expressing and working with God's laws in the service of humankind.

41.   Identify yourself with God. When you are manifesting, use the words "I Am" to begin your affirmations and, if you like, in addressing God. When you say, "I Am," you are affirming God's name which is your own.

42.   "Seek ye first the kingdom of Heaven; then shall all things be added unto thee." I think this statement is self-evident and needs no explanation.

"For what is a man profited, if he shall gain the whole world and lose his own soul?" [Mt 16: 25-26] Many people judge prosperity by the amount of money or material things you own. True prosperity is being merged with the soul and spirit, which then leads to all your needs being taken care of, in the service of God.

43. It is okay to pray for material things. Some people in the spiritual movement are confused about this point. It is perfectly all right and actually desired by the soul and monad that you utilize their help in this capacity; however, don't be greedy. Ask for what you need — no more and no less.

True abundance is not a matter of having everything, but rather of being a source through which all you need can manifest. It is being at one with the essence behind and within all things.

44. Manifestation on the level of personal power is greatly increased when your work is seen and focused upon as service to humanity. There is an ancient metaphysical saying: "When your heart is pure, you will have the strength of ten." When your work is for a noble cause, and you are doing it with a pure heart and intent, you will have a much greater amount of energy to do what is necessary, for you will be aligned with the universal force.

45. Be very specific in your visualizations and affirmations for manifestation. If you are too general, then by the laws of the universe you can manifest only a general solution or one that is too vague to manifest at all.

46. Understand that whatever you manifest is not really yours. It is really God's and you are just taking care of it. Or, to put it another way, there is no distinction between what is God's and what is yours.

47. Take good care of that which you manifest. If you manifest a new car and don't take care of it, then you are not deserving of the manifestation on the physical level. All levels need to be in alignment or manifestation can be blocked.

48. There is no way you can learn to manifest effectively without self-discipline. You must learn to discipline your mind, emotions, body, and consciousness to hold the proper vibration and to be attuned to the soul. You must not let your lower self infiltrate your mind with doubts and fears. Having discipline gives you consistency and allows you to stay continuously in Light, joy, positivity, and love, and to maintain unceasingly a consciousness of abundance.

49. Manifest from a state of consciousness of authority, knowing you are a master. There is no force more powerful than your will. To manifest effectively you must own your full power and identity as the Christ, the Buddha, the Atma, the Eternal Self. You must manifest with the full power of your self as soul and as spirit. Then the universe will instantly comply with your command.

50. Despite what your negative ego would have you believe, in reality,

you have only one need: to own the truth of your identity with God. When this need is met, then all other needs are also met as a by-product of this state of consciousness.

51. Don't regard what you are hoping to manifest as a lack. Everything, in truth, is really a part of yourself, which is God, so you lack nothing. The manifestation then becomes an opportunity to demonstrate the presence of God. When he performs his miracles of manifestation, Sai Baba describes them as simply a by-product of God's infinite nature. Manifestation is really just creativity at work.

52. When groups of people are hoping to manifest something, it is essential that all share the same vision. If not, the differing visions can cancel each other out, thus preventing the manifestation from taking place.

53. Follow your inner promptings and intuitions after praying for help. For example, let's say you have prayed for a specific dollar figure for your rent check for next month. The universe is planning to manifest it through a person you are supposed to meet at a party. You get the guidance to go to the party, but your lower self tells you that you are too tired to go; thus you could miss the manifestation that was provided for you. This is where self-discipline dovetails with being obedient to your spiritual guidance.

54. After praying, accept your prayer as having been answered. You have followed all the universal principles of manifestation. You have fulfilled the laws. Don't just believe that it has been answered; *know* that it has been answered, with every cell, molecule, and atom of your being. It is done. It is finished. So be it, for you have decreed it to be so. Your work is God made manifest. You are God, and you are one with God. You have fulfilled the law so how can your prayer not be made manifest?

55. This last law of manifestation is the law of tithing. It is related to the law of seed money. The universal law states that if you give one-tenth of your income to a charitable cause you will receive a tenfold return on your generosity. This law works with the law of karma, which states that that which you sow you reap — what you put out comes back to you. The giving of a tithe keeps the energy of money in circulation. If you are stingy with the universe, which is God, then the universe, God, will be stingy with you. If you are generous with the universe, then the universe, by law, must be generous with you.

A Course in Miracles includes many wonderful statements about the manifestation of miracles.

> There is no order of difficulty in miracles. One is not harder or bigger than another. They are all the same. All expressions of love are maximal.

Miracles are natural. When they do not occur something has gone wrong.

Prayer is the medium of miracles. It is a means of communication of the created with the Creator. Through prayer love is received, and through miracles love is expressed.

Miracles are examples of right thinking, aligning your perceptions with truth as God created it.

Miracles arise from a miraculous state of mind, or a state of miracle-readiness.

21

The Laws of Karma

*For verily I say unto you, till Heaven and
Earth pass, one jot or one tittle shall in no
wise pass from the law, till all be fulfilled*

Matthew 5:18

*And it is easier for Heaven and Earth to pass,
than one tittle of the law to fail*

Luke 16:17

The basic law of karma states that as you sow, you reap; what you put out comes back to you. This is the law of cause and effect. You might think that many people living in this world get away with a lot. I am here to tell you that no one gets away with anything. As Edgar Cayce said, "Every jot and tittle of the law is fulfilled."

The interesting thing about the law of karma is that it extends over many lives. Even if it appears that someone has unfairly taken advantage of another and escaped unscathed, it is not really so. The soul continues even if it has incarnated into another physical body. The Edgar Cayce files are filled with examples of this point. Jesus provided an excellent understanding of the law of karma when he said, "Do unto others as you would have others do unto you." This is meant more literally than you might realize.

There are different levels of karma. What I have been speaking of so far is what I would call personal karma — what you personally have set into motion with the power of your consciousness.

The second type of karma is group karma. When you incarnate onto this world you are born into a group with respect to skin color, religious affiliation, and so on. A person born into a black body in the United States has to deal with racism and prejudice, not because a black body is inferior to a white body, but because of the low level of spiritual consciousness of so many souls on this plane. A person in a black body or in any other minority takes on the karmic lessons of that group.

Another type of karma is national karma. You are born in a certain country and then indoctrinated with its egoistical identifications. If, for example, there were a war between China and the United States, inhabitants of each country would get caught up in their own national karmic lessons. You are not an island unto yourself.

Then there is planetary karma. This particular school called Earth provides lessons that are quite different from those provided by other planets in this galaxy or universe. You must deal with the planetary karma and the phase of history you are born into.

It could also be said that all karma is personal in that you, as a soul, choose your skin color, family, religion, and the country before incarnating.

The word "karma" has often been associated with bad karma, the idea that you must experience some form of suffering because of a lesson not learned. This is distinguished from the state of grace. Applying the principles in this book will allow you to avoid suffering, for what is stated here is in harmony with God's laws.

Everything in the universe is governed by laws. There are physical laws, emotional laws, mental laws, and spiritual laws. If you fall out of harmony with these laws, you suffer. Karma, hence, is not a punishment but a gift, a sign that you are out of balance.

The proper attitude toward everything that happens in life is "Not my will but thine. Thank you for the lesson." Buddhism calls this nonresistance. In psychology, it is referred to as acceptance. Instead of fighting the universe, the idea is to work with and learn from the universe. This does not mean to give up your power; just the opposite. It means to own your power and to view all that occurs as a lesson, a challenge, and an opportunity to grow. The idea is to look at the karma as a stepping stone for soul growth.

There is no need to suffer. Suffering is not God's design, it is your own. It is a sign that you are letting your negative ego, your separated, fear-based self be your guide, rather than soul or spirit.

There is no such thing as sin. A sin is supposed to be some unshakable stain on your character that cannot be removed. That is an egoistical concept, not a spiritual one. There are no sins, only mistakes. The true meaning of sin is "missing the mark." Mistakes are actually positive, not negative. The idea is to learn from them and, most of all, to forgive yourself. Perfection doesn't mean never making a mistake. True perfection is the state of always forgiving yourself for your mistake and then learning from the experience.

Another very important point with respect to karma is that all lessons are learned within self. In other words, if you are having a vicious fight with a former friend, but you choose to forgive and unconditionally love that person, letting go of your animosity, you are freed from the karma, even if the other person chooses to hold on to a grudge for the rest of the incarnation. This is a very freeing concept.

Karma comes back to you on all levels – physically, emotionally, mentally, and spiritually. How you take care of your physical body in this lifetime will determine how healthy a physical body you have in the next lifetime (if you are destined to return).

If you master your emotions in this lifetime and become peaceful, calm, joyous, and happy, then when you incarnate again, you will be a peaceful, calm, joyous, and happy baby. Some people believe in the idea of the tabula rasa, the blank slate. This is obviously absurd. You are not a blank slate when you are born. As a matter of fact, there are actually no such things as children; there are only adult souls living in babies' bodies. The average person has two hundred to two hundred and fifty past lives. The soul, with all of its twelve soul extensions, has an average of two thousand to two thousand five hundred past lives.

Another interesting point in respect to karma is the understanding that there is no such thing as linear time in the spiritual world. Time is simultaneous. Your past and future incarnations are actually happening now; the now is really all that exists.

It is possible to have karmic bleed-through from any of your eleven other soul extensions who are still in incarnation. It can come from the past or from the future. (I realize that this is a very difficult concept to understand on this plane. Try to grasp it with your right brain rather than with your left brain. Karmic bleed-through can manifest as, for example, physical symptoms that aren't in reality your own. Let's say one of your fellow soul extensions is close to death in his or her incarnation. You could be experiencing that death or running some of that person's karma through your physical body. If you want to do that for one or several of your soul extensions, you can. However, I wouldn't recommend doing it too much unless you receive clear guidance to do so.

An experience I had with Djwhal Khul one day provides a good illustration of bleed-through. He said that there was cigarette smoke in my field. I said, "Cigarette smoke? That's impossible, for I have never smoked cigarettes." I asked him if he was sure it wasn't incense, which I sometimes burn. He said, "No, it is cigarette smoke." He then searched more deeply into the cause and found it was coming from one of my soul extensions.

To understand the concept that soul extensions are guided by the soul, or oversoul, I would recommend reading one of Jane Roberts' Seth books, *The Education of Oversoul Seven*. It will help to give you a better understanding of the concepts of simultaneous time and of soul extensions' being guided by the soul.

Later I will talk more about the three permanent atoms, which are recording devices for personal karma residing in the physical, mental, and emotional bodies. The three permanent atoms record all good and bad karma, like a personal Akashic Record. These permanent atoms are also dispensers of karma. They place karmic pictures into the bloodstream, which has an enormous affect on the glandular system. This is part of God's system for implementing the law of karma fairly.

Another important point about karma is that you are given only as much as you can handle. This is controlled by your soul and monad. If all your karma were dumped upon you at the same time, it would be too much to deal with. It is possible to slow down the karma coming your way if you are feeling overwhelmed, and it is also possible to speed up your karmic lessons if you want to grow faster. This is achieved simply by praying for it to your soul or to God. It is their joy to work with you in any way you feel is comfortable.

All good karma from past lives and this one is stored in your causal body, or soul body. The building of this causal body is one of the main requirements for achieving liberation from the wheel of rebirth. To achieve ascension you need to balance only 51% of the karma of all your past lives (the karma of your personal past lives, not the karma of your eleven other soul extensions).

Much of the karma you experience in your life is not from past lives, but has been created in this life. For example, if you fall asleep at the wheel while driving and get into a serious car accident, the lesson could be as simple as learning not to be so foolish as to drive when overtired.

All karma from past lives is basically just programming in your subconscious mind and in your three permanent atoms. It can all be transformed during this life by learning to be the master of your three lower vehicles – the physical, emotional, and mental bodies – in the service of spirit and unconditional love. It is possible to completely clear your subconscious mind and three permanent atoms of all negative programming and to replace it with positive programming.

The laws of karma extend even to the type of soul you attract during intercourse and conception to be your child. The kind of soul that is attracted is largely determined by the quality of feeling and love that is being shared and made manifest during the lovemaking experience.

With respect to how karma relates to blood transfusions, organ transplants, and animal organ transplants, Djwhal Khul has said that all three are definitely not recommended and are to be avoided if at all possible.

Take, for example, the blood transfusion. Let's say that you are a third-degree initiate and have just taken your soul merge initiation. Then you go into a hospital and get a transfusion of blood from a person who hasn't stepped onto his spiritual path yet. Physically and spiritually speaking, the blood would be totally dissonant in terms of your vibration. You would be, in essence, running that person's karma through your bloodstream. An organ transplant would be even worse. And worse yet would be putting a pig's liver into a human body. They are actually doing this now!

The basic law of the universe is that your thoughts create your reality. All karma has its antecedent in some ancient thought that led to a feeling or an action. It is sometimes helpful to do hypnotic regression work to release karmic blocks from past lives or early childhood. Under hypnosis you can reexperience a past trauma, thus gaining insight into the cause of particular karmic results. Then you can very often release that program from your subconscious mind.

One final understanding about karma has to do with a master taking on the karma of one of his or her disciples. Sai Baba, the great master from India, has done this frequently for devotees. In one instance he took on the heart attack, stroke, and ruptured appendix of a devotee who would certainly have died otherwise.

Sai Baba became extremely ill for ten days. Over twenty-five of the finest doctors in India were at his bedside on the tenth day. He had turned completely black and the consensus of the twenty-five doctors was that he had only ten minutes longer to live. Sai Baba would not take medication and said that at four o'clock that day he would be giving a lecture. The doctors thought he was crazy. At the appointed hour he apparently sprinkled some water on himself and was instantly cured. From that moment forward the twenty-five doctors have prayed to Sai Baba for help before treating any patient.

Karma as It Affects the Past and the Future

I have studied the Edgar Cayce files and come up with some fascinating cases that show how the law of karma extends over past or future lives.

The first example is that of a man who lived in Rome in a past life. He was a very handsome man and he used to go around criticizing other people for being fat and not handsome like himself. In his present lifetime he has an underactive pituitary and is obese. I mentioned earlier the three permanent atoms that often release into the bloodstream karma that adversely affects the glandular system. This is one very good example of that process.

In another of Cayce's readings, a man who had knifed and killed someone in a past life is suffering from leukemia. In a similar reading, a man had killed someone and in this life he is shedding his own blood through anemia.

Some parents took their eight-year-old son to see Edgar Cayce because of a chronic bedwetting problem. It turned out that the bedwetting was a karmic lesson from a past life in Salem, Massachusetts, during the witch trials. He had been one of the men responsible for dunking the witches under water and torturing them for their beliefs. The eight-year-old boy was suffering from deep-seated guilt for having mistreated the women, and it was being manifested as bedwetting.

The cause of epilepsy in two different readings was a misuse of psychic powers in a past life, and in another reading the cause was overindulgence in sexuality. A black couple went to see Cayce and asked why it was they were black in this racist society. It turned out that in their previous lives they were white plantation owners in the South and had mistreated blacks. This reminds me of Jesus' statement to "do unto others as you would have others do unto you," for that is exactly how the law works.

A friend of mine had a fear of swimming. Two different psychics told her that she had died in the sinking of the Titanic. This same friend's three main interests in this life have been art, music, and the American Indians. One of the psychics, without knowing this, told her that her three most recent lives had been as a famous artist, a musician, and an American Indian.

A woman's fear of knives had to do with a life in Persia where she was attacked by invading forces who killed her with a knife. In another reading, a man had a very painful hip condition which the doctors said was cancer of the bone. Cayce said that it was a karmic situation from a past life in Rome where the man had been in the Coliseum laughing at the suffering of one of the people in combat.

Another reading was for a man who was suffering from severe congenital cataracts. Cayce said it was from a past life in Persia where the man had been in a tribe of barbarians who blinded other tribesmen with hot irons.

Cayce has said that hives are caused by animosities, grudges, and unkindly thoughts. Cayce also said that no one can hate his neighbor and not have stomach and liver problems.

Another reading concerned a child who was suffering from infantile paralysis at one year of age. Both of her legs were crippled and both of her feet were stunted in their growth. Cayce said that this was because of an Atlantean incarnation in which she had used drugs and hypnosis to make people weak in limb and body so they would have to follow her orders.

Another fascinating Cayce reading tells of a man who hated blacks. He was a Nazi and a member of the Ku Klux Klan. He said that blacks were like animals. This man obviously would not come for a reading, but someone who did asked how anyone could be filled with so much hate. It turned out that this soul, in a past life, had been a Phoenician in about 500 B.C. Apparently, during a war between the Phoenicians and the Carthaginians, he had been captured and made a slave on one of the ships. The ships were like the ones depicted in the movie *Ben Hur*, in which they were chained to their seats below deck and made to row. A black man would beat the drum and all the slaves would have to row to the beat of the drum. Another black man would beat the slaves who didn't keep up with the proper rowing beat. This man apparently had lived for thirty years, being transferred from ship to ship, being made to row and constantly beaten. This life is a good example of karmic bleed-through. He had built up so much hate in that lifetime that when he incarnated again it came right out.

Another reading was for a man who was born in a deformed physical body. People always wonder why one person seems blessed and another cursed. It turns out that in a past life this soul had been Nero, the Roman emperor who fiddled while Rome burned. This deluded soul had built up so much bad karma in that life, he chose to balance it out in one fell swoop by having a deformed body.

In another reading a woman had an overpowering fear of animals. This fear came from an experience in Rome when her husband had been made to fight wild beasts in one of the arenas.

Another woman had been married for nine years and had a very sweet and loving husband. The woman was still afraid to get involved sexually. It turned out that in a past life during the Crusades he had restrained her with a chastity belt which caused her to hate him. This karmic lesson still obviously hadn't been worked out.

One woman who came to see Edgar Cayce had glandular disturbances that caused an excessive menstrual flow which made it impossible for her to attend school and led to extreme depression and a nervous breakdown. Cayce said that in a past life she had been a nun in a French convent at the time of Louis XIV. She had been very stern, cold, and intolerant of human weakness. Her understanding of scripture was purely literal. She acted superior and very intolerant of others.

In another reading a woman couldn't commit to marriage. Cayce told her that her wariness sprang from a life during the Crusades when her husband had deserted her. Another woman was abnormally shy and unable to make friends. It stemmed from a life in France when she had had much talent and beauty but her husband's jealousy had caused him to try to suppress her natural impulses with cold and merciless tyranny. He had even whipped her at times.

Another reading was for a doctor who had a markedly uncommunicative nature. Cayce said it stemmed from a past life of practicing silence as a Quaker. Another person was deaf; that stemmed from closing his ears to the suffering of others in a past life. Another person had digestive problems caused by a past life of gluttony.

A motion picture producer had polio. It came from a life in Rome, again, where he had jeered and mocked others for not resisting death in the combats at the Coliseum. A man was homosexual and wanted to become a priest. This was a source of great confusion and conflict for him. In a past life he had been a satirist and gossipmonger in the French court who had taken particular delight in exposing homosexual scandals with his cartoon skill.

I have given a lot of examples of bad karma carrying over to this life. Karma can also be of a positive nature. For example, how did Mozart create piano concertos at five years of age? He had four or five lifetimes as famous musicians previous to that life.

Djwhal Khul on the Law of Karma and Rebirth

I would like to end this chapter with a series of thirteen statements by Djwhal Khul from the Alice Bailey book called *The Reappearance of the Christ*. These thirteen statements by Djwhal provide a good summation of the entire process.

1. The Law of Rebirth is a great natural law upon our planet.

2. It is a process instituted and carried forward under the Law of Evolution.

3. It is closely related to and conditioned by the Law of Cause and Effect.

4. It is a process of progressive development, enabling men to move forward from the grossest forms of unthinking materialism to a spiritual perfection and an intelligent perception which will enable a man to become a member of the Kingdom of God.

5. It accounts for the differences among men and – in connection with the Law of Cause and Effect (called the Law of Karma in the East) – it accounts for differences in circumstances and attitudes to life.

6. It is the expression of the will aspect of the soul and is not the result of any form decision; it is the soul in all forms which reincarnates, choosing and building suitable physical, emotional, and mental vehicles through which to learn the next needed lessons.

7. The Law of Rebirth (as far as humanity is concerned) comes into activity upon the soul plane. Incarnation is motivated and directed from the soul level, upon the mental plane.

8. Souls incarnate in groups, cyclically, under law and in order to achieve right relations with God and with their fellow men.

9. Progressive unfoldment, under the Law of Rebirth, is largely conditioned by the mental principle "as a man thinketh in his heart, so is he." These few brief words need most careful consideration.

10. Under the Law of Rebirth, man slowly develops mind, then mind begins to control the feeling, emotional nature, and finally reveals the soul and its nature and environment to man.

11. At that point in his development, the man begins to tread the Path of Return and orients himself gradually (after many lives) to the Kingdom of God.

12. When – through a developed mentality, wisdom, practical service and understanding – a man has learned to ask nothing for the separated self, he then renounces desire for life in the three worlds and is freed from the Law of Rebirth.

13. He is now group conscious, is aware of his soul group and of the soul in all forms and has attained, as Christ had requested, a stage of Christ-like perfection reaching unto the measure of the stature of the fullness of the Christ.

22

Children in the World Today

*The teacher has the greatest role in molding
the future of the country. Of all professions,
his is the noblest, the most difficult,
and the most important.*

Sathya Sai Baba

Education

The problems of children in the world today constitute one of the most urgent situations confronting humanity at this time in its history. The subject is very complex; however, to begin with, I want to point out how utterly inadequate the education system is.

The sole purpose of life is to achieve God-realization, immortality, and ascension in order to be of greater service to humankind. The educational system has failed in this regard. Instead of focusing on building character, on moral values, ethics, spiritual ideals, right human relationships, right living, virtue, and spiritual and soul consciousness, it has completely eliminated the soul from all facets of learning and addressed itself only to the less important half of the human being.

The situation stems from political decisions made when the Constitution was written to ensure the separation of church and state. Although meant well, the decision has caused the baby to be thrown out with the bath water. The intention was to prevent groups like the self-righteous fundamentalist Christians and "moral majority" from imposing their ego-centric values on other people in schools. In that sense, the decision was wise. The problem is that it is not acceptable to eliminate spirituality from the school altogether.

Education now is materially and egoistically oriented. The focus is on making a living, accumulating possessions, being as materially successful as possible and as comfortable as possible. The system breeds competitiveness, pride, egotism, nationalistic prejudice, separativeness, and superiority over other people, cultures, and nations. World citizenship is not emphasized. Responsibility to humankind is completely ignored.

The education system is an exercise in stuffing massive numbers of unrelated facts into youngsters' minds so they can get a good grade. It is an exercise in short-term memory development devoid of enjoyment. It is goal-oriented instead of process-oriented, functioning merely as the means to an end. If a student happens to enjoy something, it is a pleasant surprise. Most of the time schooling is a lesson in self-discipline.

College is even worse. Those who make it to the professions are often neurotic. That is the definition of success. It is nearly impossible to be a whole, complete, and balanced person and also compete successfully enough to make it to the top in a particular profession.

Sai Baba has said that the most precious gift a young person can receive in school is the gift of character. He has also said that politics without principles, education without character, science without humanity, and commerce without morality are not only useless but positively dangerous. This is the predicament in the world today in all four categories. If soul consciousness is not integrated into the education system in some universal, eclectic, nonbiased manner, the leaders of the future will be intellectually developed but spiritually retarded. Is it any wonder politicians are so corrupt, lawyers and doctors, on the whole, so egocentric, scientists so cruel to animals, businesses so willing to overcharge to make an extra buck if they can get away with it?

Children are getting degrees but they don't have inner peace or happiness. They are not right with themselves or right with God. They are ill-equipped for marriage, let alone for parenting. Is it any wonder there is so much child abuse?

There is an answer: integrate the teaching of spirituality into the classroom in the context of teaching comparative religion and emphasizing the basic oneness of all religions. In other words, all religions would be taught, with the requirement that no one religion be treated as superior to any other religion. This, of course, would require special training for the teachers.

Another way around the problem would be to teach spirituality rather than religion. There should be classes on the development of morals and ethics, on character-building, spiritual values, and right human relationships, to name just a few subjects. Schools, instead of focusing only on reading, writing, arithmetic, history, and geography, should be adding classes in self-mastery, learning to own personal power, how to develop self-love, integration of the three minds, proper diet and nutrition, meditation, the seven levels of initiation, how to integrate the monad, soul, and personality, how to balance the seven chakras, the saints of all religions, comparative religion, angels, the Spiritual Hierarchy, the evolution of minerals, plants, and animals, death and dying, the science of the bardo, the soul, how to build the antakarana, the scriptures of the world, art appreciation, music appreciation, how to transcend negative ego and duality, how to channel, how to utilize the right and left brains, mantras and words of power, ethics and moral training, psychic self-defense, extra-terrestrial civilizations, spiritual ways of doing business, how to be a spiritual politician, psychic development, balancing the four bodies, understanding the law of karma, and the story of creation from various religions.

Wouldn't school be fun if those subjects were the curriculum? I am not saying that reading, writing, and arithmetic shouldn't be taught. Of course they should. They should, however, be balanced with classes on soul development. What does it matter if people have gone through twenty years of school to get a Ph.D. if they are raving egomaniacs? Without soul consciousness in the schools, it is negative ego consciousness that is being taught.

In addition, there should be required classes on the subjects of how to maintain an effective marriage and be good parents. Most people are ill-qualified for this adventure. There should be required classes in birth control, AIDS awareness, and how to control the desires of the body in the service of unconditional love and the purposes of the soul.

It might seem unlikely that such classes will ever be incorporated into the regular school curriculum, but mark my words: in the not-too-distant future, when the Lord Maitreya makes his declaration along with the externalization of the Spiritual Hierarchy, a radical transformation will ensue which will change all the existing ego-based institutions on this planet. I prophesy that within thirty years this will take place.

Children should be taught in an atmosphere of unconditional love and firmness. These are sadly lacking in schools today. What I am suggesting requires teachers to be the embodiment of these ideals. If our teachers don't embody these ideals how can the children learn them? Education, as it is practiced today, hardens hearts and squeezes out any semblance of unconditional love and compassion. Children are taught that it is a dog-eat-dog world out there; every man for himself is the law of the jungle, so they learn only that they must get good grades and be accepted by a good college.

God doesn't care about grades or higher education if egotism is what they are used for. The key question is always, what is the purpose of life? Why have you incarnated into this physical body? The answer is so that you can achieve the realization of God. Education, as it now is practiced, most certainly does not lead children in this direction.

Religion

Why don't children receive spiritual and moral training in churches or temples? The problem is that the ego has completely infiltrated all the religious institutions. If a person isn't in right relationship with himself, he projects that wrong relationship onto everything in life, including God. The teachings of all the major religions have been distorted because scripture has been interpreted by ego rather than by spirit. When God is portrayed as a punishing and judgmental being, threatening eternal damnation in Hell, who would want to go to church? Traditional religion, in its present form, is completely bankrupt.

A child might be required to go to church only on Sunday to listen to a boring, stuffy sermon. That is not going to do the trick. Children who go to religious schools have a whole different set of psychological and spiritual problems related to the guilt, fear, and self-righteousness that are pummeled into them.

Religious institutions won't be the answer until they cleanse themselves of negative ego and accept the fact of a universal religion that recognizes many paths to God. This will happen in the not-too-distant future as the Golden Age blossoms on this planet. An axis shift from ego thinking to soul thinking is about to occur. This will mean a rebirth of all institutions within the principles of soul and the Christ consciousness.

The other institution that needs total revamping is the political system. It is sickening to watch the partisan politics in which politicians do not serve spirit. They serve their party or special interest group.

Lobbyists are basically practicing legalized bribery. Politics is a classic example of what happens to a nation when leaders are chosen who are highly developed mentally and undeveloped spiritually. Unless the educational system is thoroughly altered, more of the same can be expected from future leaders.

Children are confronted with enormous amounts of negativity and negative programming in this world.

Recent studies have ascertained that the average family watches something like six hours of television a day. Unfortunately, the soul and higher self do not guide or control television programming. Little children watch cartoons that are incredibly violent. Ninety-eight percent of the shows on television breed egoistical values. The airwaves are filled with violence, sex, machoism, and beautiful people that program children's subconscious minds. They do not have sufficiently developed conscious minds to protect themselves from negative programming. The soul doesn't even fully inhabit the mental body till the age of twenty-one. Being emotionally based and subconsciously oriented, young people are hypersuggestible. They are in hypnosis most of the time. The television programs they watch and the movies they go to see go directly into their subconscious minds.

The second negative influence that children have to deal with is the enormous amount of junk food and sugar they are exposed to. Since, by definition, they have not obtained self-mastery and are run by their desire bodies, once they have eaten junk food and sugar, they become addicted and want more. Even the schools feed them junk food and sugar. On every street corner there is a fast-food restaurant or an ice cream parlor, and the older children get, the less control parents have over this facet of their children's lives. Junk food and sugar create all kinds of chemical imbalances and a lowering of the strength of the immune system. These affect the emotional body when children and adolescents are unbalanced enough because of rapid physical growth and hormone excretion.

Children and adolescents, being emotionally based, go through many ups and downs as they are continually faced with new lessons (relationships, sexuality, dating, money, college, and so on), karmic lessons, the effects of dysfunctional families, and the fear of abuse, assault and molestation.

Parents sometimes take their adolescents to counselors or psychologists. This brings us to another problematic system in our society: 98% of all counselors, psychologists, psychiatrists, and social workers are practicing a form of psychology that is cut off from the soul and the higher self. This is not to say that they are completely ineffective; they do some good. However, it is like what Einstein said about humans using only 8% of the brain. Soul psychology is ten thousand times more effective and useful than forms of psychology that are not connected to the spiritual aspect of life. Here again, young people are confronted with a lack of the help they need.

The child is bombarded by the news the parents watch, which is filled with negativity, focusing as it does on the murder and crime that have occurred throughout the world. If God controlled the news, I am sure He would focus it on the good that occurs, also. However, the news is not based on self-realization, but on ratings. The Trilateral Commission and the secret government control the news anyway, so nothing of real interest like extraterrestrial activity gets through.

Children and adolescents have to deal with all the advertising that appeals to their desire bodies even though they are not yet in control of those bodies. If they have no spiritual training, it is inevitable that the lower self will be in control. If they cannot choose their role models from among the spiritual masters and saints of all religions, they must find them in TV shows, movies, and magazines whose stars and images fill their minds with stereotypes and addictive love. In addition, the music young people listen to is filled with lyrics of a similar type of programming, all based on egoistical principles. Music programs the subconscious mind just as a hypnosis tape does. As adolescents get a little older they are confronted with pornography, which is a creation of the lower self. Without spiritual training there is little reason not to indulge in it, which just reinforces the images in the subconscious mind and is an encouragement to treat members of the opposite sex as objects.

There are only two types of people in the world: those who are soul-attuned and those who are overidentified with matter. There are only two emotions in the world: love and fear. Which will the children choose?

Parenting

The role of parents in raising children is more important than ever now, especially because of the pervasive negativity. In my opinion as a psychotherapist and spiritual teacher, parents are much too lenient. I think they should exert strict control over their children's physical, emotional, and mental diets. Children also need to be raised in an environment of unconditional love. Firmness and love — tough love — is the ticket. In addition, at this time, it is only parents who can educate children about the universality of religions and teach them about the great saints and masters, inspiring them with noble goals and lofty ideals.

The unfortunate state of affairs in our society is that most parents are not competent to guide their children in these matters. They have been too screwed up by their own parents and the education system they have gone through. They tend to dote on the child too much or ignore him entirely and they often have reprehensible habits themselves. They smoke, drink too much, gamble, fight in the home, gossip, judge. The only hope for children is that the parents and teachers of this world transform their own consciousnesses. They can't teach that which they don't embody.

Sai Baba has said that "parents must feel that they are servants appointed by the Lord to tend the little souls that are born in their households, as the gardener tends the trees in the garden of the master."

In the future every child will receive an astrological chart at birth. (This is common practice in the Hindu culture.) In addition, parents might consider having a ray analysis and a spiritual profile done for the child by a skilled psychic or channel to determine the age of the soul, his or her place on the ladder of evolution, and mystic tendencies or lack thereof. A vocational profile is recommended for the adolescent to determine whether this soul extension would be better suited for mental or physical work.

Parents must understand that there is really no such thing as a child;

there are only adult souls living in babies' bodies. Each incarnated personality has had anywhere from two hundred to three hundred past lives. It is also important to realize that parents are not really the parents; parents are the creators of the child's physical body, while God has created the soul. In reality, each parent co-parents with God. Today, this has been forgotten.

In the Hawaiian philosophy, the higher self is called the "aumakua," the "utterly trustworthy parental self." Parents are meant to co-parent with the utterly trustworthy parental self, that incarnated personality's higher self.

Children are born with very distinct abilities, personalities, and character traits. Parents must achieve a fine balance between teaching, training, molding, and providing guidelines while at the same time allowing the child's soul to have expression. It is not an easy job.

The best thing a parent can do is learn to be right with self and right with God. It is parents who have not achieved this who create serious problems for everyone. If parents dedicate their lives to a path of God-realization, then that will be programmed into the child both energetically and by example.

Many parents are so busy that the child spends all his or her time at school, with friends, or with babysitters, and these people become the role models from whom the child learns, so it is important to choose them with care. It is also important for parents to prepare food for their children. Otherwise, they will eat junk food, and it must be remembered that such food is filled with the energy of the people who prepared it. Food you prepare will be filled with love and with your life force.

In every home there should be a little shrine of some kind, a place for prayer, meditation, repeating the name of God, reading scripture, and so on. Divine qualities such as discernment, renunciation, keenness of intellect, peace, truth, righteousness, helpfulness, nonjudgmentalness, patience, and unconditional love should be stressed and praised. Stress the equality of religions and of the great prophets and saints of all religions.

When children are very young it is a fantastic idea to talk to them while they are sleeping. Tell them how much you love them and how much God loves them. When they are sleeping they are in hypnosis. They are hypersuggestible to all programming. You can even make a tape and play it while they sleep. Fill them with thoughts of self-love, personal power, courage, strength, confidence, faith, trust, and God-attunement. You can say whatever you want as long as it is positive and uplifting. If your child is having a problem, I would recommend you do this every night for two straight months. It will work wonders.

The Responsibility of Teachers

Education in our present system is the term given to the art of collecting information in the objective world. The far more important task of education is transforming the nature of man into the divine. If this doesn't take place, the opposite takes place, and children are unconsciously taught to live like animals. Too often teachers are more concerned about being paid than about seeing the divine responsibility that has been placed within their hands. Real education is helping the child to manifest the divinity that is latent within him. It is essential that moral fiber underlie even the worldly studies that need to take place in school.

It is also essential for the teacher to create an atmosphere in the classroom of unconditional love and nonjudgmentalness. Children must be taught the true joy of learning. If the curriculum were more balanced between worldly and soul education, I am sure this would happen.

Education has, in the past, pointed the child toward the goal of earning a livelihood. In the future, that will be balanced by education to have a life worth living. It is the teacher who makes the school or harms it. The teacher shapes the manners, behavior, attitudes, and prejudices of the pupils under his or her care.

Sai Baba has described the educational system metaphorically as being like a bank. He says, "The educational system is the bank on which the nation draws a cheque whenever it wants strong, reliable, skilled workers. If it goes bankrupt, it is a national disaster." This is the situation today.

The lack of spiritual training has created large numbers of people who are not whole, balanced, and integrated. They are fragmented. They are developed intellectually and physically, but not emotionally, psychologically, and spiritually.

It is good that the educational system has at least provided intellectual and professional training, but that is not enough. It is like an apple that looks sweet and ripe but has a rotten core. If every teacher taught one hundred students the ideals I have been speaking of, the entire country would be transformed.

Djwhal Khul, in the Alice Bailey book *Problems of Humanity,* has suggested that educators lay emphasis on the following:

1. Mental control of the emotional nature;

2. Vision, or the capacity to see beyond what is to what might be;

3. Inherited, factual knowledge upon which it will be possible to superimpose the wisdom of the future;

4. The capacity to handle relationships wisely and to recognize and assume responsibility;

5. The power to use the mind in two ways:

A. As the common-sense mind that analyzes and synthesizes information conveyed to it by the five senses; and

B. As the searchlight, penetrating into the world of ideas and abstract truth.

Educators put so much importance on IQ, or the intelligence quotient. In the future they will be much more interested in the SQ, the soul quotient. I foresee a time when psychological testing might become balanced with spiritual testing in the schools, with the presence of trained astrologers, psychics, channelers, and ray analysis specialists. Educators will focus on the problems of youth from the perspective of instinctual, emotional, intellectual, and intuitional potentiality. Currently, they have made the intellectual aspect their god, to the neglect of the rest of the person.

Educators must understand that educating children for citizenship in the kingdom of God is not just a religious activity for the churches. That would be like saying that spirituality has no place in politics or the prison system. Sadly enough, this is exactly what has happened in all of the institutions on this planet. Spirituality has been separated from life itself when the whole purpose of life is to bring Heaven to Earth and integrate it in a balanced manner.

Djwhal Khul has suggested the creation of an international system of education by teachers from throughout the world. This would accelerate the potential for world peace by leaps and bounds. It would lead to a type of world democracy in which all people, regardless of race, religion, nationality, or skin color, would be seen as equals. Differences between people would be honored and respected, while the essential unity of all people would be emphasized.

The educators of the future will have to be more like psychologists and spiritual teachers, facilitating the development of the whole person, rather than just academic intellectuals cramming meaningless facts down their students' throats.

Teachers, families, principalities, parents, politicians, ministers, rabbis, counselors, and volunteer workers must all work together to correct this imbalance in the education system.

For more information, Dr. Joshua David Stone can be contacted through the publisher or at:

5252 Coldwater Canyon, #112
Van Nuys, Ca 91410
(818) 769-1181

Bibliography

A Course in Miracles. Tiburon, CA: Foundation for Inner Peace, 1975.

Bailey, Alice A. *Esoteric Psychology,* Vol. I. New York: Lucis Publishing Co., 1963.

——. *Esoteric Psychology,* Vol. II. New York: Lucis Publishing Co., 1942

——. *Glamour, A World Problem.* New York: Lucis Publishing Co., 1950

——. *Initiation, Human and Solar.* New York: Lucis Publishing Co., 1922

——. *Ponder on This.* New York: Lucis Publishing Co., 1971

——. *Serving Humanity.* New York: Lucis Publishing Co., 1972

——. *The Soul, the Quality of Life.* New York: Lucis Publishing Co., 1974

Beesley, R.P. *The Robe of Many Colors.* Kent, England: White Lodge Publications, 1968.

Brennan, Barbara. *Hands of Light.* New York: Bantam Books, 1988.

Bro, Harmon H., Ph.D. *Edgar Cayce on Dreams.* New York: Warner Books, 1968.

Cerminara, Gina. *Many Mansions.* New York: New American Library, 1988.

Edgar Cayce Foundation. *A Search for God.* Virginia Beach, VA: A.R.E. Press, 1982.

Fortune, Dion. *Psychic Self-Defense.* New York: Samuel Weiser, Inc., 1992.

Foundation for Inner Peace. *A Course in Miracles,* Volumes I, II, III. New York: 1975.

Gandhi, Mohandas K. *An Autobiography.* Boston: Beacon Press, 1957.

Hills, Nora. *You Are a Rainbow.* Boulder Creek, CA: University of the Trees Press, 1979.

Krishna, Gopi. *Kundalini – The Secret of Yoga.* Ontario, Canada: F.I.N.D. Research Trust, 1972.

Krystal, Phyllis. *Cutting the Ties that Bind.* Dorset, England: Element Press, 1982.

Sai Baba, Sathya. *Education in Human Values.* Andhra Pradesh, India: Sathya Sai Publications, 1988.

Sai Baba, Sathya. *Sathya Sai Speaks,* Vol. VII. Andhra Pradesh, India: Sathya Sai Publications, 1982.

Sechrist, Elsie. *Dreams, Your Magic Mirror.* New York: Warner Books, 1988.

Silburn, Lilian. *Kundalini, Energy of the Depths.* Albany, NY: State University of New York Press, 1988.

Sivananda, Swami. *Practice of Yoga.* India: Divine Life Society, 1984.

Solomon, Paul. Tapes. Virginia Beach, VA: Fellowship of Inner Light, 1974.

Spangler, David. *The Laws of Manifestation.* Marina del Rey, CA: DeVorss & Co., 1975.

Williamson, Marianne. *A Return to Love: Reflections on the Principles of "A Course in Miracles."* New York: HarperCollins, 1992.

Woodward, Mary Ann. *Edgar Cayce's Story of Karma.* New York: Berkley Publishing Corp., 1971.

Yogananda, Paramahansa. *Man's Eternal Quest.* Los Angeles, CA: Self-Realization Fellowship, 1975.

BOOK MARKET

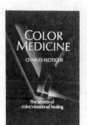

COLOR MEDICINE
The Secrets of Color Vibrational Healing

by **Charles Klotsche**

A practitioners' manual for restoring blocked energy to the body systems and organs with specific color wavelengths by the founder of "The 49th Vibrational Technique."

$11.95 Softcover 114 pp. ISBN 0-929385-27-6

MAHATMA I & II
Brian Grattan

Combined version of the original two books. Guidance to reach an evolutionary level of integration for conscious ascension. Fascinating diagrams, meditations, conversations.

$19.95 Softcover 328 pp. ISBN 0-929385-46-2

THE NEW AGE PRIMER
Spiritual Tools for Awakening

A guidebook to the changing reality, it is an overview of the concepts and techniques of mastery by authorities in their fields. Explores reincarnation, belief systems and transformative tools from astrology to crystals and healing.

$11.95 Softcover 206 pp. ISBN 0-929385-48-9

THE SEDONA VORTEX GUIDEBOOK

by **12 various channels**

200-plus pages of channeled, never-before published information on the vortex energies of Sedona and the techniques to enable you to use the vortexes as multidimensional portals to time, space and other realities.

$14.95 Softcover 236 pp. ISBN 0-929385-25-X

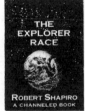

COMING SOON!
THE EXPLORER RACE
A channeled book

by **Robert Shapiro**

In this expansive overview, Zoosh explains, "You are the Explorer Race. Learn about your journey before coming to this Earth, your evolution here and what lies ahead." Topics range from ETs and UFOs to relationships.

BEHOLD A PALE HORSE

by **Bill Cooper**

Former U.S. Naval Intelligence Briefing Team Member reveals information kept secret by our government since the 1940s. UFOs, the J.F.K. assassination, the Secret Government, the war on drugs and more by the world's leading expert on UFOs.

$25.00 Softcover 500 pp. ISBN 0-929385-22-5

SHINING THE LIGHT

by **Light Technology Research**

Revelations about the Secret Government and their connections with ETs. Information about renegade ETs mining the Moon, ancient Pleiadian warships, underground alien bases and many more startling facts.

$12.95 Softcover ISBN 0-929385-66-7

SHINING THE LIGHT BOOK II

by **Light Technology Research**

Continuing the story of the Secret Government and alien involvement. Also information about the Photon Belt, cosmic holograms photographed in the sky, and a new vortex forming near Sedona.

$14.95 Softcover ISBN 0-929385-70-57

LIVING RAINBOWS

by **Gabriel H. Bain**

A fascinating "how-to" manual to make experiencing human, astral, animal and plant auras an everyday event. Series of techniques, exercises and illustrations guide the simply curious to see and hear aural energy. Spiral-bound workbook format.

$14.95 Softcover ISBN 0-929385-42-X

BOOK MARKET

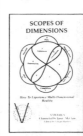

BOOK MARKET

BOOK MARKET

BOOKS BY ELWOOD BABBITT

PERFECT HEALTH
by **Elwood Babbitt**
For the first time ever, the world's most respected names in medicine and science speak through the noted trance medium. Wilhelm Reich, Einstein and others offer opinions on AIDS, nutrition, Life purpose.

$15.95 Softcover 297 pp. ISBN 1-881343-01-4

VOICES OF SPIRIT
by **Elwood Babbitt and Charles H. Hapgood**
The author discusses 15 years of work with Elwood Babbitt. This book will fascinate both the curious skeptic and the believer. Includes complete transcripts.

$13.00 Softcover 350 pp. ISBN 1-881343-00-6

PRISONERS OF EARTH
Psychic Possession and Its Release
by **Aloa Starr**
The symptoms, causes and release techniques in a documented exploration by a practitioner. A fascinating study that de-mystifies possession.

$11.95 Softcover 179 pp. ISBN 0-929385-37-3

SEDONA POWER SPOT, Vortex and Medicine Wheel Guide
by **Richard Dannelley**
An exploration of the vortex legends and their effects on the mind and spirit. Meditations, maps and photographs to guide the reader to profound transformation.

$9.95 Softcover ISBN 0-962945-2-3

THE LEGEND OF THE EAGLE CLAN
by **Cathleen M. Cramer** with **Darren A. Robb**
A remembrance out of the past, its emotional intensity pulling the Eagle Clan back together to the meeting place to hear the wake-up call and remember who they are and why they are here.

$9.95 Softcover ISBN 0-929385-68-3

THIS WORLD & THE NEXT ONE
by **Aiello**
A handbook about your life before birth and your life after death, it explains the "how" and "why" of experiences with space people and dimensions. Man in his many forms is a "puppet on the stage of creation."

$9.95 Softcover 213 pp. ISBN 0-929385-44-6

BOOKS BY ROYAL/PRIEST

PRISM OF LYRA
by **Lyssa Royal & Keith Priest**
Traces the inception of the human race back to Lyra, where the original expansion of the duality was begun, to be finally integrated on earth. Fascinating channeled information.

$11.95 Softcover 112 pp. ISBN 0-9631320-0-8

VISITORS FROM WITHIN
by **Lyssa Royal & Keith Priest**
Explores the extraterrestrial contact and abduction phenomenon in a unique and intriguing way. Narrative, precisely focussed channeling & firsthand accounts.

$12.95 Softcover 171 pp. ISBN 0-9631320-1-6

PREPARING FOR CONTACT
by **Lyssa Royal & Keith Priest**
Contact requires a metamorphosis of consciousness since it involves two species who meet on the next step of evolution. A channeled guidebook to ready us for that transformation., it is engrossing.

$12.95 Softcover 188 pp. ISBN 0-9631320-2-4

BOOKS BY DOROTHY ROEDER

THE NEXT DIMENSION IS LOVE
Ranoash through **Dorothy Roeder**
As speaker for a civilization whose species is more advanced, the entity describes the help they offer humanity by clearing the DNA. An exciting vision of our possibilities and future.

$11.95 Softcover 148 pp. ISBN 0-929385-50-0

REACH FOR US
Your Cosmic Teachers and Friends
Channeled by **Dorothy Roeder**
Messages from Teachers, Ascended Masters and the Space Command explain the role they play in bringing the Divine Plan to the earth now!

$13.00 Softcover 168 pp. ISBN 0-929385-69-1

CRYSTAL CO-CREATORS
Channeled by **Dorothy Roeder**
A fascinating exploration of 100 forms of crystals, describing specific uses and their purpose, from the spiritual to the cellular, as agents of change. It clarifies the role of crystals in our awakening.

$14.95 Softcover ISBN 0-929385-40-3

B O O K   M A R K E T   O R D E R   F O R M

BOOKS PUBLISHED BY LIGHT TECHNOLOGY PUBLISHING

		NO. COPIES	TOTAL			NO. COPIES	TOTAL
ACUPRESSURE FOR THE SOUL *Fallon*	$11.95	___	$ _____	**Wesley H. Bateman**			
ALIEN PRESENCE *Ananda*	$19.95	___	$ _____	DRAGONS AND CHARIOTS	$9.95	___	$_____
BEHOLD A PALE HORSE *Cooper*	$25.00	___	$ _____	KNOWLEDGE from the STARS	$11.95	___	$_____
CHANNELLING: Evolutionary Exercises *Vywamus/Burns*	$9.95	___	$ _____	**Lynn Buess**			
COLOR MEDICINE *Klotsche*	$11.95	___	$ _____	CHILDREN OF LIGHT ...	$8.95	___	$_____
EXPLORER RACE *Shapiro*	$24.95	___	$ _____	NUMEROLOGY: Nuances	$12.65	___	$_____
FOREVER YOUNG *Clark*	$9.95	___	$ _____	NUMEROLOGY for the NEW AGE	$9.85	___	$_____
LEGEND OF THE EAGLE CLAN *Cramer*	$9.95	___	$ _____	**Dorothy Roeder**			
LIVING RAINBOWS *Bain*	$14.95	___	$ _____	CRYSTAL CO-CREATORS	$14.95	___	$_____
MAHATMA I & II *Grattan*	$19.95	___	$ _____	NEXT DIMENSION IS LOVE	$11.95	___	$_____
NEW AGE PRIMER	$11.95	___	$ _____	REACH FOR US	$13.00	___	$_____
PRINCIPLES TO REMEMBER *Maile*	$11.95	___	$ _____	**Ruth Ryden**			
PRISONERS OF EARTH *Starr*	$11.95	___	$ _____	THE GOLDEN PATH	$11.95	___	$_____
SHINING THE LIGHT	$12.95	___	$ _____	LIVING THE GOLDEN PATH	$11.95	___	$_____
SHINING THE LIGHT — BOOK II	$12.95	___	$ _____	**Joshua David Stone, Ph.D.**			
SEDONA VORTEX GUIDE BOOK	$14.95	___	$ _____	COMPLETE ASCENSION MANUAL	$14.95	___	$_____
SHADOW OF S.F. PEAKS *Bader*	$9.95	___	$ _____	SOUL PSYCHOLOGY	$14.95	___	$_____
STORY OF THE PEOPLE *Rota*	$11.95	___	$ _____	**Vywamus/Janet Mcclure**			
THIS WORLD AND NEXT ONE *"Aiello"*	$9.95	___	$ _____	AHA! THE REALIZATION BOOK	$11.95	___	$_____
Arthur Fanning				LIGHT TECHNIQUES	$11.95	___	$_____
SOULS, EVOLUTION & the FATHER	$12.95	___	$ _____	SANAT KUMARA	$11.95	___	$_____
SIMON	$9.95	___	$ _____	SCOPES OF DIMENSIONS	$11.95	___	$_____
				THE SOURCE ADVENTURE	$11.95	___	$_____

BOOKS PRINTED OR MARKETED BY LIGHT TECHNOLOGY PUBLISHING

		NO. COPIES	TOTAL			NO. COPIES	TOTAL
ASCENSION HANDBOOK *Stubbs*	$11.95	___	$ _____	**Elwood Babbitt**			
DEDICATED TO THE SOUL ... *Vosacek*	$9.95	___	$ _____	PERFECT HEALTH	$15.95	___	$_____
E.T. 101 INSTRUCTION MANUAL *Mission Control/Luppi*	$12.00	___	$ _____	VOICES OF SPIRIT	$13.00	___	$_____
EXPLORING LIFE'S ... *Harder*	$15.95	___	$ _____	**Tom Dongo: Mysteries of Sedona**			
"I'M OK ..." *Golden Star Alliance*	$6.00	___	$ _____	MYSTERIES OF SEDONA—Book I	$6.95	___	$_____
LIFE ON THE CUTTING EDGE *Rachelle*	$14.95	___	$ _____	ALIEN TIDE—Book II	$7.95	___	$_____
OUR COSMIC ANCESTORS *Chatelaine*	$9.95	___	$ _____	QUEST—Book III	$8.95	___	$_____
OUT OF BODY EXPLORATION *Mulvin*	$8.95	___	$ _____	UNSEEN BEINGS ...	$9.95	___	$_____
REIKI A Torch in Daylight *Mitchell*	$14.95	___	$ _____	**Preston B. Nichols with Peter Moon**			
SOUL RECOVERY/EXTRACTION *Waya*	$9.95	___	$ _____	MONTAUK PROJECT	$15.95	___	$_____
TALKS WITH JONATHON *Miller*	$14.95	___	$ _____	MONTAUK REVISITED	$19.95	___	$_____
THE ARMSTRONG REPORT *Armstrong*	$11.95	___	$ _____	PYRAMIDS OF MONTAUK	$19.95	___	$ _____
SEDONA POWER SPOT/GUIDE *Dannelley*	$9.95	___	$ _____	**Lyssa Royal and Keith Priest**			
				PREPARING FOR CONTACT	$12.95	___	$_____
				PRISM OF LYRA	$11.95	___	$_____
				VISITORS FROM WITHIN	$12.95	___	$_____

ASCENSION MEDITATION TAPES

		NO. COPIES	TOTAL			NO. COPIES	TOTAL
Joshua David Stone, Ph.D.				**YHWH/Arthur Fanning**			
Ascension Activation Meditation	$10.00	___	$ _____	On Becoming	$10.00	___	$ _____
				Healing Meditations/Knowing self	$10.00	___	$ _____
Vywamus/Barbara Burns				Manifestation & Alignment w/ Poles	$10.00	___	$ _____
The Quantum Mechanical You (6 tapes)	$40.00	___	$ _____	The Art of Shutting Up	$10.00	___	$ _____
				Continuity of Consciousness	$25.00	___	$ _____
Brian Grattan				Black Hole Meditation	$10.00	___	$ _____
Seattle Seminar Resurrection 1994 (12 tapes)	$79.95	___	$ _____	Merging the Golden Light Replica of You	$10.00	___	$ _____

BOOKSTORE DISCOUNTS HONORED

SEND ☐ CHECK OR ☐ MONEY ORDER
(U.S. FUNDS ONLY) PAYABLE TO:
LIGHT TECHNOLOGY PUBLISHING
P.O. BOX 1526 ● SEDONA ● AZ 86339
(520) 282-6523 FAX: (520) 282-4130

NAME/COMPANY_____

ADDRESS_____

CITY/STATE/ZIP_____

PHONE_____CONTACT_____

All prices in US$. Higher in Canada and Europe.

SUBTOTAL: $_____

SALES TAX: $_____
(7.5% – AZ residents only)

SHIPPING/HANDLING: $_____
('3 Min.; 10% of orders over '30)

CANADA S/H: $_____
(20% of order)

TOTAL AMOUNT ENCLOSED: $_____

CANADA: Cherev Canada, Inc. 1(800) 263-2408 Fax (519) 986-3103 ● ENGLAND/EUROPE: Windrush Press Ltd. 0608 652012/652025 Fax 0608 652125